Problems of Analysis

Problems of Analysis

PHILOSOPHICAL ESSAYS

Max Black

PROFESSOR OF PHILOSOPHY
CORNELL UNIVERSITY

GREENWOOD PRESS, PUBLISHERS
WESTPORT, CONNECTICUT

The Library of Congress cataloged this book as follows:

Black, Max, 1909–
    Problems of analysis: philosophical essays.   Westport,
Conn.. Greenwood Press ₁1971. c1954₁

    xi, 304 p. 23 cm.

    Includes bibliographical references.

1. Analysis (Philosophy)—Addresses, essays, lectures.   I. Title.

B808.5.B55 1971	160	74–139124
ISBN 0–8371–5740–4		MARC
Library of Congress	72 ₁4₁	

Originally published in 1954 by Cornell University Press,
Ithaca, New York

Reprinted with the permission of the author, Max Black

Reprinted in 1971 by Greenwood Press, Inc., 51 Riverside Avenue,
Westport, Conn. 06880

Library of Congress catalog card number 74-139124
ISBN 0-8371-5740-4

Printed in the United States of America

10 9 8 7 6 5 4 3 2

One man's gnat is another man's camel.
—*Samuel Butler*

All the mistakes are there, waiting to be made.
—*S. Tartakower*

TO *Kingsley Blake Price*

Preface

SOME of these essays are technical, but I hope most of them will interest a reader who is not a professional philosopher. (Such a reader might care to read I–III, VI, and X before proceeding to the others. Essays XIII and XIV presuppose the most knowledge; XII is the only one that has any mathematics in it, but even there the calculations are easy.)

In each case I have chosen a problem that aroused my interest—partly because none of the earlier solutions seemed convincing. I shall be satisfied if I have sometimes succeeded in giving answers sufficiently plain for others to be able to profit from my mistakes.

With one exception (the last) all these essays have been written since the publication of my previous collection, *Language and Philosophy* (1949). In the case of the seven that have been previously published (I–VI, XIV), I have allowed myself the luxury of minor improvements, but no radical changes have been made.

It has been my good fortune to have the help of a number of friends, whose generous criticism has done much to improve these papers. I am especially grateful to Kurt Baier, Peter Geach, William H. Hay, Leonard Linsky, Abraham Melden, John Myhill, Frederick L. Will, Paul Ziff, and my colleagues at Cornell.

Permission to reprint some of these essays was kindly granted by the editors of *Science and Civilization, Philosophical Review, Analysis, Proceedings of the American Philosophical Association, Mind,* and *Philosophical Studies: Essays in Memory of L. Susan Stebbing.* (Further details will be found in the "Additional Notes and References" at the end of the book.) To all of these and the authors and publishers of works from which short quotations have been used I am grateful. Mr. Arnold Kapp has been of great help to me in reading proof and preparing the index.

MAX BLACK

Ithaca, New York
October, 1953

Contents

I

Problems Connected with Language

I

The Definition of Scientific Method

MY OBJECT in this essay is to clarify some of the problems involved in attempting to define scientific method. I shall argue that most writers who have tried to define scientific method have been working with a notion of definition which is too narrow for the task. I shall try to outline a pattern of definition which would be more adequate and discuss some criteria which any satisfactory definition of scientific method must satisfy. The purpose will therefore be to clear away some of the difficulties which have impeded the search for a satisfactory definition, rather than to provide a definition of my own.

Let us begin by considering some of the motives which lead us, as it has led so many philosophers and scientists in the past, to search for a definition of scientific method—or, for what is nearly the same thing, science itself.

The laziest answer will invoke that "intellectual curiosity" which so conveniently explains an interest in truth for its own sake. No doubt a thinker of precise intellectual habits will find it distasteful to be constantly using a term like "science" without having an explicit analysis of its connotation; the problem of definition may challenge his ingenuity as a chess problem might, and its solution will provide a satisfaction similar in kind. Disinterested philosophical lexicography is a harmless pursuit not to be sneered at in a world in which so few occupations are innocent. Nevertheless, we shall misconstrue the nature of our problem if we treat the definition of scientific method as a mere intellectual exercise.

When a term has a relatively well-determined denotation or application, the analysis of its connotation will, it is true, have little effect upon practice. Carpenters will continue to make

[3]

tables, in happy ignorance of the epistemologist's inability to define the term "table." The case is different when the term to be defined has controversial or problematic application. To define such a term as "justice" is to engage in a hazardous occupation, as Socrates long ago discovered. Men are firmly convinced that justice is an excellent thing, while agreeing neither in the application of the term nor on the criteria which ought to determine its use. In these circumstances, the practice of those who use the term "justice" is likely to be as inconsistent as their thought is confused, and a good philosophical analysis runs the risk of bringing such inconsistencies to public notice. To anybody who continues to believe in justice, any shift in the term's application, induced by philosophical definition, threatens to bring about a redirection of his interests. And in general, *any* definition removing inconsistencies or involving a redistribution of emphasis will redirect the interests of those who use the term, provided they can understand the definition, and have sufficient intelligence to be moved by rational considerations.

The importance of such "persuasive definitions," as they have come to be called,[1] is being increasingly recognized. We can see today, more clearly than in the past, that definition of difficult terms is usually a process not regulated simply by the character of the concept to be defined.[2] The adequacy of a persuasive definition has also to be judged in relation to the soundness of the interests which it is designed to serve; the criticism of persuasive definitions is a proceeding partly normative in character, involving considerations of an ethical as well as of a methodological and logical character. This view,

---

[1] "A 'persuasive' definition is one which gives a new conceptual meaning to a familiar word without substantially changing its emotive meaning, and which is used with the conscious or unconscious purpose of changing, by this means, the direction of people's interests" (C. L. Stevenson in *Mind*, 47 [1938]: 331). I would want to change this definition of "persuasive definition" in some respects, however. The reference to "emotive meaning," for instance, commits users of the term "persuasive" to a controversial and, in my judgment, mistaken analysis of meaning.

[2] Strictly speaking there is no determinate "concept" in such a case.

[4]

if correct, raises some difficult questions of procedure, some of which must be considered later in this essay.

Now I wish to maintain that the attempt to define scientific method or to analyze science is a search for a *persuasive* definition. I hold this to be true because I believe that the term "science" has no definite and unambiguous application. No doubt we should all agree that physics is a science par excellence, and that the atomic physicists use scientific method, whatever scientific method may prove to be. But we shall hardly agree with the remark attributed to Lord Rutherford that science consists of "physics and stamp collecting"—if this is taken to imply that nothing but physics is a science in the strict sense. Is chemistry science? Of course. But is psychology a science or the mere hope of a science? Is history a science? Or mathematics? Or ethics? Or sociology? Such questions have no answer *because they have no clear sense;* and they are asked, paradoxically enough, just *because* clear sense is lacking. For the term "science" is eulogistic, whatever science may prove to be after analysis; and these requests for classification are also clamorous demands for the recognition and material rewards which await the application of the honorific label.

If this view of the situation is correct and we are looking for a persuasive definition, the search for a definition of scientific method will require the following combination of descriptive and normative procedures.

Instances of modes of investigation provisionally identified as eminently "scientific" will be collated and compared with the hope of determining common characteristics. The instances must be such as will not be seriously disputed—and this is perhaps why a few stock instances like Kepler's investigations into planetary motion reappear so often in textbook discussions of scientific method. So long as agreement about the scientific character of the instructive examples can be preserved, the process of comparison and analysis can be treated as non-normative and descriptive; the collation of undisputed instances of scientific method is, in principle, as "objective" as taxonomy. Unfortunately, the generalizations resulting

[5]

from the examination of such undisputed instances are too indefinite to be of much use; the definitions of scientific method produced at this level are little better than banalities, and just because they codify what is commonly accepted, such definitions help not at all in resolving the burning questions of the applicability of scientific method to disputed cases. To be told that "perhaps science is after all only organized common sense, preferably derived from experiment and preferably organized on a quantitative basis" [3] helps not at all to decide whether psychical research is scientific or ethics extra-scientific. The formula elicits general agreement because it is so vague; and the vagueness covers a multitude of omissions. It is not unfair to say that the more those who write about scientific method agree, the less there is *about which* they agree.

Once we leave the area of universal agreement, we find ourselves compelled to choose criteria which are not clearly exemplified in acceptable instances: the instances are as problematic as the criteria to be employed. Our choice has to be made in the light of an interest we find to be good and is thus determined by normative considerations. It cannot be otherwise, since in this area of wider but uncertain application there is no definite denotation of the term to be analyzed. Let me make this plainer by an extreme illustration. Suppose my interest in science were to be confined exclusively to its chances of making me some financial profit (an attitude which is not altogether unheard of); in that case I might define as scientific only those investigations which, while conforming to the vague specifications achieved at our first level of analysis, *also* showed prospects of profitable exploitation by myself. The choice of my own financial interest as my *summum bonum* would be normative; but the implications of that choice would be non-normative or, in the language I have been using, descriptive. If the instance seems grotesque, it is so because we know in advance that we should refuse to accept the profit motive of a single person as determining our own interests in science. But

[3] James Bryant Conant, "The Advancement of Learning in the United States in the Post-War World," *Science*, 99 (February 4, 1944): 91.

the emphasis of theorists, from Bacon onward, on science as yielding power and mastery is not so remote from the grotesque hypothesis I have just considered. Those who single out technology for special emphasis in the definition of scientific method are committed to regarding technological advance, in that context, as a pre-eminent good. My point is that there must *be* a choice if the definition is to be worth having; it will be valuable *because* it is controversial. (The question of how such choices and value commitments are to be validated raises some of the most difficult problems of philosophy and cannot be discussed here.)

The regularizing of their own procedures is among the enduring interests of scientists. There is, in science, as in other creative human activities, a continual tension between the conservative demands of the tradition and the revolutionary activities of those who transform the tradition by revolting against it. There is something lawless in the creative process itself, and the scientists whom scientists have most wished to honor have made their discoveries by means as mysterious to themselves as to their contemporaries. But if their results are to be useful they must be communicable to those who are not themselves geniuses. Thus what begins as a brilliant discovery, as incoherent as it is dazzling, is eventually converted into a routine which the mere artisan of science can master and apply. In this way the new tradition is created but for which the later pioneers would have nothing to rebel against.

In some ways the progress of science, as here depicted, smacks too much of the marvelous and the unpredictable for comfort; and the hope has never been abandoned of reducing the process of discovery itself to a routine that can be communicated and taught. This hope has inspired investigators of scientific method from Aristotle to Descartes and from Bacon to Eddington. In one version of the legend of the Holy Grail those who sought it hoped to find a "self-acting, food-providing, talisman" [4] and this is precisely what such men as Bacon have hoped to discover. We can write off such a project as illusory

---

[4] *Encyclopaedia Britannica,* 11th ed., 12: 320.

and no more likely to succeed than the quest of the Grail itself; but it would be rash to assume that there are no principles relevant to the practice of research. However much we stress the final mystery of the art of creation, we have to admit that even the genius learns; and all learning is, necessarily, the learning of something general, reproducible, and, in theory at least, communicable. There are principles which assist the process of discovery, however insufficient in themselves to yield novel results; and if even this is not conceded, it will perhaps be granted that there are erroneous principles which constrict and hinder scientific progress. The study of scientific method may help at least to remove some of the obstacles to the development and extension of scientific thought. This alone would be sufficient justification for the most careful attempts to provide satisfactory analyses of scientific method.

I hope I have said enough to indicate something of the motives leading men to formulate definitions of scientific method; I have explained my interpretation of the procedure in which they were engaged. Now anybody who is persuaded of the importance of this enterprise may well feel some disappointment upon examining the analyses and definitions which invite his acceptance. Consider, for instance, the ancient tradition which identifies what is "really" or "pre-eminently" or "essentially" scientific with what is mathematical. This Pythagorean attitude recurs constantly in the philosophy of science; it has deep roots in Platonic metaphysics, was strong in Kepler and Galileo, Leibniz and Descartes; it was stated with unequivocal definiteness by Kant and is a living force today. Such a view can certainly not be accused of triteness or banality; it appears rather as a wild paradox which only "a fool or an advanced thinker" would seriously defend. A position which regards mathematics as the queen of the sciences, relegating the fact-finding activities of the observer and the experimenter to the role of "mere" auxiliaries, is certainly in need of a good deal of argument to render it plausible. Yet the curious inquirer, naïvely wondering at the boldness of the abstraction involved, will search in vain for such defense. What he is likely to discover instead is a claim that science is *essentially* mathematical, in spite of all appearance to the contrary.

I suppose that very few who use such language would admit that they were in search of an *essence,* in some Aristotelian sense. Yet I think it plausible that some of the defects of any definition as abstract as this are due to the use of a pattern of definition which is Aristotelian in origin. For until recent times nearly all textbooks of logic have echoed Aristotle's doctrine of definition.[5] Those who would shudder at professing Aristotelian or Thomist metaphysics continue to look for definitions *per genus et differentiam* as if no other mode of definition were conceivable.

I shall not try to make much of the point that modern generalizations of traditional logic show definition by division to be only one among many conceivable forms of definition. For this is not of much importance here, except as helping to encourage an attitude of sensible irreverence in respect of any claims of finality for Aristotelian logical doctrine.

What is more important to stress is that definition by genus and differentia is always definition of a *determinate* and *immutable species.* What we define in this manner is a *kind* of thing, capable of having repeated instances alike in character; and the kind of thing that we define must have precise and constant boundaries. So long as this type of definition is used, it is impossible to define the name of a unique entity, say "Napoleon"; nor can we define a general term such as "bald" which, being vague, admits of a fringe of borderline cases; nor a term such as "music" whose criteria change in time. Definition is of something generic, determinate, and unchanging; and it follows that definitions are final, in the sense of never calling for

[5] "The traditional theory of definition is based upon the theory of the predicables. It can be summed up in the rule: definition should be *per genus et differentiam* (i.e., by assigning the genus and the distinguishing characteristic). This rule expresses Aristotle's view that definition states the essence of what is defined. . . . Everything, it is assumed, has a determinate essence and there is one and only one definition appropriate to it, viz., that which expresses the essence" (L. S. Stebbing, *A Modern Introduction to Logic* [1st ed.; New York, 1930], p. 432).

[9]

revision. We may make a mistake in defining "science" or "scientific method," but if we find the correct definition it will stand for all time; to characterize a definition as "provisional" or "approximate" is to talk nonsense. Again, if "science" is a vague term, the boundaries of which are *not* precisely determined, it is insofar recalcitrant to this kind of definition: the best we can do is to substitute for the vague term some more precise substitute which *can* be defined. If the progress of science is in some respects a unique historical phenomenon, definition is impossible; if the "nature" of science is not constant, there is nothing that we can properly define.

These assumptions of the generality, definiteness, and constancy of the object of definition will seem to most people too obvious to be questioned; and we may as well grant that definition is most easily accomplished where the assumptions are justified. I wish to urge, however, that when the object of definition is "science" or "scientific method" we are not justified in postulating generality, definiteness, and constancy. We ought at least to consider seriously the possibility that the "scientific method" which is worth defining is in some respects historically unique, is continuous with its contraries, and is appreciably variable with time.

If serious account is taken of the uniqueness, indeterminateness, and variability of scientific method, it will be a matter of relative unimportance whether the process of analysis is called "definition." For those who conform most faithfully to the Aristotelian canons of definition will permit *some* kind of investigation into the connotation of individual, indeterminate, or variable terms. Rather than talk of definition in such cases they may prefer to say that the individual can be *described*, the indeterminate can be rendered determinate (by elimination of vagueness), and the variable can be subsumed under unchanging laws of change. Such ways of describing the task to be performed are not to be recommended; for they blur the important point that what we have to do is not so much to describe an object or to invent a new notation *as to clarify the language we now have and the thoughts we express by means of it.* I see no good reason not to call this "definition." Whether it can be effectively practiced remains to be seen.

My quarrel with the traditional mode of definition is, in short, that it takes for granted certain conditions of generality, definiteness, and fixity which are not always, or always completely, satisfied; that rigid adherence to these assumptions narrowly limits the range of what can be "properly" defined; and entails that "scientific method," *qua* unique, indeterminate, and subject to change, is indefinable.

So far, you may complain, no shred of evidence has been given of the contention that "science" and "scientific method" are recalcitrant to definition in the Aristotelian mode. I can think of no better means of persuasion than to invite you to contemplate in imagination the totality of the activities involved in and relevant to what we call "science."

Consider, if you will, the vast variety of activities of a scientific character which must have occurred yesterday—the glass blowing and the dissecting; the manipulation of rulers, stop watches, test tubes, bunsen burners, cyclotrons, questionnaires; men fishing in swamps, solving differential equations, polishing lenses, composing manuscripts, developing photographic plates, writing a polemic against vitalism, modifying an axiom system; handling, manufacturing, observing, experimenting, calculating, theorizing, speculating. Is not the resulting impression one of the extreme diversity, not to say heterogeneity, of the activities which we are naturally inclined to regard as scientific? Yet there is something more than a mere aggregate here; we know that this congeries of observations, manipulations, experimentations, explanations, calculations, predictions, speculations is unified by an extremely fine network of relationships. There *is* a pattern, but an extremely complex one.

The activities I have distinguished are not conducted independently and in isolation; the prosperity of one depends upon the success of all: calculation is performed for the sake of experimental and observational test; experiment is conducted in the service of generalization, which in turn uses theory, which provokes speculation, which invites systematization, which is controlled by experiment . . . and so on, without end, in a maze of cross connections and mutual dependencies. Science is an organic system of activities; and the pattern of its development is also organic.

We have imagined ourselves taking the latest cross section of scientific activity. To do justice to our subject we must extend our survey in imagination to cover the history and development of scientific activity no less than its present condition. We shall then see that this vast symphony of activities displays superordinate rhythms of development and change; there will be brought vividly to our notice the striking variety of motives and circumstances which have fostered or hindered the progress of science, the changes in instruments, modes of calculation, theories, underlying methodologies, and philosophies. For sheer complexity of texture and incident, science is like life itself and as little to be reduced to formula.

Some scientists regard an interest in the history of their subject as mere antiquarianism, and it may be that the very remote past consists largely of mistakes to be avoided. But it deserves to be remembered that the history of any scientific discipline intimately determines the current modes of investigation. The frames of reference which appear eligible to any given epoch, the instruments accepted as respectable, and the types of "fact" taken to have evidential value are historically conditioned. To pretend otherwise is to claim for human reason, as manifested in scientific progress, a universality and fixity it has never manifested. We may justly call the pattern of development organic, since the causal pattern is not analyzable into a set of independent causal strands; there is constant interaction across the temporal dimension.

A lively awareness of the complexity of science, regarded as a historical phenomenon, will make it seem unlikely that we shall succeed in finding a relatively simple and immutable essence underlying the confusing procession of accidents. We seem to have not a coherent nexus of well-defined and fully cognizable universals, but rather a concentration and overlap-

[12]

ping of characteristics of variable degree. None of the characters which we recognize in the scientific process are independently necessary or sufficient, but all, supporting and jointly reinforcing one another, give rise to the unique historical phenomenon.

Neither observation, nor generalization, nor the hypothetico-deductive use of assumptions, nor measurement, nor the use of instruments, nor mathematical construction—nor all of them together—can be regarded as essential to science. For branches of science can easily be found where any one of these criteria is either absent or has so little influence as to be negligible. Astronomy makes no experiments, mathematics uses no observation, geography is mainly descriptive, archaeology hardly uses measurement, much taxonomy frames no abstract generalizations, and biology is hardly beginning to use mathematical idealization and formalization. The characters mentioned are neither necessary nor sufficient, but they may be present in higher or lower degree and they contribute to what we recognize as science. Their diminution removes from an activity the feature we apprehend as scientific; their joint presence in high degree creates conditions recognized as pre-eminently scientific.

This line of thought will lead us to abandon the search for a timeless and immutable essence in favor of the identification of a system of overlapping and interacting criteria. I propose to call this "range definition." [6] I am proposing, in fact, that we take seriously the organic and historical aspects of science. I propose that we treat "scientific method" as a historical expression meaning, among other things, "those procedures which, as a matter of historical fact, have proved most fruitful in the acquisition of systematic and comprehensive knowledge." On this approach, the methodological problems involved in the definition of scientific method closely parallel those arising in an attempt to define Napoleon, the industrial revolution, slavery, or any other person or institution having historical actuality. In each such case, what we recognize as the

[6] For further discussion of this kind of definition, see the next essay.

[13]

idiosyncrasy of the unique historical phenomenon is constituted by a growing together, a concrescence, of variable factors, interacting to produce the degree of unification and contrast with an environment which leads us to recognize a distinct entity.

The technical problems which arise in range definitions are similar in character to those encountered in the specification of biological or psychological "types." And logicians have already begun to consider the methods of formalization appropriate.[7] To provide a satisfactory range definition we shall need (a) a description of the main factors engaged, (b) determination of their relative "weight" or importance, and (c) an account of their mode of interaction.

In trying to carry out such a program as this the pervasive difficulty will be that of choosing a proper level of abstraction. The greater formal complexity of range definition will not exempt it automatically from the danger of overabstraction; the result of our labors may still prove to be a sterile formula, unable, for all its complexity, to influence practice. There is, however, a kind of formulation of principle which is able to avoid this danger. I shall try to show how this happens by considering an illuminating illustration of the formulation of principles of scientific method.

Claude Bernard's *Introduction to the Study of Experimental Medicine,* first published in 1865,[8] is a classic of the philosophy of science which deserves to be better known in the English-speaking countries. Its title may have misled readers into expecting a technical treatise on physiology; it is in fact an essay on method not unworthy to be classed with that of Descartes. We shall not find here the pretensions to system, arrangement, and thoroughness of more elaborate treatises on scientific method. Here everything is said directly, simply,

[7] See C. G. Hempel and P. Oppenheim, *Der Typusbegriff im Lichte der neuen Logik* (Leyden, 1936).

[8] I shall quote from H. D. Greene's translation, published by Macmillan in 1927.

without pretentiousness or pseudo profundity; we can almost hear the harpsichord playing in the background. But there is nothing forced or contrived in this elegance; every page is informed with the judgment and educated memory of a superb experimenter. We seem to be always in the presence of a *person*, meditating upon a lifetime's experience of creative research.

The reflections of such a man deserve respect. I shall select for special attention two aspects of his doctrine which are directly relevant to my present purpose. First, Bernard's fallibilism [9] with respect to scientific theory—a doctrine held by many but never, to my knowledge stated better—will point the way for a more radical fallibilism with respect to the principles of scientific method. Second, Bernard's use of determinism as an instrument of criticism and discovery may throw light upon the manner in which principles of method can, in favorable cases, contribute to the progress and extension of science.

Bernard's views about the uncertainty of all scientific theory arise from his analysis of the distinction between experiment and observation and of the part played in both by hypothesis. Experiment, he says, differs from observation in demanding artificially induced variation for the sake of comparison and reasoning.[10] Experiment is relatively active, observation relatively passive; but the most elaborately artificial experiment terminates in simple observation, a submission to the verdict of experience. It is important to notice that because the ex-

[9] The term is Peirce's. See *Collected Papers of Charles Sanders Peirce,* ed. Charles Hartshorne and Paul Weiss (6 vols.; Cambridge, 1931–1935), 1: 13, 141–152.

[10] "We give the name observer to the man who applies methods of investigation, whether simple or complex, to the study of phenomena which he does not vary and which he therefore gathers as nature offers them. We give the name experimenter to the man who applies methods of investigation, whether simple or complex, so as to make natural phenomena vary, or so as to alter them with some purpose or other, and to make them present themselves in circumstances or conditions in which nature does not show them." Bernard, *Experimental Medicine,* p. 15.

perimenter *interrogates* nature, every experiment is based upon a "preconceived idea," a hypothesis to be tested.[11] But once the experimental conditions have been set up, the scientist must turn passive again. "Observers, then, must be photographers of phenomena; their observations must accurately represent nature. We must observe without any preconceived idea; the observer's mind must be passive, must hold its peace; it listens to nature and writes at its dictation." [12] Without hypotheses or "preconceived ideas" we should never discover the observations—so that even an erroneous theory is better than none at all.[13] But we must always "be ready to abandon, to alter or to supplant" [14] the hypothesis in the light of the decisive judgment of the observations by which it is tested.

To a generation successfully weaned from Baconian empiricism, Bernard's insistence upon the primacy of fact and the need for theoretical "preconceptions" in research may seem too elementary to call for praise. But a successful marriage of rationalism and empiricism is hard to arrange; and it is of great interest to see how Bernard manages to reconcile his great respect for fact with a thorough belief in the intelligibility of phenomena. He is a rationalist to the finger tips; observation, he says, is *always* made for the sake of generalization and explanation; the disproof of a theory must always be an incentive to theoretical explanation of the discrepancy—"negative facts when considered alone never teach us anything." [15] So it is that, in spite of his confidence in the senses,[16] he does not hesitate to outlaw a fact, if necessary. He says, of a particu-

[11] "It is impossible to devise an experiment without a preconceived idea; devising an experiment, we said, is putting a question; we never conceive a question without an idea which invites an answer" (*ibid.*, p. 23).

[12] *Ibid.*, p. 22. See p. 192: "We must never go beyond facts and must be, as it were, photographers of nature."

[13] "Even mistaken hypotheses and theories are of use in leading to discoveries. . . . It seems, indeed a necessary weakness of our mind to be able to reach truth only across a multitude of errors and obstacles" (*ibid.*, 170).

[14] *Ibid.*, p. 23.   [15] *Ibid.*, p. 174.   [16] *Ibid.*, p. 177.

lar instance, "The irrationality of the fact, therefore, led me to see *a priori* that it must be false, and that it could not be used as a basis for scientific reasoning." [17] Yet faith in the ultimate intelligibility and rationality of the universe is controlled and moderated in him by an abiding scepticism concerning *particular* explanations and reasons. Because every theory is an imperfect, and partly arbitrary, extrapolation from observation, we must never place unqualified trust in *any* theory. "When we propound a general theory in our sciences, we are sure only that, literally speaking, all such theories are false." [18] "Even when we have a theory that seems sound, it is never more than relatively sound, and it always includes a certain proportion of the unknown." [19] This paradoxical attitude of active scepticism, of an undogmatic and corrigible faith, Bernard sums up in a striking phrase: "We must have robust faith," he says, "and not believe." [20] We must not believe wholeheartedly in any body of scientific theory; the object of our robust faith is determinism. Determinism, he says, "is the absolute principle of science" [21] and to abandon it is to renounce the hope of being scientific. "In science we must firmly believe in principles, but must question formulae; on the one hand, indeed, we are sure that determinism exists, but we are never certain we have attained it." [22]

It might be supposed that a determinism such as Bernard espoused would be too pliable to serve as a guide and a stimu-

[17] *Ibid.,* p. 179.   [18] *Ibid.,* p. 36.   [19] *Ibid.,* p. 162.

[20] *Ibid.,* p. 168. We may be reminded here of Huxley's notion of "tätige skepsis" that he adapted from Goethe. For a similar more recent statement see Morris R. Cohen, *Studies in Philosophy and Science* (New York, 1949), p. 50: "We may define science as a self-corrective system . . . *science invites doubt.* It can grow or make progress, not only because it is fragmentary, but also because no one proposition in it is in itself absolutely certain, and so the process of correction can operate when we find more adequate evidence. But note, however, that the doubt and the correction are always in accordance with the canons of the scientific method, so that the latter is the bond of continuity."

[21] Bernard, *Experimental Medicine,* p. 39.

[22] *Ibid.,* p. 168.

lant to research. It has often been pointed out that determinism, construed as the principle that laws exist of no matter what degree of complexity, is irrefutable in principle. Faced with no matter how much confusion and irregularity of appearance, a determinist can always continue to *look* for laws. Is Bernard's major principle anything more than an expression of his determination to continue to look and to theorize? Does his determinism do any work, or is it merely a regrettable lapse into metaphysics?

Now I am inclined to think that Bernard's determinism, *as he used it,* can be shown to have been an active instrument of research and criticism. His practice repeatedly shows his faith in ultimate rationality lighting the path to original discovery. When the physicians of his day invoked the tact and intuition of the medical practitioner, Bernard counters with a stubborn search for causal sequences; when other theorists hid their ignorance of biological laws by appealing to some mysterious "vitality" or vital force, he condemns them for irrationality and continues to experiment; and in more specific contexts where less clearheaded experimenters blunder, Bernard's robust faith in a deterministic order of nature fortifies him in a laborious but successful search for rational explanation. Belief in determinism was, to him, a light for the darkness, not a mere obeisance to an imputed order of nature.

Such an interpretation might easily be wrong; and it is conceivable, though I find myself unable to believe it, that Bernard read his philosophical principles back into earlier researches which at the time of their performance required no better support than the luck and cunning of the investigator. Those who prefer to think that the experimenter is guided mainly by intuition may do so if they can persuade themselves that the term is something better than a disguise for our own ignorance of the creative process. But the general point is sound, and could be supported by ample illustrations from the history of science. As the individual experiment itself would be nothing without a preconceived idea, however crude and faulty in detail, so would the whole course of research be a mere random succession of fumbles but for the co-ordination of leading ideas. It seems implausible to me that any regulative principle as abstract as determinism in its most general formulation can have decisive influences upon research; and I think it demonstrable that in any epoch of experimental research the leading ideas take more specific forms, varying with the climate of philosophical opinion and the earlier fortunes of the science.[23]

I have been citing Claude Bernard's philosophy of science in support of my contention that cautious extrapolation of methodological principles may be a valuable guide to scientific research. There is, however, much in Bernard's doctrines themselves that would seem open to serious objection.

His conception of the fact of observation as simply given, the observer himself acting as a passive photographer of nature, is hardly adequate. The image itself betrays the intention; for a photograph is not an identical reproduction of the scene it portrays and must itself be correctly interpreted if it is to be a suitable datum for inference. The insistence upon the primacy of what is presented is valuable, but it must be reconciled with the principle of opposite tendency, to the effect that there is no observation without interpretation; pure observation is a myth. What shall *count* as a fact in any well-developed science is already largely determined by theory embodied in the disposition of the scientific instruments, the selection of "competent" scientists, and the postures of "correct" observation. That Bernard needed to take no account of such complications is explained by the simplicity of his observations.

We cannot share, today, his unqualified faith in determinism. If we are to continue to search for laws, we must be prepared to find them complex beyond all the expectations of earlier scientists. Bernard's distrust of statistical generaliza-

---

[23] I take this to explain in part Bernard's success in using determinism. Given the special context of physiological experiment in the last century, I think he had robust faith, not in general determinism, but rather in the existence of laws and explanations of *a certain kind*.

tion—thoroughly justified in his own context—must seem old-fashioned to a generation educated in statistical physics. We must be prepared to mix a little more scepticism with our faith than Bernard was prepared for.

One of the major contributions of this century's philosophy of science has been the clarification and analysis of the symbolic aspects of science. We are beginning to understand how very far from being a literal generalization about observable features of observable phenomena the theories of any advanced science must be taken to be. The more advanced the science, the greater the part played in its theories by unobservables; and the more urgent the task of elucidating the deductive paths connecting such abstruse and recondite entities with the experiences to which, however indirectly, they refer. A well-developed philosophy of science will have much to say in this chapter of its investigations.

We can now begin to see some hope of solving our problem about the choice of overlapping criteria for a definition of science. It will be remembered that I claimed that science, as a historical process, resembled an organism in being a manifestation of variable, interacting factors. Now we have to add that analysis of the character of this process, as it shows itself in the formulation of an explicit methodology, may itself become a factor in the further development. Principles abstracted from the past history may be put to work to help determine its future and themselves become subjected in this way to continuing experimental test. And the same holds for the goals, standards, and ideals which determine the choice, acceptance, and rejection of principles in the light of continuing experimental tests. Looking back at the history of science, we choose such principles of method as will seem to answer best to the search for knowledge of the world—as in the light of that examination we feel constrained to envisage what we now call the world and knowledge of it. If our choice is wise, the principles can be set to work to assist in the acquisition of more knowledge; and if the application, however successful, changes our conceptions of what should be the right method—

[20]

indeed, of what we should regard as "nature," "the world," "fact," "evidence," and the other terms of our philosophical discourse—that is no more than we should be wise to expect.

I am advocating an attitude of active scepticism, of faith without belief, toward the very principles of investigation themselves. No doubt, to renounce the support of determinism or any other immutable theoretical certainty is to call for an attitude of mind difficult to sustain. There will be some to object that in the absence of some such underpinning the program is condemned to a futile relativism and, if it be wholehearted, a complete scepticism. "What," it will be said, "in the last analysis, justifies your choice of standards, ideals, criteria, and principles? If the justification lies in the future, then your choice of a scientific method is no better *now* than a blind guess. To be rational *now*, it must itself be based on rational first principles necessarily incapable of justification empirically. You want the advantage of a metaphysics while shirking the labor required to establish it."

The question is too large to be argued fully here. Let me be content to affirm that in the last analysis there is *no* last analysis. If the search for a definition of scientific method is more than an exercise in platitudinous verity or epigrammatic falsity, it is a serious attempt to clarify the relation of our culture to its past in order to bring into sharper focus our commitments to its future. This means starting from the standpoint not of a detached rational being exempt from the influence of his history but from our own standpoint in space and time. We start with given notions, preconceptions, and prejudices about knowledge, evidence, method, and science which it is mere folly to pretend to ignore. What we can do is to render these philosophical preconceptions more rational by testing them against past history and future experience. This is as far removed from blind guessing as the calculations of the meteorologist are from the casual weather predictions of the man in the street. But the philosopher of science may be sufficiently humble to expect no higher ratio of success than the weather forecaster; his one advantage in the long run over the advocate of intuition or guesswork is that he may hope to learn from his mistakes.

Since we have introduced the salutary virtue of humility, let me repeat that at best we have here the mere outline of a program. The detailed execution of the program, by which its merits must eventually be judged, is by far the harder undertaking. When we compare our present conception of scientific method with those of Herschel, Whewell, Jevons, Bernard, John Stuart Mill, and the other nineteenth-century writers we may take pride in having made marked advances. Certainly we have a much sounder grasp of the character and importance of the symbolic aspects of scientific method; our conceptions of statistical method, the nature of mathematics, of measurement, and the use of nonobservable theoretical entities have advanced in a way which would astound our not-so-distant predecessors. It would be self-deception, however, to pretend that light shines everywhere in those intensely cultivated regions, and it is safe to predict that theorists who venture already to lay down definite prescriptions for research in economics, psychology, or the still embryonic social sciences will seem entertainingly doctrinaire to their not-so-distant successors. The wisest philosophers of science have shown their wisdom not least in shrouding their first principles in protective ambiguity. The best we can hope for is some useful second principles that will prove to be not so vague as to be exempt from refutation by experience still to come, or so hopelessly wrong as to deserve outright rejection when science has suffered its next benign convulsion.

So much ground has been covered in this paper that a summary may be welcome. I began by characterizing definitions of "scientific method" as "persuasive," in a technical sense of that term. "Scientific method," it was contended, is a term of such controversial application that a definition universally acceptable can be expected to be platitudinous. A useful definition will be a controversial one, determined by a choice made, more or less wisely, in the hope of codifying and influencing scientific procedures. It is too much to expect infallible recipes for conducting research, but most definitions in the literature fail to satisfy the more modest demand of helping to determine the development and extension of scientific method. A common defect is excessive abstraction; it was suggested that this arises from conformity to a pattern of definition Aristotelian in origin. The search for an immutable and determinate essence underlying the plentitude of the historical process can result only in epigrammatic paradox. We may do better, I urged, to think of science as a concrescence, a growing together of variable, interacting, mutually reinforcing factors contributing to a development organic in character. The type of definition appropriate takes the form of a description of the constitutive factors, together with an indication of their relative weight or importance and their mutual relationships.

For further light upon the kind of definition that would be satisfactory I turned to Claude Bernard's philosophy of science. He was found to be advocating a blend of rationalism and empiricism, marked by submission to the authority of the results of observation, and an unflagging confidence in the causal structure of the universe. His scepticism with regard to the finality of scientific theory was congenial to the more radical fallibilism advocated in this paper. Though his robust faith in determinism cannot be shared without reservation, the use he made of it as an instrument of criticism encouraged us to hope that methodological principles might have a useful regulative function.

My own contention was that the very principles of scientific method are themselves to be regarded as provisional and subject to later correction, so that a definition of "scientific method" would be verifiable, in some wide sense of the term. To the degree that the definition is framed in the light of our best reflection about past knowledge-seeking activities, with the intention that it shall guide our further pursuit of knowledge in the future, we can properly claim that the procedure is rational. For to be rational is to be always in a position to learn more from experience.

[23]

II

Definition, Presupposition, and Assertion

1. WHENEVER I speak of "definition" in this essay, I shall mean an explanation of the uses of some word or expression. In one case to be considered, the definition is a way of teaching somebody how to use the *definiendum;* in another the intention is to give an explicit description or analysis of the meaning of some word or expression with whose uses one is already familiar.

When logicians speak of the definition of a term, they usually have in mind analysis or description of that term's connotation. A characteristic statement is "To define a term is to state its connotation, or to enumerate the attributes it implies. Thus we define a parallelogram as a quadrilateral figure whose sides are parallel." [1] In this type of definition, we are supposed to "state" the connotation by successively dividing an inclusive genus into progressively narrower subspecies. Such a definition provides a necessary and sufficient condition for the application of the term: thus a thing is properly called a parallelogram if and only if that thing is a quadrilateral figure and also has parallel sides. Another way of putting the matter is that the things to which the term applies (i.e., its extension) constitute a sharply delineated class: everything that exists must be either wholly inside the class of parallelograms or wholly outside it. The necessary and sufficient criterion for application of the term "parallelogram" provides a conclusive test for membership in the extension of that term, i.e., for membership in the corresponding class.

It is no accident that favorite examples of this traditional

[1] J. E. Creighton and H. R. Smart, *An Introductory Logic* (New York, 1932), p. 81.

type of definition *per genus et differentiam* are drawn from mathematics. For in a calculus such definitions are often practicable and useful. Because the terms of such a calculus are "uninterpreted," the rules connecting them can be as clearcut as the rules of chess. But as soon as we pass from "pure" to "applied" mathematics, it is hard to find a single accurate and useful definition of the traditional type. The kind of definition that consists in giving the connotation of a term in the form of a necessary and sufficient condition determining a class, far from being normal or customary, is something exceptional and remarkable.

Consider the problems that arise in defining the meaning of a name for some breed of animal. Suppose we had to explain the meaning of the word "dachshund" to somebody not already acquainted with those agreeable little beasts or with the name applied to them. It is unlikely that a dictionary definition like "one of a German breed of small hounds with a long body and very short legs" would be satisfactory. For a man who had mastered this definition could hardly be expected to recognize a dachshund when he met one. At first sight, a basset hound may resemble a dachshund, and the dictionary definition of the former as "a long-bodied short-legged dog resembling a dachshund but larger and heavier" will not help us much in distinguishing between an oversized dachshund and an undersized basset.

Somebody might be inclined to say that the dictionary definitions are simply poor as definitions and that sufficient ingenuity would provide a satisfactory definition of the traditional type. But if we really wanted to teach the use of the word, a more fruitful procedure would surely be the *exhibition of specimens;* this is how all of us in fact learn to use words like "dachshund," "spaniel," or "bulldog." A successful explanation of this kind will usually require the presentation of a wide range of variation in the specimens, in order to diminish the risk that adventitious common features might be supposed significant. On the other hand, it will be unwise to exhibit abnormal or exceptional specimens: the object is to have an extensive range of variation grouped around some *clear cases*.[2]

The "clear cases" may themselves show considerable variation. The learner may be shown a wire-haired or a smooth dachshund or, again, dachshunds of various colors, all of them being presented as equally good "clear cases."

Part of such a definition of the word "dachshund" might take the following form: "This dog and that one and that one are *clear cases* of a dachshund. This one is very nearly a clear case, but has such and such a deviation. This other one is still further removed from being a perfectly clear case. And this one is a borderline specimen and could be called a dachshund or a basset indifferently." The specimens by means of which the meaning of the label "dachshund" is explained are presented in an *order*, determined by the degree of deviation from one or more specimens that are introduced as typical or "clear cases."

Such exhibition of specimens is usually intended to result in the knowledge of *criteria* for application of the word "dachshund," for otherwise the learner will find it hard to apply the label to new cases.[3] However, the demand for a *necessary and sufficient* criterion is too exacting.

All kinds of features are relevant to the claim that a particular dog is a dachshund—its length, weight, the texture and color of its coat, the relative proportion of its legs to the rest

---

[2] Occasionally it might seem more natural to speak of "normal," "standard," "central," "perfect," or "ideal" specimens. I shall not consider the different varieties of definition that some of these words suggest. I shall use "typical case," throughout, as a synonym for "clear case."

[3] By a "criterion" I mean a test which can be used in determining whether the word in question should be rightly applied to a given specimen. Such a test will normally mention some character (or "constitutive factor" as we shall later call it) that the specimen is required to have. Thus, one criterion for the application of the word "dachshund" is that the specimen be within a given size range. In the case of some relatively simple words, however, it would be inappropriate to speak of criteria. It seems impossible to formulate any criterion for the use of the word "mauve" or other color words.

[26]

of its body, and so on. If *all* these features are within certain ranges of variation, we have a typical dachshund (a "clear case"); if any of them are outside the corresponding range of variation, the animal falls short, in that respect, of complete conformity to the type. No one of these criteria is by itself necessary, nor is any one of them sufficient, and the same is true of any simple conjunctive or disjunctive combination of the criteria. The animals we call "dachshunds" have no common "attribute," and there is, strictly speaking, no class of dachshunds. Instead of a sharp boundary between dachshunds and other animals, we have what has been called a "borderline region"—a kind of no-man's-land where deviation from typical specimens of the breed is so great that the question whether given animals belong to the breed is no longer determinate. But there is no sharp line between the "borderline region" and the field of clear application.

It is customary to represent the relation of a class of things to the rest of the universe by a circle or some other closed curve. Points inside the circle and on its circumference represent members of the class in question, while points outside the circle represent things excluded from that class. The fact that every point in the diagram is either inside or outside the circle accurately reflects the conception of a class as determined by a strict dichotomy.

For a spatial representation of the mutual relations of the things referred to by a word like "dachshund," we may think of the way in which a mountain range gradually merges into the plains to which it descends. The summits may be taken to correspond to the typical or "clear" cases, while the region where the mountain eventually becomes indistinguishable from the surrounding plains represents the "borderline region." The corresponding geometrical diagram will be a *surface*. Among the many forms which such a surface might take, the case of a "tableland" or "mesa" with precipitous bounding faces will correspond to the special case of a *class term*. I propose to say that the individual dachshunds constitute a *range*, rather than a class, of instances.

[27]

It might be thought that the reason there is no necessary and sufficient criterion for the application of the word "dachshund" is its imprecise use by laymen who lack the specialized knowledge needed for the substitution of a more precise word. But the more detailed specifications formulated by breeders reveal essentially the same logical situation. In place of my vague references to length, weight, and so on (which betrayed my own ignorance of the breed in question) we find more detailed instructions concerning the traits and features that must be displayed by a satisfactory specimen of the breed. These criteria, however, are still very numerous, admit of variation in the degree to which they are met, and no simple conjunctive or disjunctive combination [4] of them is both necessary and sufficient. Nor is this due to ineptitude on the part of breeders and dog fanciers. The quest for a definition *per genus et differentiam* would be futile in view of the purposes the definition has to serve. The flexibility of even the technical use of the breed name is demanded by the complexity and variability of the phenomena to be described. Absence of a necessary and sufficient criterion is not a symptom of inadequacy of the language, but accurately reflects the complexity and continuous variability of the subject matter to which the language refers.

The nonexistence of rigidly demarcated classes is not a special and peculiar by-product of canine promiscuity. If we examine instances of the application of any biological term, we shall find ranges, not classes—specimens arranged according to the degree of their variation from certain typical or "clear" cases. And the same is true, so far as I can see, of all the familiar terms of the arts and crafts, of law, politics, education, and aesthetics. Nor are the technical terms of philosophy different in this respect. Variability of joint criteria of application, the existence of ranges, not classes, of instances seems to me to be the rule, not the exception.

---

[4] It may be that *some* complex truth function of the desired characters will prove roughly adequate. But such a combination of characters will hardly answer to the demands of the traditional classificatory definition, nor will it include any indication of the relative "weight" of the factors.

According to the account I have been giving, "range definition," as I propose to call it, requires the exhibition or delineation of one or more typical, or "clear" cases. Such cases I propose to call *"paradigms."* The traits or features or properties that vary from instance to instance, and are described in what I have been calling the "criteria" for application of the term, I shall call *"constitutive factors."* I have already proposed that the things to which the term is applied be called a "range"; it will be convenient to say that a word whose instances constitute a range is a *"range word."*

Range words may sometimes be combined to provide what at first sight appears to be a traditional classificatory definition. For a suitable hearer, "bitch" might be simply defined as "female dog." Since both "dog" and "female" are range terms, their combination determines a range also, not a class. The definition tells us, very roughly, how to combine the criteria used in identifying the two ranges, in such a way as to provide criteria for the subrange "bitch." (We notice, however, that if A is a criterion for "dog" and B a criterion for "female," the conjunction $A.B$ is not necessarily a criterion—or a criterion with the same "weight"—for "bitch." For the nature and relative importance of the criteria by which sex is determined vary with different species of animals.)

A formal range definition of a word W might take the following form: (a) one or more paradigms, $P_1, P_2, P_3, \ldots P_m$ are presented or described, (b) a set of constitutive factors, $F_1, F_2, F_3, \ldots F_m$, all capable of variation and all present in one or other of the paradigms, are indicated or described, (c) rules are formulated for determining how variations in the constitutive factors determine the degree of "distance" from the various paradigms.

This is an idealized description of what would usually be regarded as a satisfactory range definition. In actual practice, we are content with something less precise. Not all the relevant constitutive factors will be explicitly symbolized or described; nor will it usually be possible to give very exact instructions for arranging instances in the order of their distance from the paradigms. In short, the expression "range definition" is itself a range term.[5]

I hope the example of the word "dachshund" will have sufficiently indicated what I would accept as a clear case of a range definition.

2. When we teach a man the meaning of the word "dachshund," we take it for granted that he has a good deal of elementary but relevant knowledge about the behavior of dogs and other animals. For example, we expect him to know that the traits of an animal vary continuously during its lifetime —that leopards do not change their spots, and lions never change into tigers. So far as I can see, no *reference* to such approximate constancy of traits is part of the meaning of the

[5] The only previous discussion I have been able to find of something approximating this kind of definition is in J. N. Keynes's *Formal Logic* (Cambridge, 1928): "Men form classes out of vaguely recognised resemblances long before they are able to give an intensive definition of the class-name, and in such a case if they are asked to explain their use of the name, their reply will be to enumerate typical examples of the class. This would no doubt ordinarily be done in an unscientific manner, but it would be possible to work it out scientifically. The extensive definition of a name will take the form: *X is the name of the class of which* Q_1, Q_2, . . . , Q_n *are typical.* This primitive form of definition may also be called *definition by type*" (p. 34). L. S. Stebbing objects to this: "It may, however, be doubted whether the giving of typical examples can be rightly regarded as a process of defining" (*A Modern Introduction to Logic* [London, 1930], p. 422).

Cf. also the following statement: "The conformity of an individual to the type of a particular species depends on the fulfilment of an infinity of correlated peculiarities, structural and functional, many of which, so far as we can see (like keenness of scent and the property of perspiring through the tongue in dogs), have no connexion one with another. There may be deviations from the type, to a greater or less degree, in endless directions; and we cannot fix by any hard-and-fast rule the amount of deviation consistent with their being of that species, nor can we enumerate all the points, of function or structure, that in reality enter into the determination of things of a kind. Hence for definition, such as we have it in geometry, we must substitute classification; and for the demonstration of properties, the discovery of laws" (H. W. B. Joseph, *Introduction to Logic* [2d ed.; Oxford, 1925], p. 103).

[30]

word "dachshund" or other breed names. Yet this fact about the continuity of traits plays an important part in determining the application of the range term "dachshund," as the following considerations will show.

Consider what we should say if a dog that satisfied all the tests for being a clear case of a dachshund were gradually to change until it were indistinguishable from a poodle, and then back again until it looked exactly like a dachshund! Should we feel justified in continuing to call it a dachshund? And should we be speaking correctly if we did? If I am right in thinking that reference to the continuity and constancy of traits is not part of the meaning of "dachshund," we can hardly regard this queer kind of a dog as a "borderline case." Our dachshund-poodle or poodle-dachshund still exemplifies in eminent degree all the constitutive factors we have in mind in using the word "dachshund"; and the case is unlike that of a deformed puppy or "sport," deviating so far from the "clear cases" as to fall within the penumbra of vagueness. If we forget its curious history, we have an animal that ought to rank as an excellent specimen of the breed. Nevertheless, I think we should be right to refuse to apply the word "dachshund" in this type of case.[6]

The uses of the word "dachshund" were taught to us on the assumption that the fantastic case I have just been describing never happens. And if such a case were to happen, the correct verdict would be that no provision was made for it in the original process of definition. It would be wrong to say of such an extraordinary freak, "This *is* a dachshund," and equally wrong to say, "This is *not* a dachshund"—unless the negative statement was used to mean that the word "dachshund" had no application to the situation. (Of course, a man might say, "This *is* a dachshund," in an attempt to enforce a change in the meaning of the word, but I am excluding this type of case.)

The correct judgment would be that such a freak, not hav-

---

[6] But contrast Locke's discussion of monsters in Bk. III, ch. vi, sec. 27, of the *Essay*. Also Leibniz' *New Essays Concerning the Human Understanding*, Bk. III, ch. vi (e.g., p. 344 of the Open Court edition).

ing been considered when the definition was framed, falls on that account *outside the jurisdiction* of the definition. The question whether or not such an extraordinary object is a dachshund *does not arise,* because anybody who uses the term "dachshund" according to the usual definition is committed to taking for granted that such extraordinary cases do not occur. (It would be rather odd to say that we normally *believe* in the absence of such aberrant cases, since we very likely have not considered the question. But *if* the question were put, it would be answered unhesitatingly.)

Suppose I bet a dollar that a certain coin will show heads after being flipped into the air, i.e., promise to pay a dollar if it shows tails, in consideration of receiving a dollar if it shows heads. We can imagine that, by some extraordinary chance, the coin in question lands and remains *on edge.* Is either party then obligated to pay any sum? Clearly not. This type of case was not considered in the framing of the conditions regulating the bet. The terms of the wager were framed upon the supposition that the coin would show either heads or tails upon landing. If the coin lands on its edge, or is swallowed by some hungry bird, or explodes in mid air, or suffers one of the other fantastic and unlikely mischances that were too absurd to have been discussed when we made the bet—why then the bet "is off," as we say. The terms of the wager become null and void, for failure of one of the suppositions whose truth had been taken for granted. It has long been recognized that bets, promises, commands, and other such linguistic acts may depend upon suppositions, in the sense that they become "null and void" if those suppositions prove false. It has not been so clearly recognized that definitions also may become null and void for precisely similar reasons. The example I have given provides a case of this kind, I believe, in which the form of words "This is a dachshund" fails to have a good use, not because it contains a nonsense word like "Snark," and not on account of overt or concealed contradiction, and not, finally, because the instance in question is a borderline specimen. The expression "This is a dachshund" fails to have a predetermined use because the case in question violates one of the conditions determining the kind of case in which either that expression or its logical negation is properly applicable.

The example I have been using was one in which the assumption or supposition upon which the definition was based took the form of a claim about a certain regularity of occurrence in the constitutive factors (the physical traits of a dachshund). The following example illustrates the case of a supposition concerning relations between two or more of the constitutive factors.

In diagnosing a disease, a physician will pay attention both to the observable condition of the patient's body (his temperature, pulse rate, and so on) and to the feelings of pain or discomfort reported by the patient. Features of the conditions of the patient's body and features of his experiences are constitutive factors of such a term as "scarlet fever." Consider now the predicament of a physician who finds a patient exhibiting all the *outward* symptoms of an acute case of scarlet fever, while professing to feel in perfect health. The doctor might be inclined to cry out, incredulously, "This kind of thing just doesn't happen!"—as indeed it does not. And this is one reason why it is a case outside the scope of the name "scarlet fever." It would be wrong to say the patient had scarlet fever, and wrong to say he did not have scarlet fever—just as wrong as to answer the question "Have you stopped beating your mother?" either in the affirmative or in the negative.

Part of the medical definition of scarlet fever might be put in the form: "Scarlet fever is shown by the presence of such and such feelings, and such and such bodily manifestations, *the two occurring together*." Here the words "the two occurring together" express what I have been calling a "supposition" of the definition—the assumption violated in the instance I have conjured up.

Consider, for a last example, the case of a student of theology who believes that there is a Being who is omnipotent *because* he is omniscient. And let us suppose that he gives the name "God" to this Being, so that the definition of that word as he uses it is "the Being who is omnipotent because omniscient." Such a man would believe, I am supposing, that omniscience necessarily confers omnipotence and that omnipotence is impossible without omniscience. He would, therefore, use omniscience or omnipotence indifferently as criteria for application of the word "God." Now let us suppose that further studies led the theologian to revise his original belief by substituting for it the belief that there was a Being who was omniscient but not, however, omnipotent. This discovery might easily appear as a logical contradiction. Qua omniscient, the Being whose existence has now been discovered should be called "God," but qua non-omnipotent he is not "God." However, there is no contradiction. The situation is that a supposition for the use of the name "God" (viz., that a Being who is omniscient will necessarily also be omnipotent) has here been abandoned, and the name no longer has its original use. Whenever a supposition as to the correlation of constitutive factors is falsified, a self-contradiction will seem to result. This appearance is produced by an effort to apply a word in its original meaning to a case outside the scope of that meaning.

Normally, the "suppositions" involved in a range definition are not explicitly stated. When they are accepted by both parties, it is unnecessary to allude to them, and only the new stipulations needed for the definition are stated in so many words. But if the suppositions were explicitly formulated, they would naturally be expressed in a kind of *preamble*. Such an explicit definition would then have the form: "Whereas such and such is the case, therefore the word *W* shall be applied in such and such ways." Here the first clause ("Whereas such and such is the case") is what I have called the preamble.

The proposition expressed by the preamble and any logical consequences of that proposition I propose to call, from now on, *presuppositions* of the word in question. Thus it is a presupposition of the word "dachshund" that breed characters are approximately constant; it is a presupposition of the name "scarlet fever" that the condition of a patient's body is correlated with that patient's feelings; it was a presupposition of the term "God," in the use described, that any Being who was omniscient would be omnipotent. It will be noticed that, according to the above definition, a presupposition of a word is always a proposition, i.e., something that is true or false—and not itself a word.

Of course, the relation expressed by the words "Whereas . . . therefore," is quite different from the relations of material implication or entailment. The words following "Whereas," i.e., the "preamble," express a practical consideration or reason for framing the definition as we do. The definition does not *follow* from the presuppositions of the word defined, nor do the presuppositions follow from the definition.

Though I introduced the foregoing analysis by referring to a case in which a word, "dachshund," was supposed to need explanation for the benefit of somebody unacquainted with its meaning, I have gradually shifted to talking about definitions describing the meaning of a name such as "scarlet fever" or "God" whose use is already known. Indeed, the distinctions proposed will apply just as well to the latter type of case as to the former. In the case of any range word whose use we know, say the word "happiness," we may ask such questions as: "What would be paradigms (or clear cases) of happiness?" "By what criteria do we judge the relative degrees of deviation from these paradigms?" "How are these criteria related?" "What are the presuppositions of the word *happiness?*" In the case of a word like "happiness," the answers to such questions as these might be said—at any rate by some philosophers—to constitute an analysis rather than a definition. But this distinction is unimportant for the present discussion.

Questions may arise as to the meaning of whole sentences, as well as the words composing such sentences; and some words are of such a character that their meaning can be explained only by reference to the meaning of sentences in which those words can occur. Our account can be easily adapted to apply to sentences, as well as to words. The "ranges" will now be ranges of situations, rather than things. By the presuppositions of a sentence will be meant a proposition expressed by the "preamble" of an explanation of the meaning of that sentence and all the logical consequences of that proposition. If a presupposition of a word W is falsified, it becomes impossible to say, of the instance falsifying it, either that it is W or that it is not W. Similarly, if a presupposition of a sentence is falsified in a given situation, it becomes impossible in that situation either to say that the sentence expresses a true proposition or that it does not; the question of truth or falsity simply fails to arise.

Some of the presuppositions of a sentence are sometimes shown by explicit symbolic devices. Thus among the presuppositions of the sentence "Napoleon met the Czar of Russia" are the propositions *that somebody called "Napoleon" once existed, that there is a country called "Russia," that Russia had one and only one Czar,* and so on. Of these presuppositions, the last is explicitly symbolized by the occurrence of a descriptive phrase of the form "the so and so." [7]

In criticizing a particular philosophical argument, it may be more important to examine the presuppositions of the terms used than to try to refute the considerations advanced in support of the conclusion. Indeed, if the preferred terminology of the author is accepted by the critic, there may remain little scope for radical disagreement about the position in question. Consider, for instance, the difference between arguing about logical topics (a) in terms of "*L*-truth," (b) in terms of "warranted assertibility." Can this be one reason why philosophers so often complain that their critics have failed to understand them? [8]

[7] Cf. P. F. Strawson, "On Referring," *Mind,* 59 (1950): 320–344, and especially p. 330.

[8] It is instructive to read in this connection Royce's article, "On Definitions and Debates" in *Journal of Philosophy,* 9 (1912), reprinted in *Royce's Logical Essays,* ed. D. S. Robinson (Dubuque, Iowa, 1951). The American Philosophical Association had set up a distinguished "Committee on Definitions" to fix the terms of a general discussion, "The Relation of Consciousness and Object in Sense Perception." Royce argues, in persuasive and sometimes amusing detail, that the definitions chosen all presuppose that a "complex of physical qualities" could be "given in some

In order to simplify the discussion, I have sometimes spoken as if the words, expressions, and sentences used for illustration had the same meaning for all their users, so that we might properly speak of "*the* definition" or "*the* analysis" of *the* meaning of the words in question. Of course, the true situation is usually more complicated. Even a relatively unambiguous word like "dachshund" will be used by different speakers at the same time, or by the same speaker at different times, in divergent senses.

When different users of the word succeed in defining a term according to the pattern I have been describing, any divergences in their uses will result in divergences between the various definitions. These may take a number of alternative forms. There may be disagreement about the choice of paradigms, or about the nature of the relevant constitutive factors, or about the rules determining the contribution of the factors to the ordering of specimens with regard to the paradigms, or finally with regard to the choice of presuppositions of the word or sentence in question. In order to have a determinate answer to the question "What is the definition of the word W?" we must specify *what usage* of the word W we have in mind. Conversely, a range definition is a way of rendering more specific one use among many of the word in question.

3. I want now to use the foregoing theory in trying to become clearer about the notion of "assertion." The word "assertion," and the related and equally troublesome word "proposition," are constantly used by philosophers, but it is not clear what is meant, or intended to be meant, by either word.

The technical term "assert" is connected with the more inclusive layman's word "say." To assert something is to *say* something, in one use of the elusive term "say." I propose, therefore, to begin by making some obvious distinctions in the meaning of the latter word.

---

particular perception." Since Royce, like many other philosophers, could not accept this presupposition, it became impossible for him to participate in the discussion.

When a man says that fish are mammals, he may be doing one of four things:

(i) He may be simply uttering a set of noises which we should recognize as an instance of the sentence "Fish are mammals," without necessarily even understanding what he is saying. In this sense of "say," a man might say, "Fish are mammals," in his sleep, and a foreigner can say that fish are mammals without knowing the meaning of a single English word. A parrot might say the same thing, and perhaps even a phonograph. (For the sake of simplicity, I shall neglect, throughout this essay, the case of *written* discourse.)

(ii) A man may pronounce the words "Fish are mammals" as in (i) above and also understand what the words mean (i.e., mean something *by* them) and yet not be using the sentence to make any assertion. If a student has said, in class, "It is my opinion that fish are mammals," the lecturer may echo part of his remark, saying, with the same intonation and expression, "Fish are mammals. Let us consider this." Unlike the student, he is not *claiming* that fish are mammals. Or a man may practice a speech he has promised to make by saying aloud, with the intonation and expression appropriate to an assertion, the words "All men are equal!" Not until he actually makes the speech will he *claim* that all men are equal. An actor in a play understands what he says, but he is not taken by the audience to be claiming that anything is really the case. (All examples in the following discussion will be *declarative* sentences, but parallel distinctions could be made for commands, requests, questions, prayers, and other forms of speech. A man can utter the words "Open the door" without giving a command; he may utter the words "Is Pakistan a sovereign state?" without asking a question.)

(iii) Sometimes a man may utter the sentence "Fish are mammals" while disbelieving what he says, in order to deceive his hearers. He is then making a truth claim, though of course lying. It is customary to say of such a case as this that the speaker *asserts* that fish are mammals, whether he is lying or speaking truthfully.

[38]

(iv) Finally, men often make statements seriously, in good faith, knowing or believing what they say, or, at any rate, not disbelieving it. In such a case as this, I shall say the speaker *honestly asserts* that fish are mammals.

In talking about a man "saying" something, we may mean either that he is merely pronouncing a form of words, or uttering them with understanding, or making a truth claim by their means, or finally, making an honest assertion. Here we have four progressively narrower senses of "saying." I want to consider, in more detail, what we mean by an *honest* assertion. And for this purpose I shall begin by describing a paradigm for the application of the sentence "Tom honestly asserted that it had begun to rain."

The following simple train of events would certainly justify us in saying that Tom had honestly asserted it had begun to rain:

Mary, sitting with her back to the window, asks Tom, "How is the weather now?" Tom walks over to the window, draws the curtain, sees that rain is falling, and says, "It has begun to rain."

This is as clear and unproblematic a case of honest assertion as we can hope to find. But if we now try to analyze what we *mean* by calling it a case of honest assertion and begin by listing all the factors in the domestic episode that might plausibly be taken to be relevant, we may well be surprised at the number and variety of factors resulting. We shall certainly have to include, besides the mere pronouncing of the words in question, the speaker's linguistic background and knowledge of the particular setting. And these in turn can be broken down into a surprisingly large number of factors.

At the risk of being pedantic, we might obtain some such list as the following:

(1) Tom pronounced the words "It has begun to rain," (2) which were words belonging to the English language, (3) making up a complete sentence, (4) indeed a declarative sentence, (5) whose meaning he understood. (6) Those words meant that it had begun to rain, (7) and it had begun to rain. (8) Another per-

[39]

son, Mary, was present, (9) who had asked Tom a question, (10) to which his remark was an answer. (11) The speaker, Tom, remembered the question, (12) knew that his hearer, Mary, was in the room, (13) believed that Mary could hear him, (14) intended to use the words "It has begun to rain," (15) intended them to mean what they usually mean, (16) intended to be heard, (17) believed that it had begun to rain, (18) intended his words to be understood, (19) in the sense in which he used them, (20) and intended to be believed.

One might be reluctant to believe that all these listed factors could be relevant to the truth claim we make when we say that Tom honestly asserted it had begun to rain. For example, some people might say that the prior question addressed to the speaker was merely a cause or reason for his assertion, and no part of what we mean when we say that he made the assertion in question. I am far from wanting to argue that an honest assertion must always be preceded by a question to which it is an answer. But *if* such a question has been asked, it is then relevant to our verdict that a subsequent assertion *has* been made.

Suppose, for example, that after Mary has asked, "How is the weather now?" Tom, walking over to the window as before, says, "Tomorrow is Tuesday." The fact that what he said was *not* an answer to the preceding question would make it appear doubtful that he *was* honestly asserting anything. His hearer would naturally suppose that he could not have heard the question right, or that he was joking or indulging in a piece of silly mystification. Or consider a case in which two men have been walking in the rain for a good hour after the rain has started, and one of them then turns to the other, saying, "It has begun to rain." The hearer would not know what to make of this remark—its inappropriateness to the general context would lead him to question whether anything could have been honestly asserted. He would fail to understand what had been said, in one important sense of "understand," though in another sense of "understand" he would perfectly well understand the meaning of the words used.

[40]

I hope enough has been said to indicate, at least in outline, how I would go about trying to show that a great many factors were relevant to the claim that Tom had honestly asserted that it had begun to rain.

So far we have been talking about a single, relatively determinate, situation and the features of the situation that are relevant to the claim that an honest assertion has been made. If, however, we say, "Tom honestly asserted that it had begun to rain," without specifying any particular context of utterance, any one of a wide range of situations would justify our claim. Tom might not have used just those words, "It has begun to rain," but some other sentence; he might have used the single word "Rain!" and not a sentence at all; might have made the corresponding remark in French or some other language; or might simply have used some prearranged signal or gesture. No preceding question need have been asked; the speaker might have made a mistake in supposing somebody was present or that he could have been heard; indeed nobody but the speaker need have been present. The speaker might not have intended to say anything, but found himself blurting out the words; might have been telling the truth while knowing it would inevitably deceive his hearer; and so on, through a whole gamut of variations.

This is how I would try to show that none of the relevant factors is *necessary* for there to be a situation which we should want to describe as one in which Tom honestly asserted that it had begun to rain. However, I do not wish to overemphasize the variety of these situations. My chief contention is that these various, yet related, situations can be organized in terms of their deviation from central cases or "paradigms."

It may be objected that I have not *proved* there is no necessary and sufficient factor present in all cases of honest assertion that it has begun to rain. But if anybody thinks there *is* such an invariable index of honest assertion, he may be challenged to describe it. There is, of course, a certain conventional way of pronouncing a sentence—an "assertive tone of voice," as we might say—which we often use as a reliable sign that something has been asserted. But a man can assert that it has begun to rain without using words at all, and hence without using an assertive tone of voice. On the other hand, one may say, "The boojum is a snark," in an assertive tone of voice and be making no assertion whatever.

The attempt to find a necessary and sufficient factor in a supposed characteristic attitude on the part of the speaker is equally doomed to failure. Suppose somebody said, "To assert that it has begun to rain is to pronounce the words, 'It has begun to rain,' or some sign having the same meaning, in an assertive tone of voice and *with intention*. The speaker has to intend or 'mean' what he says. To assert honestly is to assert while believing what one is asserting." The chief difficulty about this objection to the view I am advocating is that "intending," like all other psychological words, is itself what I have previously called a range word. The word refers not to a class of cases having a common identifiable character, but to a whole spectrum of instances related to one another by gradually shifting criteria.

A clear case of intending to say, "It has begun to rain," would be the following. Our old friends, Tom and Mary, have quarreled so violently that they have not spoken to one another for several days. Now Tom wants to heal the breach and says to himself, "The very first time Mary asks a question, I intend to answer it." Then Mary asks, "How is the weather now?" and the action proceeds as before.

Here is a clear case of intention, a paradigm. Tom has considered the matter, formulated a prior resolution, and has carried that resolution into effect. But now suppose somebody simply asks me, in a more normal situation, what the weather is. I would probably reply, "It has begun to rain," without taking any particular thought and certainly without needing to screw my resolution to the sticking point. Here there is nothing, over and above my honestly making the assertion, that could properly be called my *intending* to make the assertion. I simply said what I did, and the fact that I did say it in the circumstances in question is a proof that I "intended" to say it, in the peculiar sense of "intended" that is relevant. We do not usually say that a child who alters the position of a chess piece on a chess board, but knows nothing about the purpose or the rules of the game of chess, has "really" made a move. But when an experienced chess player is playing a game, his making *exactly the same maneuver* as the child counts as a move. There is no reason to believe that each move in a game of chess is accompanied by a specific attitude or intention on the part of the player who makes the move. Similarly, given certain surrounding circumstances, the proof that a man made an assertion may be that he simply pronounced certain words; and whether or not he had any concomitant mental attitude may be irrelevant.

I want to consider now some of the presuppositions governing the usage of the expression "honestly asserts." Examination of the factors relevant to the correct application of the sentence "Tom asserted that it had begun to rain" would show that these factors could be roughly separated into three groups. In the first group we can put whatever the speaker finally *did*, i.e., in this case his pronouncing the words in question in an assertive tone of voice. Let us call this his *performance*. In the second group let us put all factors which refer to the speaker's feelings, memories, intentions, at the time of his performance, insofar as they are relevant. Let us call these factors, collectively, the speaker's *mental state*. (This is not a very happy term, but I think its meaning here will be sufficiently understood.) Finally, let us lump together everything else, relevant to the claim that Tom asserted it had begun to rain, by calling the remaining factors, collectively, the *context*. The context of our original paradigm included, e.g., Tom's having been asked a question, the fact that it was raining, and so on.

Now while the speaker's performance, his mental state, and the context are all relevant to the claim that he honestly made a certain assertion, I think we commonly expect there to be certain causal connections between them. We normally suppose that if a man pronounces the words "It is raining now" in an assertive tone of voice, and in the context previously described, that is a sufficient sign that he is in the corresponding mental state. It would seem pointless in this familiar type of case to require additional evidence that he has the beliefs, intentions, purposes, and so on, which would be appropriate; his performance in that context is excellent evidence that he is in the requisite mental state. Only in abnormal cases where the performance is very remote from our paradigms, or the context is of a character with which we are unfamiliar, do we find it necessary to inquire into the speaker's mental state. Only in such atypical cases do we find it necessary to ask questions like "What was he trying to say?" "What could he have had in mind?" "What could he have supposed to be the case?" "What was his purpose?"—all directed toward elucidating what I have called the speaker's "state of mind."

One general presupposition of the term "honestly assert" accordingly takes the form "Given such and such a context, the speaker's performance will signify that he is in such and such a mental state." Accordingly the criteria we use in central and typical cases have reference mainly to performance and context, and not to the mental state that is supposed to be correlated with them.[9]

So far, I have been discussing the meaning of the term *"honestly* assert." I have chosen to do this rather than to begin by considering the term "assert," because I think assertion can easily be explained in terms of honest assertion, while the reverse is not the case. A speaker who asserts, but does not honestly assert, what he says is lying. He is *pretending* to make an honest assertion in a case in which he disbelieves what he is saying. If we understand what it is to make an honest assertion, and what it is to pretend to do something, we can derive a sufficiently clear notion of what it is to make a show of honestly asserting, that is to say, what it is to lie. On the other hand, the expression "honest assertion" does suggest that "honest assertion" stands for a subrange of a wider range of situa-

[9] When this presupposition is violated, we get paradoxical utterances, as in the case of a man who says something of the form "p, but I don't believe it." See the next essay.

tion called "assertion." If this suggestion were correct, it ought to be possible *first* to describe a range of situations that are what we would want to call assertions (whether honest or dishonest) and then to select from these a subrange to which we give the name "honest assertion." This, however, seems to me to be an inversion of the proper order of definition of the two terms. I cannot see how to describe what we mean when we talk about cases of lying except by saying something like, "Lying occurs when a man tries to give the illusion that he is telling the truth, i.e., that he is honestly asserting something." If this is correct, we need to understand what it is to speak truthfully before we can understand what it is to lie; we must define "honestly assert" before we can define "assert."

We do, in fact, learn to understand language in our infancy because adults begin by telling the truth to us, however much they may afterward use language for deception. A society in which parents constantly lied to their children from the outset, and in unpredictable ways, would be one in which, so far as I could see, it would be logically impossible for the next generation to learn the language. The connection between the words, the environment, and the normal human purposes of the speakers would be destroyed, and for those newcomers to the society who had no previous memories of truthtelling to fall back upon, the words they heard could have no meaning.

III

Saying and Disbelieving

IF THOMAS were to say, "Mushrooms are poisonous, but I don't believe it," would he be contradicting himself? This question has been discussed by many writers,[1] all of whom agree that no self-contradiction would occur. According to them Thomas expresses the very same proposition that would be expressed if somebody else were to say, "Mushrooms are poisonous, but Thomas does not believe that they are." The latter proposition is obviously not self-contradictory, and might very well be true; mushrooms might really be poisonous and Thomas need not believe that they are.

Those who have discussed the question agree, however, that it would be "perfectly absurd"[2] for Thomas to make such a remark, and they give a number of explanations of the source of this absurdity. It seems to me that all these accounts contain the same mistake: in arguing that Thomas would be expressing the same proposition that would be expressed by the sentence referring to Thomas by his name, they all assume that he would be expressing *some* proposition, and that he would, therefore, be making an *assertion*. I think this is wrong, and I shall try to show why.

I shall begin by considering what Moore says. His view is that when Thomas pronounces the words "Mushrooms are

---

[1] A. M. MacIver, "Some Questions about 'Know' and 'Think,'" *Analysis*, 5 (1937–1938): 43–50. G. E. Moore, *Ethics* (London, 1912), p. 125. *The Philosophy of G. E. Moore*, ed. P. A. Schilpp (Evanston, Ill., 1942), pp. 541–543. *The Philosophy of Bertrand Russell*, ed. P. A. Schilpp (Evanston, Ill., 1944), pp. 203–204. See also, C. H. Langford in *The Philosophy of G. E. Moore*, pp. 332–333, Y. Bar-Hillel in *Mind*, 55 (1946): 333–337, P. F. Strawson in *Mind*, 59 (1950): 330–333, Norman Malcolm in *Philosophical Analysis*, ed. M. Black (Ithaca, N.Y., 1950): pp. 259–261.

[2] See the next quotation from Moore.

poisonous" his words "imply" that Thomas believes mushrooms to be poisonous. What the word "imply" means, Moore explains as follows:

There seems to be nothing mysterious about this sense of "imply" in which if you assert that you went to the pictures last Tuesday, you *imply*, though you don't *assert*, that you *believe* or know that you did; and in which, if you assert that Brutus' action was right, you *imply*, but don't *assert*, that you approve of Brutus' action. In the first case, that you do imply this proposition about your present attitude, although it is not implied by (i.e., does not follow from) *what* you assert, simply arises from the fact, which we all learn by experience, that in the immense majority of cases a man who makes such an assertion as this does believe or know what he asserts: lying, though common enough, is vastly exceptional. And this is why to say such a thing as "I went to the pictures last Tuesday, but I don't believe that I did" is a perfectly absurd thing to say, although what is asserted is something perfectly possible logically . . .[3]

In an earlier discussion, Moore says:

There is an important distinction, which is not always observed, between what a man *means* by a given assertion and what he *expresses* by it. Whenever we make any assertion whatever (unless we do not mean what we say) we are always *expressing* one or other of two things—namely, either that we *think* the thing in question to be so, or that we *know* it to be so.

And a few lines later, he adds:

Even when I do not mean what I say, my words may be said to *imply* either that I think that A is B or that I know it, since they will commonly lead people to suppose that one or other of these things is the case.[4]

Moore's latest statement of the point is as follows:

To say such a thing as "I believe he has gone out, but he has not" is absurd. This, though absurd, is not self-contradictory; for it may quite well be true. But it is absurd, because, by saying "he

[3] *The Philosophy of G. E. Moore*, pp. 542–543.

[4] *Ethics*, p. 125.

has not gone out" we *imply* that we do *not* believe that he has gone out, though we neither assert this, nor does it follow from anything we do assert. That we *imply* it means only, I think, something which results from the fact that people, in general, do not make a positive assertion, unless they do not believe that the opposite is true: people, in general, would not assert positively "he has not gone out", if they believed that he had gone out. And it results from this general truth, that a hearer who hears me say "he has not gone out", will, in general, assume that I don't believe he has gone out, although I have neither asserted that I don't, nor does it follow, from what I have asserted, that I don't. Since people will, in general, assume this, I may be said to *imply* it by saying "he has not gone out", since the effect of my saying so will, in general, be to make people believe it, and since I know quite well that my saying it will have this effect.[5]

From these remarks of Moore, we can derive the following explanation of the way in which he is here using the word "imply": Suppose (a) a speaker is using an expression, E, (b) people do not generally use E unless some related proposition p_E is true, (c) people hearing the speaker use the expression E will generally believe p_E to be true, and finally (d) the speaker knows all this—then if these four conditions are met, the speaker's words may be said to imply p_E.

The following examples will fit this explanation:

(i) A man will not normally say "Damn!" unless he is annoyed, and people hearing him swear will normally believe him to be annoyed, and he knows this; so if a man says "Damn!" he *implies* that he is annoyed.

(ii) Only a woman will normally say, "I am going to have my dress lengthened," and anybody hearing these words will believe that a woman is speaking, and the speaker herself knows this; so anybody using those words implies that she is a woman.

(iii) Nobody who utters an English sentence is usually unable to speak English, and this is a matter of common knowledge, both to the speaker and to his hearers; hence anybody

[5] *The Philosophy of Bertrand Russell,* p. 204.

who utters an English sentence *implies* that he can speak English.

(iv) If anybody makes any remark at all, he is normally awake, and people will know him to be awake and he knows that they will know it; so if I make any remark at all, I *imply* that I am awake.

If any of these implications happens to be false, then we must say that some more or less unusual event has occurred and that is all there is to it—a man has used an oath without being annoyed, or has talked about "my dress" although he is a man, or has uttered an English sentence without being able to speak English, or has been talking in his sleep.

On this view, what Thomas said, when he said, "Mushrooms are poisonous, but I don't believe it," was not self-contradictory, but only wildly implausible and contrary to what experience would lead us to expect. The absurdity of his remark is a *factual* absurdity, such as would be involved in saying: "I know my Christian name, but I simply cannot remember my surname" or "I feel perfectly well, yet I never sleep at all" or "The inside of my body is a vacuum." All of these remarks are wildly implausible; they are all absurd because they are incredible and known by the speaker to be incredible.

Moore said that lying—and we might add, joking—is "vastly exceptional." But the speaker might be a congenital liar like Pecksniff, so that we would be really amazed to find him telling the *truth*. Of course a man who says, "*p,* but I don't believe *p,*" immediately blows the gaff upon himself, and this is no doubt rarer than unabashed and unqualified lying—as rare, perhaps, as the spectacle of a man's walking on his hands. We might say that the absurdity of a man's walking on his hands arose from the apparent *pointlessness* of the performance; but if the man in question said that he was practicing acrobatics, we would understand the point of what he was doing, and would no longer describe his performance as absurd. But can we even imagine what it would be like for the utterance in good faith of "*p*, but I don't believe *p*" to have a point? If Moore is right, the mistake made by Thomas is in spinning a yarn which we normally have every reason to disbelieve; there is no logical discrepancy between the two clauses of Thomas' statement. In practice, however, we do treat the apparent discrepancy between "*p*" and "I believe that not-*p*" as a logical discrepancy. Suppose we hear a public speaker say, at one point in his remarks, "There will be another World War within a decade," and then hear the same speaker say, later on, "I believe there will not be another World War within the next ten years." It would be natural, and reasonable, to ask him to *reconcile* these two remarks; we treat each as telling against the truth of the other, and we assume that both ought not to be asserted simultaneously. Suppose now the speaker in question were to answer our demand by saying, "You know how irresponsible I am! I said there would be a war within ten years in order to shock the audience. But I don't really believe what I said, you know!" This explanation would tell us *why* he said what he did, and remove the surprise we may have felt at his saying it. Yet it would confer no license upon him to continue to assert both "*p*" and "I believe that not-*p*" in the future. To the charge that one assertion contradicts another, it is no defense to say, "I was lying when I said '*p*'." This may explain how the speaker came to say "*p*," and also "not-*p*"; it has no tendency at all to show the two propositions are consistent.

Moore's account assumed that somebody could at any rate *assert,* "I went to the pictures last Tuesday, but I don't believe that I did." This assumption needs to be examined. Let us first consider what our response would be if we heard somebody pronounce these words in an assertive tone of voice.

The first difficulty is to imagine any context in which this performance would not leave us flabbergasted and utterly at a loss to know what to think. Of course, philosophers can say anything, and if a member of the Aristotelian Society were overheard intoning these words, we might be sympathetic rather than surprised. But if an ordinary man in ordinary circumstances were to burst out with, "I went to the pictures last Tuesday, but I don't believe that I did," our best surmise might be that he was reciting a line of verse, or pulling our leg, or "simply saying the words" without meaning what he said. If he assured us that he was in earnest, however, and that he meant what he said; and if he even repeated the extraordinary remark with added vehemence, we might think a further effort of interpretation worth making.

Now ordinary language is so pliable that almost any sentence can be *made* to bear a meaning. A man who seriously said, "I went to the pictures yesterday, but I don't believe it," might mean something like this: "There is evidence to show that I went to the pictures yesterday (people claim to have seen me there, here is my ticket stub, etc.)—I suppose I must have been there—yet I can't remember a thing about it. I seem to remember playing chess that night—I still can't believe it."

In this interpretation, the words "I went to the pictures yesterday" have been replaced by the weaker sentence "I suppose I must have gone to the pictures yesterday," which *falls short* of making the original assertion. By weakening the first clause of the original paradoxical remark (and by changing "I don't" into "I can't"), we succeed in making good though unusual sense of that remark.

A psychologist or a philosopher might offer a second interpretation, somewhat on the following lines: "Yes, I went to the pictures yesterday. But I would hardly dignify my attitude toward that fact by using the impressive word 'belief.' I take the fact for granted, act as though it were a fact, but there's none of the effort and tension that are a sign of genuine active belief." In this interpretation, the second clause of the original paradoxical remark (i.e., "I don't believe I went to the pictures yesterday") has been given a weaker meaning than it would normally have. "I don't believe" has been construed as meaning the same as "I don't *actively* believe." This second interpretation, like the first, makes good, though still more unusual, sense of the original paradoxical remark.

[51]

Both interpretations are strained or forced. If we were to impose them on the speaker's words, we should be entertaining extraordinary hypotheses about what the speaker was trying to say. Only if we had some good independent reason to suppose he was speaking responsibly, would we feel justified in making such extraordinary efforts to make sense of what, on first hearing, was quite unintelligible.

Imagine now that the speaker rejects all such ingenious attempts to put a reasonable, if far-fetched, interpretation upon his language. Perhaps he retorts: "This is all very ingenious, but quite irrelevant. I meant exactly what I said, and I was using words in their familiar ordinary meanings. There is no question of mere evidence that I went to the pictures yesterday—I actually went. And I don't assume or take for granted that I did—I don't believe it, I actively *dis*believe it!" If this should happen, all that would be left for us to say would be the exasperated "He *can't* be serious." This is not an expression of incredulity, like the "I don't believe it" of the man who first met a giraffe. My contention is that it would be *wrong* to say that the original paradoxical remark was an assertion at all.

Let us consider, for the sake of comparison and contrast, the following case. A man, of average height, on being asked how tall he is, replies, apparently in all seriousness, "Two feet." Further investigation seems to show that he is not joking, that he means his words to be understood literally, in their familiar nonmetaphorical senses, that he clearly understood the original question, knows what he is saying, and so on. These considerations would incline us to say he *is* honestly asserting that he is two feet tall. On the other hand we would be just as strongly disinclined to say that he could be honestly asserting what he seemed to be asserting.

I have argued above [6] 'that it is a "presupposition" of the expression "honest assertion" that there shall be a certain accord between the speaker's performance (the words he uses) and his "state of mind" (among other things, his knowledge

[6] See the second essay of this book.

that he is not two feet tall). In an abnormal case like the present one in which the presupposition is falsified, the expression lacks a use, and the question whether or not an honest assertion was made fails to arise. This is what happens when a man of normal height says he is two feet tall.

Thus the sentence "He honestly asserted that he was two feet tall" has no application in the situation described. It would be wrong either to say that the speaker did honestly assert that he was two feet tall or that he did not honestly assert that he was two feet tall. It would be wrong to *use* the expression "honestly assert" at all in this case. (If we like, we can say that a case of a man's uttering the paradoxical sentence in the situation described is *not* a case of an honest assertion—provided we understand this to mean only that we cannot use the expression "honest assertion" for that type of case.)

If all else failed, we should probably say of a man who seemed to be honestly asserting he was two feet tall, in the circumstances described, that he must be insane. But this judgment would not be a clinical diagnosis (though the speaker's extraordinary remark might be the first entry in a medical dossier). Even if he never behaved otherwise than normally on all subsequent occasions, we should be tempted to say that he must have been *momentarily* insane. This is like saying that an act for which we have no explanation is "due to chance," where we provide only the illusion of an explanation. By shrugging the speaker off as insane, we excuse ourselves from having to choose between "He asserted" and "He did not assert"; we banish the instance from the realm of logical adjudication.

Parallel considerations apply to the case of a speaker who seems to be honestly asserting something expressed by the words "I went to the pictures yesterday, but I don't believe that I did" and to be using those words, nonfiguratively, in their ordinary senses. If evidence points to the man's being in earnest, understanding what he says, and so on, a presupposition of the term "honestly asserts" is falsified. It would be wrong to say that he made an honest assertion and wrong to deny that he made an honest assertion. And to say he must have been insane would be simply a way of parrying a demand to choose between the two judgments.

It seems to me that the meaning of the word "assertion" is to be understood in terms of the meaning of the expression "honest assertion," and not *vice versa*.[7] A man who lies is try-ing to deceive his hearers by behaving like somebody who makes an honest assertion. Now if it is improper to say that a man could make an honest assertion by means of a certain sentence, it would seem to follow that it must be improper to say that a man could lie when using that sentence. I hold, therefore, that it would be wrong to describe a normal man who said, "I am two feet tall," as lying, or, indeed, as making an assertion at all.

The sentence "I am two feet tall" might be used, in excep-tional circumstances, to make an honest assertion. A midget might say it, and a philosopher, who followed Alice down the rabbit hole, might have to say it. No circumstances can be described, however, in which it would be proper to make an honest assertion by means of the words "Oysters are edible, but I don't believe it"—to change the illustration—so long as those words were being used in their familiar ordinary senses.

I think we can see why the form of words "Oysters are edible, but I don't believe it" is always improper. When the words "Oysters are edible" are pronounced assertively, the tone of voice used, together with the choice of the appropriate copula ("are," not "may be," or "conceivably might be" or one of the other alternatives available) is a *conventional sign* of what we might call "good faith." In order to use the English language correctly, one has to learn that to pronounce the sentence "Oysters are edible" in a certain tone of voice is to *represent oneself* as knowing, or believing, or at least not dis-believing what is being said. (To write a check is to represent oneself as having money in the bank to honor the check.) Perhaps the tone in question was once the natural and un-

[7] See above, end of essay II.

[54]

tutored way in which conviction would manifest itself. But whether this is so or not, that tone has become a *conventional* sign. So that, whether the man who asserts "Oysters are edible" in fact believes what he is saying or is deliberately lying, he signifies that he knows, or believes, or at least does not disbelieve what he says. (If this were not so, lying would be more difficult than it is. A liar trades upon the conventional signification of his linguistic act to produce a deceptive impression.)

In saying that an utterance in a certain tone of voice *conventionally* signifies "good faith" on the speaker's part, I mean that the making of such an utterance in the absence of the corresponding knowledge or belief is properly treated as a violation of the language. If a man began a sentence with the words "After Columbus landed at San Salvador," while believing that Columbus never did land at San Salvador, he would be misusing the words as much as if he deliberately used the word "red" to describe something blue. A liar who speaks earnestly is faking a manifestation of belief (like a man who tries to appear younger by wearing a wig); but a man who says "*p*" while disbelieving *p* is misusing a conventional sign (like an unmarried woman who wears a wedding ring).

I have said that the speaker's words *signify* that he does not disbelieve what he says. It would be incorrect to say that he *asserts* this, since in such contexts we commonly use the word "assert" to refer only to what is explicitly formulated by a declarative sentence—or what is entailed by the proposition expressed. The speaker says (i.e., asserts) that oysters are edible (and whatever logically follows from the truth of that proposition) but nothing more. In this sense of "say," a man who utters a command has "said" nothing whatever, for he has not explicitly formulated any declarative sentence. Yet he has certainly *communicated* a certain wish by the use of a conventional sign. A certain tone of voice in conjunction with the choice of the imperative mood conventionally signifies that the speaker desires the action he is describing to be performed.

Logicians have almost invariably neglected the *significa-*

tion, as distinct from the *meaning*, of utterances, with the result that they have been led to overlook the possibility of conflicts between significations. If I say, "Close that door, but don't close it!" it would be improper to say that I am uttering a self-contradiction in the logician's sense of that term. Yet the utterance "Close that door!" contains a conventional sign whose signification is incompatible with the signification of "Do *not* close that door!" If I had said, "I want you to close that door, but I do not want you to close that door," there would be a plain logical contradiction in what I was saying. But part of the signification conventionally conveyed by the utterance "Close that door, but don't close it!" is exactly the same as would be conveyed by the self-contradictory indicative sentence. The two imperatives have *incompatible* significations.

Consider now our response to the words "Close that door! I don't want you to do it, however." Here we would properly regard the indicative sentence ("I don't want you to do it") as canceling the imperative—and if the command were to be reiterated we should be unable to make sense of the communication. There is a conflict here between the conventional signification of the imperative tone and the meaning of what is said by the indicative sentence that follows; the signification of the sign is incompatible with the meaning of the words. A similar case occurs when an attempt is made to use the words "Oysters are edible, but I don't believe that they are." The pronouncing of the first three words conventionally signifies that the speaker does not disbelieve what he says; this signification is incompatible with what is explicitly asserted by the clause that follows; hence the whole sentence fails to have a use.

It follows that to pronounce, in an assertive tone of voice, the sentence "Jones honestly asserted that he went to the pictures but that he did not believe that he went," without the intention of giving the words an unusual meaning, would be to *misuse* language. It would not be the kind of misuse involved in pronouncing assertively the words "Runcibles are chuffable"; nor the kind of misuse involved in saying, "Every triangle has exactly two sides"; nor the kind of misuse involved in announcing without qualification, "A virus is non-animate." It is not a case of nonsense, or logical contradiction, or unqualified application of a term to a borderline case. The sentence in question might be called "inoperative," because its truth would require the falsification of one of its own presuppositions. We could *give* it a sense, if we chose. But that would require a change in our language.

IV

The Language of Sense-Data

ALTHOUGH the term "sense-datum" has been in common use for forty years, its meaning is not altogether clear, even now. And this must be my excuse for this essay.

I shall try to explain how the use of a certain kind of "sense-datum language" might be taught. This will allow me to show some of the limitations of such a "language" and to express some doubts about its usefulness in discussing phenomenalism or other controversial topics in the theory of knowledge. Unhappily, sense-datum theorists do not agree among themselves, and I shall no doubt misrepresent some of their doctrines, in spite of my best endeavors to concentrate attention upon the common elements in their views.

I am going to suppose, then, that a sense-datum theorist has agreed to teach the uses of the term "sense-datum" to some layman—John Doe, let us say—who is quite unacquainted with the technical terms of epistemology. Before describing the form that such instruction might take, I shall digress, in order to remind my readers of some well-known features of the procedures involved in trying to teach somebody the use of a new and unfamiliar word. These reflections will provide us with a useful test of the extent to which the subsequent instructions for the use of "sense-datum" can be regarded as satisfactory.

Suppose one had to teach somebody how to use the word "jerboa." My dictionary contains the definition, "a small jumping rodent with long hind legs and a long tail." This is somewhat indefinite, and might perhaps be improved. No matter how good a definition were supplied, however, we would not be prepared to say that anybody had fully mastered the use of "jerboa" unless he could *recognize* a jerboa if he had occasion to see one. This might be tested at the zoo, or, if

[58]

this were too inconvenient, by a demonstration of ability to identify stuffed specimens or photographs. Given the appropriate situation, a man who knows how to use "jerboa" correctly should be able to say *"That* is a jerboa."

A man might be able to point out, recognize, or identify jerboas, after a fashion, without having mastered all the uses of "jerboa." He might be able to say, *"That* is a jerboa," with fair success, and yet have only the vaguest notion of what he *meant* by "jerboa." (Foreigners "pick up" many words in this way.) He might be helpless to define "jerboa"; perhaps he would not know the verbal contexts into which "jerboa" can be inserted without producing nonsense, or the kinds of inference to be drawn from true statements containing that word. In short, he might be able to point to jerboas, without having linked the word "jerboa" to the remainder of his working vocabulary. Let us say that he has learned an *ostensive rule* for the use of "jerboa," without having yet mastered the *syntactical rules* for the use of the word. (For brevity, I shall sometimes say "the grammar of *W,"* instead of "the syntactical rules for the use of *W."*)

In learning an ostensive rule for the use of a word, one inevitably learns a little of that word's grammar. An intelligent child whose elders point at a cage, saying, "That is a jerboa," will at once understand that they are pointing at an *animal,* and not at a tuft of grass or a rock. And this tells him something about the grammar of "jerboa," since to say, "A jerboa is a species of animal," would be to provide a syntactic rule. Again, the very form of words used with the pointing gesture (not to speak of the form of that gesture itself) tells him something about how the new word is to be combined with others. The formula, "That is a jerboa," stamps "jerboa" as a class-name and thus supplies a small item of information about that word's grammar.

Even though there is no such thing as a purely ostensive use of a word, in isolation from all other words or symbolic gestures, the ostensive and syntactical rules are relatively independent of each other. A man might know a good deal about

[59]

the grammar of "jerboa" while still unable to point to jerboas. On the other hand, he might be good at pointing to jerboas, while knowing very little about the linguistic connections of the word "jerboa." Similarly for the word "sense-datum." Our test of proper and full understanding of that word's meaning must be mastery of both ostensive and syntactical rules of usage. We need to know not only when to say, "That is a sense-datum," but also the verbal contexts into which "sense-datum" may be inserted without producing nonsense, and the kinds of inferences that may correctly be drawn from "sense-datum statements."

Let us return, then, to John Doe's first lesson in sense-datum language, and let us suppose that the instructor begins with *ostensive* rules.

I suggest that the instructions might properly take some such form as the following imaginary lesson:

If I were to ask you, at some time, what you saw at that time, you might reply, truthfully, "I see a red flash"—or, again, on another occasion, "I see a tree." Somebody else might say you were not telling the truth. He might object, "You couldn't have seen a red flash, for I was watching and saw nothing." Or, on the second occasion, "That's not a *tree*—look, it's only a piece of scenery." If you had spoken truthfully, as I supposed, each of these objections must have been unjustified, but they were at any rate *relevant*. If you were to say, "I see a red flash" or "I see a tree," in the circumstances I have described, you would expect that the truth of certain statements about the experiences of others or about material things *could* upset your own statements.

But now, in the very same situations I have described, I want you to speak in a special and extracautious way—to try confining yourself to what is *immediately given*, i.e., to what you can be sure of, no matter what may be the truth about material things or about what other people see. In order to do this, you might perhaps say, "I see what *looks to me* like a red flash" or "I *seem to see* a tree," using these new sentences in such a way that no statements about other men's experiences or about material things could have any relevance. You will then be making what I shall call *basic statements*. I think you will easily be able to apply what

I have been saying to the cases of feeling, touching, tasting, smelling, or hearing, as well as the case of seeing, with which I have started.

Next, I want you to try transforming your basic statements in the following way: Instead of saying, "I see what looks to me like a red flash," say, "I see a red-flashy-sense-datum." Instead of saying, "I seem to see a tree," say, "I see a tree-y (or, for euphony's sake, treelike) sense-datum." Whenever this is possible, I shall say that you are making a *pure observation statement*. The word "sense-datum" is used in making pure observation statements (though also in other ways). I hope you now understand how to use "sense-datum" in making pure observation statements.

In outlining these hypothetical instructions for the use of "sense-datum," I have made the following suppositions: (a) John Doe already knows how to describe perceptual situations, whether veridical or delusive, in ordinary language. The exact form taken by such ordinary descriptions is unimportant. (b) We can make plain to him the kinds of ordinary descriptions we have in mind. (c) He can understand what we mean when we tell him to try to confine himself to a statement about the "immediately given." (We so construe the "immediately given" that any statement exclusively about the immediately given is logically independent of statements about material things or the experience of others.) (d) Doe learns to use "sense-datum" by learning how to transform *some* ordinary descriptions of perceptual situations into sentences containing the word "sense-datum." Later on, I shall discuss what is involved in introducing more abstract and general uses of "sense-datum."

Our hypothetical layman, John Doe, might reed further explanation before he could use these instructions. The expression "statements about material things" might be sufficiently puzzling to need the further explanation that it covered statements about rainbows, lightning flashes, shadows, and optical images, as well as more substantial things like tables and chairs. Still more important would it be to make clear to him the kind of case in which the transition from "I

[61]

see (hear, smell, feel, etc.) *X*" to "I see (hear, smell, feel, etc.) an *X*-like-sense-datum" is permissible. It was not intended that "I see nothing" should be convertible into "I see a nothing-like-sense-datum," or that "I feel depressed" should be replaceable by "I feel a depression-like-sense-datum." Roughly speaking, the sentence to be transformed must contain a transitive verb followed by an accusative in the form of a noun or a noun clause. This condition could be made more precise, if necessary, but I hope I have said enough to indicate at any rate the general form that the instructions would take.

Perhaps the way of introducing "sense-datum" that I have sketched will seem unnecessarily roundabout. The learner was taught to restrict the meanings of familiar sentences, like "I see a red flash" and "I see a tree," by confining them to the "immediately given," and only then to transform the sentences in such a way as to include the word "sense-datum." Contrast this with the definition of "jerboa." We would not introduce the word "jerboa" by reference to situations in which a man *says*, "I am seeing a small jumping rodent, etc."; if we had to describe situations for the ostensive use of "jerboa" (in lieu of pointing to specimens of the breed) we should describe the situations *directly*, not as situations corresponding to the correct use of familiar sentences. Why not do the same in the case of "sense-datum"?

My answer is that no unmetaphorical sense attaches to "pointing at" or "picking out" sense-data, so that our only recourse is indeed to define the use of "sense-datum" in terms of some pre-existent use of *words*.

Sense-datum theorists may have thought otherwise, and they have certainly written as though it were sensible to speak literally of "pointing out" or "picking out" sense-data. A good example is a passage in which G. E. Moore tried to explain how he was using the word "sense-datum," by giving his readers elaborate instructions for "picking out" at least one sense-datum.

Moore wrote:

[62]

In order to *point out* to the reader what sort of thing I mean by sense-data, I need only ask him to look at his own right hand. If he does this he will be able to pick out something (and unless he is seeing double, only one thing) with regard to which he will see that it is, at first sight, a natural view to take that that thing is identical, not indeed, with his whole right hand, but with that part of its surface which he is actually seeing . . .[1]

(The roundabout description used by Moore is due to his attempt to make "sense-datum" a noncommittal or "neutral" term.) In similar vein, Moore writes, elsewhere, that whenever we see a physical object "we are directly aware of and can easily *pick out* or discriminate with no appreciable degree of indefiniteness, one object and only one that is a sense-datum." [2]

In the case of material things like jerboas, there is a perfectly familiar procedure called "picking out." If a man points to a jerboa, saying, "*That* is a jerboa," and I correctly grasp his meaning, I may be said to have picked out or discriminated a jerboa. This usually calls for an effort of attention: I look at the animals or other material things before me, search for the object of reference, and decide which of them was intended. Is there anything corresponding to this in the case of sense-datum?

There is, of course, no question of literally pointing to a sense-datum. Can it be that all I am required to do in order to follow Moore's instructions is to look at my hand? If I do, I shall probably *stare* at it, as a painter might who wanted to copy it on canvas. Perhaps I shall then be surprised to notice the color of the shadows, perhaps it will look larger than I had realized—perhaps I shall see it in relief, as though the background were blotted out by a mask of black paper. These are special and unusual ways of looking at a hand: as I see my hand "from the corner of my eye" while writing, the way it looks answers to none of these descriptions. But it cannot be

---

[1] G. E. Moore, "A Defence of Common Sense," in *Contemporary British Philosophy*, Second Series (London, 1925), p. 218. Italics added.

[2] G. E. Moore, "The Nature of Sensible Appearances," *Aristotelian Society Proceedings*, Supplementary Volume 6 (1926): 181. Italics added.

essential to Moore's instructions that I take up an aesthetic attitude—I do not really have to concentrate and stare in order to see the sense-datum he was trying to describe. (According to sense-datum theorist I cannot help being acquainted with sense-data in profusion, just so long as I remain conscious. There is no need to peer at my thumb or to stare at a tomato while trying to doubt that it really is a tomato—no need, it seems, to do anything. Even dozing off will do no harm, so long as I can be sure of dreaming. No wonder they think only a lunatic could doubt that sense-data exist.) When Moore asks us to "pick out" the sense-datum he is not really asking us, however much his words may suggest to the contrary, to perform any act of attention or to do *anything* at the time we look at the hand. We "pick out" the sense-datum when and only when we know what answers to Moore's roundabout description. But the description is insufficient. To "pick out" a jerboa is to distinguish it from other animals or material things. I know what it is to search for an animal of a certain kind, but I do not know what is is to search for a *thing*. "Thing" is not a genus word.

There are a few cases in which a more direct description of a sense-datum does seem possible. We may be told, for instance, that an after-image or any of the spots dancing before our eyes (*muscae volitantes*) are sense-data. But this serves at best for cases of "delusive" perception and does not establish the usage for veridical situations. Whenever sense-datum theorists have claimed to be picking out, in cases of veridical perception, things that were instances of sense-data, it will be found that they have only been tying the use of the word "sense-datum" to uses of more-or-less well-understood phrases like "red patch" and "squeaky noise."

To return to John Doe's first lesson in talking sense-datum language. Anybody of average intelligence could learn to obey the instructions, up to a point. It is easy enough to pick up the trick of converting "I see a dog" into "I see a doglike sense-datum," or passing from "I hear a noise" to "I am acquainted with an auditory sense-datum." (The second transition pre-supposes some extension of the training procedure previously described.) This kind of usage is *mechanical;* it might be learned blindly by somebody who had not the least idea of what "sense-datum" was intended to signify. But what *does* the word signify when used by a man who fully understands the original instructions and intends to obey them?

So far as I can see, the function of the word in this use is wholly *privative:* it is a device for depriving ordinary language of some of its ordinary meaning. When the word "sense-datum" is used in the way previously explained, its occurrence is a *signal* or *index* that the speaker is using language in a special and restricted way: it shows the hearer that the speaker is trying (with whatever success) to talk only about the "im-mediately given." The speaker uses ordinary language, in a more or less distorted form, together with a signal that serves notice of his intention to strip away some of the customary meaning. Exactly the same result might be achieved by using an appropriate exclamation ("I see a horse—sense-datum talk!") or by a special tone of voice. The man who has learned to use "sense-datum" in this fashion is, as it were, waving a flag of incorrigibility while he speaks. If the speaker were to say *that* he is talking about the immediately given, he would not be confining himself to the immediately given but talking about his intentions in speaking. We have to suppose, there-fore, that he is not talking about his intentions but rather evincing them by the use of the technical term.

Let us consider, next, the consequences of attempting to communicate by means of pure observation statements. We stipulated that such statements should be exempt from refu-tation by statements about other persons' experiences or about material things. Or to speak in the material mode of speech, our stipulation amounted to demanding that pure observa-tion statements should remain uncorrected no matter what proved to be the case about the external world or the experi-ences of others.

It follows, easily enough, that no statements about the ex-

[65]

periences of others or about material things could *establish* John Doe's pure observation statements. For if a statement about material things could establish the pure observation statement "I see there a red-expanse-sense-datum," it would *dis*establish the pure observation statement "I see there a green-expanse-sense-datum." And so in general: The making of any pure observation statement *A* will exclude the making of at least one other pure observation statement, *B*. Any evidence for *A* will be evidence against *B*. Indeed, we shall soon see that John Doe's pure observation statements are, according to our stipulations, bereft of *all* logical connection with *any* statement that another person could make.

Suppose Doe says, "I see a red-flashy-sense-datum," using the sentence, as he was taught, to refer only to what was "immediately given" to him. It might be supposed that his pure observation statement would be refuted if another person were able to say truthfully, "When Doe spoke just now, he saw nothing red at all." But this is a statement about a material thing, since the speaker identified Doe as the person whose *body* he can see. So, even if this latter statement were true, and Doe really did see nothing red at all, and all of us knew it, we should have no reason to brand Doe's original statement as false. Again, it is obvious that another person's pure observation statements could neither conflict with, nor support, Doe's pure observation statement. We are left with the conclusion that nothing that another person could say, whether about Doe's physical environment, his known reliability as a reporter, the common uses of the words used by Doe—or indeed about anything whatsoever—could have the least tendency either to support or to demolish what Doe intended to say.

This being so, it is plain that others could not take Doe's observation statements seriously as *communications*. The vaunted incorrigibility of the sense-datum language can be achieved only at the cost of its perfect futility as a means of communication. And it would be pointless to retort, "Quite so. The sense-datum language is a *private* language." If it is logically impossible to communicate anything by using words in a certain way, it seems to me misleading, to say the least, to continue to describe that way of using words as a "language." (Of course, if anybody wants to talk about "private language" there can be no objection so long as it is clear both to himself and his audience that he means a "language" which it is logically impossible for anybody other than the speaker to understand. Would anybody want to use the expression "private language" on these terms?)

These conclusions cannot be evaded by supposing relations of probability to hold between pure observation statements and the statements of others. It might at first seem plausible to contend that even if it is *logically possible* for Doe to be speaking truthfully in saying, "I see a red-flashy-sense-datum," in a case where we are right in saying that he is seeing nothing red whatever, that we might nevertheless have good reasons for thinking this *highly unlikely*. If his pure observation statement were to be true, it might be said, there must have occurred a slip of the tongue on his part, and we might have very good evidence to show that the *probability* of this hypothesis was negligible.

This will not do at all. We might be inclined to regard as excellent evidence that Doe had really said what he meant, his saying subsequently that he *had* really meant what he originally said. But this is a statement about the words he previously used (among other things). It is, therefore, a statement about material things and therefore has no bearing upon the truth of the original pure observation statement.

A more general consideration is this: In order to know that X is probably telling the truth now, we must have evidence that X has told the truth in similar circumstances in the past. It follows from what was said earlier that it is logically impossible to provide such evidence: there never is even a single occasion on which others can bring evidence to show that X is making a true pure observation statement on that occasion. Hence, others are never justified in making the weaker statement that he is *probably* making a true pure observation statement on any occasion. (It might be worth considering what evidence they could have that he was making a pure observation statement at all.)

Even if others refused to treat John Doe's pure observation statements as genuine statements, there are two ways in which they could continue to make good use of them. (a) They could simply neglect the sense-datum signal used in making pure observation statements. This means treating Doe's remarks as if he were simply using the language of everyday life. When we hear Doe say, "I see a red-flashy-sense-datum," we say, "If he were talking in a less peculiar way, he would simply say 'I see a red flash.' We know how to bring evidence for and against *this* assertion. So let us suppose this *is* what he is saying." This retranslation into ordinary language refuses to take Doe's use of the word "sense-datum" seriously: it simply ignores the flag of incorrigibility that he is waving. If this is the best that can be done, use of the word "sense-datum" in talking to others is just a waste of time. (b) Doe's hearers might take the sense-datum signal seriously, by treating the *whole* utterance as a deliberate *manifestation* or *symptom*. A doctor can learn something from a patient's groans without raising any question of truth or falsity; and we can read a barometer without supposing it to *assert* anything. Similarly, we might find it useful to treat Doe's alleged "pure observation statements" as a special kind of behavior, to which questions of truth or falsity were simply not relevant. We could, then, draw inferences from the fact that he had uttered certain words, while attaching no sense to the supposition that what he was saying was true or false. If we are to take the use of "sense-datum" by Doe as anything more than a redundant flourish, this mode of interpretation seems the only one left open to us. If John Doe uses "sense-datum," as taught in his first lesson, in talking to others, he is simply inviting them to treat his words as they would a groan or an exclamation on his part.

This second mode of interpretation of the "pure observation statement" of others is not very different from the first. If we treat Doe's utterance of the words "I see a red-flashy-sense-datum" as a reliable signal, our interpretation of that signal is that he is seeing a red flash. On the first interpretation we take him to be *saying* this. On the second interpretation we treat his utterance simply as behavior and *we* say that he must be seeing a red flash.

Could not the question of the truth of a pure observation statement have meaning for the speaker himself? If others can do no better than regard his utterance as an articulated exclamation, cannot he himself know what he is stating? Let us see.

Consider the following two statements that one and the same person might make: (a) "I see a red-flashy-sense-datum," (b) "In a moment I shall say in good faith 'I can remember clearly that I did not see any red flash just now.'" It is clear that (b) is a statement about "material things," as we are using that phrase, since it refers to a certain event involving the uttering of words. According to our conventions for the use of (a), it follows that the truth of (b) has not the slightest tendency to show that (a) is false, or even that (a) is probably false. Suppose, then, that the speaker first writes down the words used in making statement (a) and later makes the statement, in good faith, "I can remember clearly that I did not see any red flash just now." So long as he abides by the conventions he was taught for the use of "sense-datum," this provides no ground at all for questioning, let alone correcting, (a). Indeed, in relation to his own previous pure observation statements, the speaker is in as parlous a plight as everybody else. If he does not treat his own earlier remarks as mere symptoms, or manifestations—as mere behavior—they are no use to him, either. But what reason does he then have for continuing to treat them as statements? None at all, so far as I can see. By destroying all connection between pure observation statements and even his own subsequent experiences, the speaker succeeds in destroying their utility as statements even for his own "private" purposes.

It is worth noticing, finally, that on this exclamatory interpretation of pure observation statements, it becomes impossible to subject them to the customary logical operations of

[69]

negation, generalization, etc. It is no more possible to contradict a pure observation statement than it is to contradict a command or an expletive. (Of course, we may have negative commands, and we might make provision for negative observation statements. But a negative observation statement in the sense-datum language would not be in logical conflict with the correlated positive.) Similarly, the form of words "If I see a red-flashy sense-datum, I also hear a loud-squeaky sense-datum" has been given no more sense, as yet, than the form of words "If Ouch! then Alas!"

Some of these unpleasant consequences could be avoided if the stipulation that pure observation statements shall refer only to the "immediately given" be allowed a weaker sense than the one I have adopted. But such gains would be achieved only at the expense of the incorrigibility that sense-datum theorists have wanted the simplest sense-datum statements to have. As soon as we allow such statements to be logically connected with statements about the external world, or others' experiences, or the speaker's own experiences in the past or the future, we cease to talk exclusively about what is "present" at the time of utterance, and admit the logical possibility of "correction" by reference to what happens elsewhere or at other times. I do not know how to give a weaker interpretation of the "immediately given," and I shall leave it to those who have higher hopes of "sense-datum language" to provide it, if they can.

So far, we have been examining the mere ABC of sense-datum language, as determined by approximately "ostensive" uses of "sense-datum." We are left with the task of stating "syntactical" uses for that term. The ostensive rules, whether in the form I have outlined, or in some variant answering better to the purposes of sense-datum theories, would not sufficiently determine the distinctively philosophical uses of sense-datum language. Failure to see this is, perhaps, responsible for the mistaken claim that sense-datum terminologies are "neutral" with respect to alternative epistemological positions.

The following are characteristic statements by sense-datum theorists. Professor Price said: "The term 'sense-datum' is meant to be a *neutral* one. The use of it does not imply the acceptance of any particular theory. The term is meant to stand for something whose existence is indubitable (however fleeting), something from which all theories of perception ought to start, however much they may diverge later." [3] No doubt Professor Broad thought the same when he wrote: "There can be no doubt whatever of the existence of such things as sense-data: it is practically a mere matter of definition." [4] We shall see before long how extraordinarily complicated the definition needs to be, and how far from obvious it is that anything can answer to the definition.

The line of thought that convinces those who believe the existence of sense-data to be so indubitable is simple enough. Surely, they think, nobody can seriously doubt the existence of red patches and squeaky noises. And surely we must take account of *these* "sense-data" at least, no matter what specific form of a theory of perception we proceed to adopt.

We have to bear in mind, however, that phrases like "red patch" or "squeaky noise," when used without elaborate supplementation, fail to convey to the hearer the sense they are intended to bear when used as a part of sense-datum language. When the full explanation is given, it is bound to respect the etymology of "sense-datum" sufficiently to characterize the specimen sense-data as examples of things *given* in sensation. To say that there *are* sense-data in this sense is to commit oneself to a view (whether a "theory" or not we need not pause to consider) as controversial as anything else in epistemology.

Closely connected with inattention to the need of syntactical as well as ostensive rules for the use of "sense-datum" is the

[3] H. H. Price, *Perception* (rev. ed.; London, 1950), p. 19.

[4] C. D. Broad, "Phenomenalism," *Aristotelian Society Proceedings,* 15 (1914–1915): 231.

common view, that philosophers have always been talking about sense-data, though without using precisely that word. Price, for instance, has held that expressions like "sensible species," "ideas of sensation," "impressions," and "Vorstellungen" (as used by Kant) have been synonyms for "sense-data." Indeed he has traced the genealogy of the expression "sense-datum" back to the very beginnings of philosophy. He has said: "The Sense-Datum Philosophy . . . is as old as Plato himself, for something very like it occurs both in the *Republic* and the *Theaetetus*. Philosophers have been talking about 'phantasmata,' 'ideas of sense,' 'sense-impressions,' 'presentations,' for ages. It is only the *phrase* 'sense-datum' which is new: the linguistic conventions (and these are what matter) were essentially the same." [5]

Among the "linguistic conventions" to which Price refers are what I have called the "syntactical rules for the use of 'sense-datum.' " We need not consider what Plato meant. The usages of English-speaking philosophers in the forty years since Russell introduced the term "sense-datum" in *The Problems of Philosophy* are enough to show the bewildering variety of "linguistic conventions" regulating the use of "sense-datum." Some have used it to stand for a particular; others, like Russell, Dawes Hicks, and Prichard,[6] for a universal. Some have wanted to stipulate that the distinction between appearance and reality should have no application to sense-data; others have wanted to be able to raise questions about the real, though unperceived, properties of sense-data.[7] Moore wants to leave it an open question whether sense-data are parts of material things; Ayer, on the other hand, so uses "sense-datum" that it is logi-

[5] H. H. Price, "Critical Discussion of Ayer's *Foundations of Empirical Knowledge*," Mind, 50 (1941): 283. For a similar statement see Price's *Perception*, p. 19.

[6] Bertrand Russell, *The Problems of Philosophy* (London, 1912), p. 17. G. Dawes Hicks, *Critical Realism* (London, 1938), p. 71. H. A. Prichard, *Knowledge and Perception* (Oxford, 1950), p. 201.

[7] Contrast A. J. Ayer, *The Foundations of Empirical Knowledge* (New York, 1940), p. 123, with Bertrand Russell, *Our Knowledge of the External World* (London, 1926), p. 141.

cally impossible for a sense-datum to be a part of a material thing.[8]

Such disagreements in usage of what must be regarded as a shamefully ambiguous term are not trivial, for the choice made of the linguistic conventions determines in large measure the kind of answer that can be given to the traditional epistemological questions. All the philosophers I have cited agree in the intention to speak about what they take to be "given" in "immediate experience." But since their views about the given and about experience differ, their technical terminologies naturally reflect these differences.

We need not invoke such disagreements in usage in order to see the need for further specifications of the meaning of "sense-datum." It is obvious enough that if "sense-datum" were to be formally defined as "that red patch, that squeaky noise, *and so on,*" we should be left quite in the dark as to the significance of the crucial words, "and so on." The term "sense-datum" is intended to be a *general* term, and if we are to use it with understanding we need to be told what it is in general that *qualifies* anything to rank as a sense-datum. We need syntactical rules as well as ostensive ones.

Fortunately, Professor Broad has recently provided an exceptionally clear account of the connotation of "sense-datum" as *he* uses that term. He writes:

We can now give a description of the technical term 'sensum' or 'sense-datum.' We give this name to that particular which a person *really is* prehending in any experience in which he *appears to himself* to be prehending a physical event or a part of a surface of a body. We give it on the double assumption (i) that he *is* prehending a particular of some kind, and (ii) that he is *not* prehending a physical event or a part of the surface of a body. If this account of the meaning of the term be accepted, one thing at least is certain. The use of it presupposes a positive doctrine, viz., that experiences of seeing, feeling, and hearing do consist in or involve *prehending* a particular of *some kind,* which has, and is

---

[8] See G. E. Moore, "Reply to My Critics," in *The Philosophy of G. E. Moore* (Evanston, Ill., 1942), p. 643, and A. J. Ayer, *op. cit.,* p. 71.

prehended as having a certain intrinsic quality, e.g., redness or hotness or squeakiness. Unless this assumption is true there is nothing answering to the above description of a 'sensum' or a 'sense-datum.' [9]

Broad proceeds to explain that by "S prehends x as red" he means precisely the same as "x sensibly presents itself to S as red." He further elucidates the meaning of "prehending" by stating seven conditions that prehension must satisfy. The last three of these are the following:

(5) It is *logically* possible that a particular, which was in fact prehended on a certain occasion by a certain person as having a certain quality, should have existed and had that quality at that time even though it had not been prehended by him or anyone else. (6) It is *logically* possible that there should be particulars which are never prehended by anyone, but are of the same kinds as those which are actually perhended. Thus, e.g., it is logically possible that there should be particulars which are squeaky, in the sense in which the word is used in the sentence 'That sounds squeaky,' but which are not prehended by anyone. (7) It is *logically* possible that a particular, which was in fact prehended on a certain occasion by a certain person, should then have been prehended by *another* person, either instead of, or in addition to the one that actually prehended it.[10]

Could it have been anything as elaborate as this that Broad earlier had in mind when he said, in the quotations I have already used, that the existence of such things as sense-data is "practically a mere matter of definition"? As Churchill might say, "Some definition!"

Let us see how far Broad's stipulation for the use of "sense-datum" can be met by our procedure.

Broad requires that "sense-datum" shall refer to a *particular,* and not to a universal capable of having instances. This condition has been met by the form adopted in our earlier instructions for the construction of "pure observation state-

[9] C. D. Broad, "Some Elementary Reflexions on Sense-Perception," *Philosophy,* 27 (1952): 12–13.

[10] *Ibid.,* p. 15.

ments." Indeed the form we chose for such statements automatically satisfies other conditions that are sometimes stipulated for the use of sense-datum language. For instance, by demanding that such statements be expressed by sentences of the form "I feel a *hard-sense-datum*" we have satisfied a common demand that a sensing situation be "analyzed into an act and an object." By giving no sense to statements like "I saw a sense-datum which looked red but was really blue" or "I saw a sense-datum which looked red but was really scarlet," we have ensured that the sense-datum shall have all and only the properties it seems to have. (This, however, disagrees with Broad's usage.)

A good many such specifications of the grammar of "sense-datum" can be made without any important modification of the instructions given in our first lesson in speaking sense-datum language. But the philosophical consequences of such conventions are correspondingly trivial. If the outcome of the adoption of sense-datum language were simply the squeezing of bits of ordinary language into a special linguistic form, it would hardly be worth the trouble of learning it.

For what, after all, is the point of introducing a sense-datum language? I hope nobody is going to argue that a language of this kind would enable us to avoid mistakes made by ordinary men whenever they suppose themselves to be perceiving material things. Epistemologists have, of course, often argued that ordinary language embodies such mistakes. Prichard said that "what is ordinarily called perception consists in *taking*, i.e., really *mis*taking, something that we see or feel for something else." [11] And Broad has said that "the primitive belief which accompanies all perceptual situations is certainly to a very large extent false." [12]

But the alleged mistakes are not empirical ones like that of mistaking a waxwork figure at Madame Tussaud's for a real

[11] H. A. Prichard, *op. cit.*, p. 52.

[12] C. D. Broad, *The Mind and Its Place in Nature* (London, 1925), p. 185.

[75]

policeman. If the man who uses sense-datum language is safe from being deceived by illusions or hallucinations, it will be only because he abstains from making statements about material things. And if he uses a richer language containing translations (supposing them to be possible) of the statements made in ordinary life, he will immediately risk making the same kind of mistake that ordinary people do in delusive perception. Nor is there any advantage for ordinary purposes in confining statements about observation to a special grammatical form (the actor-act-accusative construction); everything we say about our experiences could be said in language having a very different grammar—for instance in a language having no first person and no verbs. If we found some American Indians referring to perceptual situations by forms which we should find it natural to translate as "I see redly" or "I see in-a-spreading-chestnut-tree-way" or, in general, by sentences in which the verb was followed by an adverb or adverbial clause, we should have no difficulty in understanding them. Just so long as different perceptual situations were described by different sentences—so that there was the same "multiplicity" in their language as in our own—their way of talking would do as well as any other. The advantages of sense-datum language must be sought exclusively in its philosophical uses.

The philosophically interesting uses of "sense-datum" first arise when questions are asked like, "Could a sense-datum have existed even if it had never been sensed?" and "Could one and the same sense-datum be sensed by more than one person?" These are distinctively philosophical questions and it was in order to be able to ask them that sense-datum language was invented.

Broad, as we have seen, demands that it shall be "logically possible" for an affirmative answer to be given to the question whether a sense-datum exists unsensed. This commits him to a certain syntactical convention, viz., that the question "Do unsensed sense-data exist?" shall make sense.

This condition, however, I cannot satisfy. It was an important part of the conditions introduced earlier for the use of "sense-datum" that the use of the term be accompanied by some indication of the identity of the speaker. In order to understand a statement of the form "I see a red-flashy-sense-datum," it is essential that we know *who* utters the words; the meaning of the statement (or the significance of the signal, if we decide not to count it as a statement) depends upon the context in which it is uttered. A pure observation statement is in this important respect unlike a statement like "all men are mortal" which can be made by anyone at any time without change of reference. Now the questions that Broad wishes to be significant call for a violation of this contextual requirement. He asks us to treat as significant questions like, "Are there any unsensed red flashes?" for which no provision has been made in ordinary language; the attempt to connect the philosophical question with any pre-existent use of language for the discussion of perceptual situations fails at the very outset.

Sense-datum theorists have constantly talked as if they understood such questions as the one about the existence of unsensed sense-data. But it is no accident that arguments about such alleged questions are interminable and inconclusive. It is no accident that the only reasons Moore can give for supposing unsensed "sensibles" to exist are (a) that there is no contradiction in so supposing, and (b) that he has "in Hume's phrase . . . a strong propensity to believe it." [18] We might as well say there is no logical contradiction in supposing that the grin on the Cheshire Cat's face continues to exist when the cat has disappeared—or that we have a strong propensity to disbelieve it. The reason why there is no logical contradiction is that no use has been given to the words expressing the "supposition" in question. The only use that sense-datum theorists actually make of such "questions" is to transform them, by the rules of formal logic, into similar questions, for which it is equally hopeless to expect any answer. The fact that sense-datum theorists reason about such ques-

[18] G. E. Moore, "The Status of Sense-data," *Aristotelian Society Proceedings,* 14 (1913–1914): 367.

tions is no proof that the "questions" have meaning. For it is well known that logical transformations can be performed upon sentence forms containing variables, or upon the same sentences with nonsense-words substituted for the variables.

The same may be said of Broad's demand that it be logically possible for two persons to sense one and the same sense-datum. When are we going to *say* that two persons have prehended the same sense-datum? Neither Broad, nor any other sense-datum theorist can tell us. They simply assume that "questions" about the identity of the sense-data of different persons have a meaning, when they have really failed to give those alleged questions any meaning at all. If we are willing to use the sense-datum language we expose ourselves to the danger of perpetuating the confusions that have been in the minds of its inventors.

The following have been some of my chief points in this essay:

(1) There is no settled sense-datum terminology. If we want to talk sense-datum language, *we* shall have to supply an adequate description of that language.

(2) The task will consist of giving both "ostensive" and "syntactical" rules for the use of "sense-datum."

(3) Ostensive rules for "sense-datum" can be given by trying the use of that word, in the fashion outlined in the paper, with certain ordinary ways of describing perceptual situations.

(4) This procedure makes "sense-datum" a *signal* of a special and restricted way of using ordinary language.

(5) Utterances so restricted have to be regarded as a kind of exclamation, to which questions of truth or falsity are inapplicable.

(6) Such utterances are "incorrigible," but only because the notions of verification or falsification do not apply to them.

(7) The incorrigibility of the pure observation statements is achieved at the cost of their utter futility for the purposes of communication or inference.

(8) A sense-datum language that includes syntactical rules

[78]

of the sort assumed by sense-datum theorists in the past is not "neutral," but presupposes a positive and controversial doctrine.

(9) If we formulate syntactical rules conforming to the intentions of sense-datum theorists, we find ourselves either violating the ostensive rules, or using "sense-datum" in utterances for which no verification procedures have been provided.

(10) No good purpose is served by using a sense-datum language in philosophical discussion.

V

The Identity of Indiscernibles

A. THE PRINCIPLE of the Identity of Indiscernibles seems to me obviously true. And I don't see how we are going to define identity or establish the connection between mathematics and logic without using it.

B. It seems to me obviously false. And your troubles as a mathematical logician are beside the point. If the principle is false you have no right to use it.

A. You simply *say* it's false—and even if you said so three times that wouldn't make it so.

B. Well, you haven't done anything more yourself than assert the principle to be true. As Bradley once said, "Assertion can demand no more than counter-assertion; and what is affirmed on the one side, we on the other can simply deny."

A. How will this do for an argument? If two things, *a* and *b*, are given, the first has the property of being identical with *a*. Now *b* cannot have this property, for else *b* would be *a*, and we should have only one thing, not two as assumed. Hence *a* has at least one property, which *b* does not have, that is to say the property of being identical with *a*.

B. This is a roundabout way of saying nothing, for "*a* has the property of being identical with *a*" means no more than "*a* is *a*." When you begin to say "*a* is . . ." I am supposed to know what thing you are referring to as "*a*" and I expect to be told something about that thing. But when you end the sentence with the words ". . . is *a*" I am left still waiting. The sentence "*a* is *a*" is a useless tautology.

A. Are you as scornful about difference as about identity? For *a* also has, and *b* does not have, the property of being different from *b*. This is a second property that the one thing has but not the other.

B. All you are saying is that *b* is different from *a*. I think the

[80]

form of words "*a* is different from *b*" does have the advantage over "*a* is *a*" that it might be used to give information. I might learn from hearing it used that "*a*" and "*b*" were applied to different things. But this is not what you want to say, since you are trying to use the names, not mention them. When I already know what "*a*" and "*b*" stand for, "*a* is different from *b*" tells me nothing. It, too, is a useless tautology.

A. I wouldn't have expected you to treat "tautology" as a term of abuse. Tautology or not, the sentence has a philosophical use. It expresses the necessary truth that different things have at least one property not in common. Thus different things must be discernible; and hence, by contraposition, indiscernible things must be identical. Q.E.D.

B. Why obscure matters by this old-fashioned language? By "indiscernible" I suppose you mean the same as "having all properties in common." Do you claim to have proved that two things having all their properties in common are identical?

A. Exactly.

B. Then this is a poor way of stating your conclusion. If *a* and *b* are identical, there is just one thing having the two names "*a*" and "*b*"; and in that case it is absurd to say that *a* and *b* are two. Conversely, once you have supposed there are *two* things having all their properties in common, you can't without contradicting yourself say that *they* are "identical."

A. I can't believe you were really misled. I simply meant to say it is logically impossible for two things to have all their properties in common. I showed that *a* must have at least two properties—the property of being identical with *a,* and the property of being different from *b*—neither of which can be a property of *b.* Doesn't this prove the principle of Identity of Indiscernibles?

B. Perhaps you have proved something. If so, the nature of your proof should show us exactly what you have proved. If you want to call "being identical with *a*" a "property" I suppose I can't prevent you. But you must then accept the consequences of this way of talking. All you mean when you say "*a* has the property of being identical with *a*" is that *a* is *a.* And

[81]

all you mean when you say "*b* does not have the property of being identical with *a*" is that *b* is not *a*. So what you have "proved" is that *a* is *a* and *b* is not *a*, that is to say, *b* and *a* are different. Similarly, when you said that *a*, but not *b*, had the property of being different from *b*, you were simply saying that *a* and *b* were different. In fact you are merely redescribing the hypothesis that *a* and *b* are different by calling it a case of "difference of properties." Drop the misleading description and your famous principle reduces to the truism that different things are different. How true! And how uninteresting!

A. Well, the properties of identity and difference may be uninteresting, but they *are* properties. If I had shown that grass was green, I suppose you would say I hadn't shown that grass was colored.

B. You certainly would not have shown that grass had any color *other than* green.

A. What it comes to is that you object to the conclusion of my argument following from the premise that *a* and *b* are different.

B. No, I object to the triviality of the conclusion. If you want to have an interesting principle to defend, you must interpret "property" more narrowly—enough so, at any rate, for "identity" and "difference" not to count as properties.

A. Your notion of an interesting principle seems to be one which I shall have difficulty in establishing. Will you at least allow me to include among "properties" what are sometimes called "relational characteristics"—like *being married to Caesar* or *being at a distance from London?*

B. Why not? If you are going to defend the principle, it is for you to decide what version you wish to defend.

A. In that case, I don't need to count identity and difference as properties. Here is a different argument that seems to me quite conclusive. The only way we can discover that two different things exist is by finding out that one has a quality not possessed by the other or else that one has a relational characteristic that the other hasn't.

If *both* are blue and hard and sweet and so on, and have the

[82]

same shape and dimensions and are in the same relations to everything in the universe, it is logically impossible to tell them apart. The supposition that in such a case there might really be two things would be unverifiable *in principle*. Hence it would be meaningless.

B. You are going too fast for me.

A. Think of it this way. If the principle were false, the fact that I can see only two of your hands would be no proof that you had just two. And even if every conceivable test agreed with the supposition that you had two hands, you might all the time have three, four, or any number. You might have nine hands, different from one another and all indistinguishable from your left hand, and nine more all different from each other but indistinguishable from your right hand. And even if you really did have just two hands, and no more, neither you nor I nor anybody else could ever know that fact. This is too much for me to swallow. This is the kind of absurdity you get into, as soon as you abandon verifiability as a test of meaning.

B. Far be it from me to abandon anything you hold so sacred. Before I give you a direct answer, let me try to describe a counterexample.

Isn't it logically possible that the universe should have contained nothing but two exactly similar spheres? We might suppose that each was made of chemically pure iron, had a diameter of one mile, that they had the same temperature, color, and so on, and that nothing else existed. Then every quality and relational characteristic of the one would also be a property of the other. Now if what I am describing is logically possible, it is not impossible for two things to have all their properties in common. This seems to me to *refute* the Principle.

A. Your supposition, I repeat, isn't verifiable and therefore can't be regarded as meaningful. But supposing you *have* described a possible world, I still don't see that you have refuted the principle. Consider one of the spheres, *a* . . .

B. How can I, since there is no way of telling them apart? *Which* one do you want me to consider?

A. This is very foolish. I mean *either* of the two spheres, leaving you to decide which one you wished to consider. If I were to say to you, "Take any book off the shelf," it would be foolish on your part to reply, "Which?"

B. It's a poor analogy. I know how to take a book off a shelf, but I don't know how to identify one of two spheres supposed to be alone in space and so symmetrically placed with respect to each other that neither has any quality or character the other does not also have.

A. All of which goes to show as I said before, the unverifiability of your supposition. Can't you imagine that one sphere has been designated as *"a"*?

B. I can imagine only what is logically possible. Now it is logically possible that somebody should enter the universe I have described, see one of the spheres on his left hand and proceed to call it *"a."* I can imagine that all right, if that's enough to satisfy you.

A. Very well, now let me try to finish what I began to say about *a* . . .

B. I still can't let you, because *you,* in your present situation, have no right to talk about *a.* All I have conceded is that if something were to happen to introduce a change into my universe, so that an observer entered and could see the two spheres, one of them could then have a name. But this would be a different supposition from the one I wanted to consider. My spheres don't yet have names. If an observer were to enter the scene, he could perhaps put a red mark on one of the spheres. You might just as well say, "By '*a*' I mean the sphere which would be the first to be marked by a red mark if anyone were to arrive and were to proceed to make a red mark!" You might just as well ask me to consider the first daisy in my lawn that would be picked by a child, if a child were to come along and do the picking. This doesn't now distinguish any daisy from the others. You are just pretending to use a name.

A. And I think you are just pretending not to understand me. All I am asking you to do is to think of one of your spheres, no matter which, so that I may go on to say something about it when you give me a chance.

B. You talk as if naming an object and then thinking about it were the easiest thing in the world. But it isn't so easy. Suppose I tell you to name any spider in my garden: if you can catch one first or describe one uniquely you can name it easily enough. But you can't pick one out, let alone "name" it, by just thinking. You remind me of the mathematicians who thought that talking about an Axiom of Choice would really allow them to choose a single member of a collection when they had no criterion of choice.

A. At this rate you will never give me a chance to say anything. Let me try to make my point without using names. Each of the spheres will surely differ from the other in being at some distance from that other one, but at no distance from itself—that is to say, it will bear at least one relation to itself— *being at no distance from,* or *being in the same place as*—that it does not bear to the other. And this will serve to distinguish it from the other.

B. Not at all. *Each* will have the relational characteristic *being at a distance of two miles,* say, *from the center of a sphere one mile in diameter,* etc. And each will have the relational characteristic (if you want to call it that) of *being in the same place as itself.* The two are alike in this respect as in all others.

A. But look here. Each sphere occupies a different place; and this at least will distinguish them from one another.

B. This sounds as if you thought the places had some independent existence, though I don't suppose you really think so. To say the spheres are in "different places" is just to say that there is a distance between the two spheres; and we have already seen that this will not serve to distinguish them. Each is at a distance—indeed the same distance—from the other.

A. When I said they were at different places I didn't mean simply that they were at some distance from one another. That one sphere is in a certain place does not entail the existence of any *other* sphere. So to say that one sphere is in its place, and the other in its place, and then to add that these places are different seems to me different from saying the spheres are at a distance from one another.

B. What does it mean to say "a sphere is in its place"? Nothing at all, so far as I can see. Where else could it be? *All* you are saying is that the spheres are in different places.

A. Then my retort is, What does it mean to say, "Two spheres are in different places"? Or, as you so neatly put it, "Where else could they be?"

B. You have a point. What I should have said was that your assertion that the spheres occupied different places said nothing at all, unless you were drawing attention to the necessary truth that different physical objects must be in different places. Now if two spheres must be in different places, as indeed they must, to say that the spheres occupy different places is to say no more than that they are two spheres.

A. This is like a point you made before. You won't allow me to deduce anything from the supposition that there are two spheres.

B. Let me put it another way. In the two-sphere universe, the only reason for saying that the places occupied are different would be that different things occupied them. So in order to show the places were different you would first have to show, in some other way, that the spheres were different. You will never be able to distinguish the spheres by means of the places they occupy.

A. A minute ago, you were willing to allow that somebody might give your spheres different names. Will you let me suppose that some traveler has visited your monotonous "universe" and has named one sphere "Castor" and the other "Pollux"?

B. All right—provided you don't try to use those names yourself.

A. Wouldn't the traveler, at least, have to recognize that *being at a distance of two miles from Castor* was not the same property as being at a distance of two miles *from Pollux?*

B. I don't see why. If he were to see that Castor and Pollux had exactly the same properties, he would see that "being at a distance of two miles from Castor" meant exactly the same as "being at a distance of two miles from Pollux."

A. They couldn't mean the same. If they did, *"being at a distance of two miles from Castor and at the same time not being at a distance of two miles from Pollux"* would be a self-contradictory description. But plenty of bodies could answer to this description. Again if the two expressions meant the same, anything which was two miles from Castor would have to be two miles from Pollux—which is clearly false. So the two expressions don't mean the same and the two spheres have at least two properties not in common.

B. Which?

A. *Being at a distance of two miles from Castor* and *being at a distance of two miles from Pollux.*

B. But now you are *using* the words "Castor" and "Pollux" as if they really stood for something. They are just our old friends *"a"* and *"b"* in disguise.

A. You surely don't want to say that the arrival of the name-giving traveler creates spatial properties? Perhaps we can't name your spheres and therefore can't name the corresponding properties; but the properties must be there.

B. What can this mean? The traveler has not visited the spheres, and the spheres have no names—neither "Castor," nor "Pollux," nor *"a,"* nor *"b,"* nor any others. Yet you still want to say they have certain properties which cannot be referred to without using names for the spheres. You want to say "the property of being at a distance from Castor" though it is logically impossible for you to talk in this way. You can't speak, but you won't be silent.

A. How eloquent, and how unconvincing! But since you seem to have convinced yourself, at least, perhaps you can explain another thing that bothers me: I don't see that you have a right to talk as you do about places or spatial relations in connection with your so-called "universe." So long as we are talking about our own universe—*the* universe—I know what you mean by "distance," "diameter," "place," and so on. But in what you want to call a universe, even though it contains only two objects, I don't see what such words could mean. So far as I can see, you are applying these spatial terms in their present usage to a hypothetical situation which contradicts the preconditions of that usage.

B. What do you mean by "precondition"?

A. Well, you spoke of measured distances, for one thing. Now this assumes some means of measurement. Hence your "universe" must contain at least a third thing—a ruler or some other measuring device.

B. Are you claiming that a universe must have at least three things in it? What is the least number of things required to make a world?

A. No, all I am saying is that you cannot describe a configuration as *spatial* unless it includes at least three objects. This is part of the meaning of "spatial"—and it is no more mysterious than saying you can't have a game of chess without there existing at least thirty-five things (thirty-two pieces, a chessboard, and two players).

B. If this is all that bothers you, I can easily provide for three or any number of things without changing the force of my counter-example. The important thing, for my purpose, was that the configuration of two spheres was symmetrical. So long as we preserve this feature of the imaginary universe, we can now allow any number of objects to be found in it.

A. You mean any *even* number of objects.

B. Quite right. Why not imagine a plane running clear through space, with everything that happens on one side of it always exactly duplicated at an equal distance in the other side.

A. A kind of cosmic mirror producing real images.

B. Yes, except that there wouldn't be any mirror! The point is that in *this* world we can imagine any degree of complexity and change to occur. No reason to exclude rulers, compasses, and weighing machines. No reason, for that matter, why the Battle of Waterloo shouldn't happen.

A. Twice over, you mean—with Napoleon surrendering later in two different places simultaneously!

B. Provided you wanted to call both of them "Napoleon."

A. So your point is that everything could be duplicated on the other side of the nonexistent Looking Glass. I suppose whenever a man got married, his identical twin would be marrying the identical twin of the first man's fiancée?

B. Exactly.

A. Except that "identical twins" wouldn't be *numerically* identical?

B. You seem to be agreeing with me.

A. Far from it. This is just a piece of gratuitous metaphysics. If the inhabitants of your world had enough sense to know what was sense and what wasn't, they would never suppose all the events in their world were duplicated. It would be much more sensible for them to regard the "second" Napoleon as a mere mirror image—and similarly for all the other supposed "duplicates."

B. But they could walk through the "mirror" and find water just as wet, sugar just as sweet, and grass just as green on the other side.

A. You don't understand me. They would not postulate "another side." A man looking at the "mirror" would be seeing *himself*, not a duplicate. If he walked in a straight line toward the "mirror" he would eventually find himself back at his starting point, not at a duplicate of his starting point. This would involve their having a different geometry from ours—but that would be preferable to the logician's nightmare of the reduplicated universe.

B. They might think so—until the twins really began to behave differently for the first time!

A. Now it's you who are tinkering with your supposition. You can't have your universe and change it too.

B. All right, I retract.

A. The more I think about your "universe" the queerer it seems. What would happen when a man crossed your invisible "mirror"? While he was actually crossing, his body would have to change shape, in order to preserve the symmetry. Would it gradually shrink to nothing and then expand again?

[89]

B. I confess I hadn't thought of that.

A. And here is something that explodes the whole notion. Would you say that one of the two Napoleons in your universe had his heart in the right place—literally, I mean?

B. Why, of course.

A. In that case his "mirror-image" twin would have the heart on the opposite side of the body. One Napoleon would have his heart on the left of his body, and the other would have it on the right of his body.

B. It's a good point, though it would still make objects like spheres indistinguishable. But let me try again. Let me abandon the original idea of a *plane* of symmetry and to suppose instead that we have only a *center* of symmetry. I mean that everything that happened at any place would be exactly duplicated at a place an equal distance on the opposite side of the center of symmetry. In short, the universe would be what the mathematicians call "radially symmetrical." And to avoid complications we could suppose that the center of symmetry itself was physically inaccessible, so that it would be impossible for any material body to pass through it. Now in *this* universe, identical twins would have to be either both right-handed or both left-handed.

A. Your universes are beginning to be as plentiful as blackberries. You are too ingenious to see the force of my argument about verifiability. Can't you see that your supposed description of a universe in which everything has its "identical twin" doesn't describe anything verifiably different from a corresponding universe without such duplication? This must be so, no matter what kind of symmetry your universe manifested.

B. You are assuming that in order to verify that there are two things of a certain kind, it must be possible to show that one has a property not possessed by the other. But this is not so. A pair of very close but similar magnetic poles produce a characteristic field of force which assures me that there are two poles, even if I have no way of examining them separately. The presence of two exactly similar stars at a great distance might be detected by some resultant gravitational effect or by optical interference—or in some such similar way—even though we had no way of inspecting one in isolation from the other. Don't physicists say something like this about the electrons inside an atom? We can verify *that* there are two, that is to say a certain property of the whole configuration, even though there is no way of detecting any character that uniquely characterizes any element of the configuration.

A. But if you were to approach your two stars one would have to be on your left and one on the right. And this would distinguish them.

B. I agree. Why shouldn't we say that the two stars are distinguishable—meaning that it would be possible for an observer to see one on his left and the other on his right, or more generally, that it would be *possible* for one star to come to have a relation to a third object that the second star would not have to that third object.

A. So you agree with me after all.

B. Not if you mean that the two stars do not have all their properties in common. All I said was that it was logically possible for them to enter into different relationships with a third object. But this would be a change in the universe.

A. If you are right, nothing unobserved would be observable. For the presence of an observer would always change it, and the observation would always be an observation of something else.

B. I don't say that every observation changes what is observed. My point is that there isn't any *being to the right* or *being to the left* in the two-sphere universe until an observer is introduced, that is to say until a real change is made.

A. But the spheres themselves wouldn't have changed.

B. Indeed they would: they would have acquired new relational characteristics. In the absence of any asymmetric observer, I repeat, the spheres would have all their properties in common (including, if you like, the power to enter into different relations with other objects). Hence the Principle of Identity of Indiscernibles is false.

A. So perhaps you really do have twenty hands after all?

B. Not a bit of it. Nothing that I have said prevents me from holding that we can verify *that* there are exactly two. But we could know *that* two things existed without there being any way to distinguish one from the other. The Principle is false.

A. I am not surprised that you ended in this way, since you assumed it in the description of your fantastic "universe." Of course, if you began by assuming that the spheres were numerically different though qualitatively alike, you could end by "proving" what you first assumed.

B. But I wasn't "proving" anything. I tried to support my contention that it is logically possible for two things to have all their properties in common by giving an illustrative description. (Similarly, if I had to show it is logically possible for nothing at all to be seen I would ask you to imagine a universe in which everybody was blind.) It was for you to show that my description concealed some hidden contradiction. And you haven't done so.

A. All the same I am not convinced.

B. Well, then, you ought to be.

2

Zeno's Paradoxes

Zénon! Cruel Zénon! Zénon d'Elée
M'as-tu percé de cette flèche ailée
Qui vibre, vole, et qui ne vole pas!
Le son m'enfante et la flèche me tue!
Ah! le Soleil . . . Quelle ombre de tortue
Pour l'âme, Achille immobile à grands pas!
—Paul Valéry

VI

Achilles and the Tortoise

1. SUPPOSE Achilles runs ten times as fast as the tortoise and gives him a hundred yards' start. In order to win the race Achilles must first make up for his initial handicap by running a hundred yards; but when he has done this and has reached the point where the tortoise started, the animal has had time to advance ten yards. While Achilles runs these ten yards, the tortoise gets one yard ahead; when Achilles has run this yard, the tortoise is a tenth of a yard ahead; and so on, without end. Achilles never catches the tortoise, because the tortoise always holds a lead, however small.

This is approximately the form in which the so-called "Achilles" paradox has come down to us. Aristotle, who is our primary source for this and the other paradoxes attributed to Zeno, summarizes the argument as follows: "In a race the quickest runner can never overtake the slowest, since the pursuer must first reach the point whence the pursued started, so that the slower must always hold a lead" (Physics, 239b).[1]

[1] Aristotle's solution seems to be based upon a distinction between two meanings of "infinite"—(a) as meaning "infinite in extent," (b) as meaning "infinitely divisible." "For there are two senses in which length and time and generally anything continuous are called 'infinite': they are called so either in respect of divisibility or in respect of their extremities. So while a thing in a finite time cannot come in contact with things quantitatively infinite, it can come in contact with things infinite in respect of divisibility; for in this sense the time itself is also infinite . . ." (*Physics*, 233a). This type of answer has been popular (cf., e.g., J. S. Mill, *System of Logic* [5th ed.; London, 1862], pp. 389–390). Several writers object that infinite divisibility of the line implies its actually having an infinite number of elements—and so leaves the puzzle unresolved. But see H. R. King, "Aristotle and the Paradoxes of Zeno," *Journal of Philosophy*, 46 (1949): 657–670.

For references to the vast literature on this and the other arguments of Zeno, see F. Cajori, "The History of Zeno's Arguments on Motion," *Amer-*

2. It would be a waste of time to prove, by independent argument, that Achilles *will* pass the tortoise. Everybody knows this already, and the puzzle arises because the conclusion of Zeno's argument is known to be absurd. We must try to find out, if we can, exactly what mistake is committed in this argument.[2]

3. A plausible answer that has been repeatedly offered [3] takes the line that "this paradox of Zeno is based upon a mathematical fallacy" (A. N. Whitehead, *Process and Reality* [New York, 1929], p. 107).

Consider the lengths that Achilles has to cover, according to our version of the paradox. They are, successively, a hundred yards, ten yards, one yard, a tenth of a yard, and so on. So the total number of yards he must travel in order to catch the tortoise is

$$100 + 10 + 1 + 1/10 + \ldots$$

This is a convergent geometrical series whose sum can be expressed in decimal notation as 111. i, that is to say exactly 111⅑. When Achilles has run this number of yards, he will be dead level with his competitor; and at any time thereafter he will be actually ahead.

---

ican Mathematical Monthly, 22 (1915): 1–6, 39–47, 77–82, 109–115, 143–149, 179–186, 253–258, 292–297.

[2] It has sometimes been held (e.g., by Paul Tannery in *Revue Philosophique,* 20 (1885), that Zeno's arguments were sound. "Tannery's explanation of four arguments, particularly of the 'Arrow' and 'Stade' raises these paradoxes from childish arguments to arguments with conclusions which follow with compelling force . . . it exhibits Zeno as a logician of the first rank" (Cajori, *op. cit.,* p. 6).

Cf. Russell's remark that the arguments of Zeno "are not, however, on any view, mere foolish quibbles: they are serious arguments, raising difficulties which it has taken two thousand years to answer, and which even now are fatal to the teachings of most philosophers" (*Our Knowledge of the External World* [London, 1926], p. 175).

[3] In addition to the reference to Whitehead, see for instance Descartes (letter to Clerselier, Adam and Tannery ed. of *Works,* 4 [Paris, 1897]: 445–447), and Peirce (*Collected Papers* [Cambridge, Mass., 1931] 6.177–6.182). Peirce says ". . . this silly little catch presents no difficulty at all to a mind adequately trained in mathematics and in logic . . ." (6.177).

A similar argument applies to the time needed for Achilles to catch the tortoise. If we suppose that Achilles can run a hundred yards in ten seconds, the number of seconds he needs in order to draw level is

$$10 + 1 + 1/10 + 1/100 + \ldots$$

This, too, is a convergent geometrical series, whose sum is expressed in decimal notation as 11. i, that is to say exactly 11⅑. This, as we should expect, is one tenth of the number we previously obtained for the length of the race. (For Achilles was running at ten yards per second.)

We can check the calculation without using infinite series at all. The relative velocity with which Achilles overtakes the tortoise is nine yards per second. Now the number of seconds needed to cancel the initial gap of a hundred yards at a relative velocity of pursuit of nine yards per second is 100 divided by 9, i.e., 11⅑. This is exactly the number we previously obtained by summing the geometrical series representing the times needed by Achilles. Achilles is actually running at ten yards per second, so the actual distance he travels is 10 × 11⅑, or 111⅑, as before. Thus we have confirmed our first calculations by an argument not involving the summation of infinite series.

4. According to this type of solution, the fallacy in Zeno's argument is due to the use of the words "never" and "always." Given the premise that "the pursuer must first reach the point whence the pursued started," it does *not* follow, as alleged, that the quickest runner "never" overtakes the slower: Achilles does catch the tortoise at some time—that is to say at a time exactly 11⅑ seconds from the start. It is wrong to say that the tortoise is "always" in front: there is a place—a place exactly 111⅑ yards from Achilles' starting point—where the two are dead level. Our calculations have shown this, and Zeno failed to see that only a finite time and finite space are needed for the infinite series of steps that Achilles is called upon to make.

5. This kind of mathematical solution has behind it the authority of Descartes and Peirce and Whitehead [4]—to mention no lesser names—yet I cannot see that it goes to the heart

---

[4] See the last footnote.

of the matter. It tells us, correctly, when and where Achilles and the tortoise will meet, *if* they meet; but it fails to show that Zeno was wrong in claiming they *could not* meet.

Let us be clear about what is meant by the assertion that the sum of the infinite series

$$100 + 10 + 1 + 1/10 + 1/100 + \ldots$$

is $111\frac{1}{9}$. It does not mean, as the naïve might suppose, that mathematicians have succeeded in adding together an infinite number of terms. As Frege pointed out in a similar connection,[5] this remarkable feat would require an infinite supply of paper, an infinite quantity of ink, and an infinite amount of time. If we had to add all the terms together, we could never prove that the series had a finite sum. To say that the sum of the series is $111\frac{1}{9}$ is to say that if enough terms of the series are taken, the difference between the sum of that *finite number* of terms and the number $111\frac{1}{9}$ becomes, and stays, as small as we please. (Or to put it another way: Let n be any number less than $111\frac{1}{9}$. We can always find a finite number of terms of the series whose sum will be less than $111\frac{1}{9}$ but greater than n.)

Since this is all that is meant by saying that the infinite series has a sum, it follows that the "summation" of all the terms of an infinite series is not the same thing as the summation of a finite set of numbers. In one case we can get the answers by working out a finite number of additions; in the other case we *must* "perform a limit operation," that is to say, we must prove that there is a number whose difference from the sum of the initial members of the series can be made to remain as small as we please.

6. Now let us apply this to the race. The series of distances traversed by Achilles is convergent. This means that if Achilles takes enough steps whose sizes are given by the series one hundred yards, ten yards, one yard, one-tenth yard, etc., the distance *still to go* to the meeting point eventually becomes, and stays, as small as we please. After the first step he still has $11\frac{1}{9}$ yards to go; after the second, only $1\frac{1}{9}$ yard; after the third, no

[5] *Grundgesetze der Arithmetik*, 2 (1903): §124. Or see my translation in *Translations from the Philosophical Writings of Gottlob Frege* (Oxford, 1952), p. 219.

more than $\frac{1}{9}$ yard; and so on. The distance still to go is reduced by nine-tenths at each move.

But the distance, however much reduced, still remains to be covered; and after each step there are infinitely many steps still to be taken. The logical difficulty is that Achilles seems called upon to perform *an infinite series of tasks;* and it does not help to be told that the tasks become easier and easier, or need progressively less and less time in the doing. Achilles may get nearer to the place and time of his rendezvous, but his task remains just as hard, for he still has to perform what seems to be logically impossible. It is just as hard to draw a very small square circle as it is to draw an enormous one: we might say both tasks are infinitely hard. The logical difficulty is not in the extent of the distance Achilles has to cover but in the apparent impossibility of his traveling any distance whatsoever. I think Zeno had enough mathematical knowledge to understand that if Achilles could run $111\frac{1}{9}$ yards—that is to say, keep going for $11\frac{1}{9}$ seconds—he would indeed have caught the tortoise. The difficulty is to understand how Achilles could arrive anywhere at all without first having performed an infinite series of acts.

7. The nature of the difficulty is made plainer by a second argument of Zeno, known as the "Dichotomy" which, according to Aristotle, is "the same in principle" (*Physics,* 239b). In order to get from one point to another, Achilles must first reach a third point midway between the two; similarly, in order to reach this third point he must first reach a fourth point; to reach this point he must first reach another point; and so on, without end. To reach *any* point, he must first reach a nearer one. So, in order to be moving at all, Achilles must already have performed an infinite series of acts—must, as it were, have traveled along the series of points from the infinitely distant and *open* "end." [6] This is an even more astound-

---

[6] This, at any rate, is the usual interpretation, though I cannot see that Aristotle was thinking of anything more than an argument resembling the "Achilles" in all respects except that of the ratio in which the distance is divided. For the contrary view see, for instance, Sir Thomas Heath, *Mathematics in Aristotle* (Oxford, 1949), pp. 135–136.

ing feat than the one he accomplishes in winning the race against the tortoise.

The two arguments are complementary: the "Achilles" shows that the runner cannot reach any place, even if he gets started; while the "Dichotomy" shows that he cannot get started, i.e., cannot leave any place he has reached.

8. Mathematicians have sometimes said that the difficulty of conceiving the performance of an infinite series of tasks is factitious. All it shows, they say, is the weakness of human imagination and the folly of the attempt to make a mental image of mathematical relationships.[7] The line really does have infinitely many points, and there is no logical impediment to Achilles' making an infinite number of steps in a finite time. I shall try to show that this way of thinking about the race is untenable.

9. I am going to argue that the expression, "infinite series of acts," is self-contradictory, and that failure to see this arises from confusing a series of acts with a series of numbers generated by some mathematical law. (By an "act" I mean something marked off from its surroundings by having a definite beginning and end.)

In order to establish this by means of an illustration I shall try to make plain some of the absurd consequences of talking about "counting an infinite number of marbles." And in order to do this I shall find it convenient to talk about counting an infinite number of marbles as if I supposed it was sensible to talk in this way. But I want it to be understood all the time that I do not think it sensible to talk in this way, and that my aim in so talking is to show how absurd this way of talking is. Counting may seem a very special kind of "act" to choose, but I hope to be able to show that the same considerations apply to an infinite series of any kind of acts.

[7] "La perception sensible n'embrasse que le fini; l'imagination atteint encore les infiniment grands et les infiniment petits, tant qu'ils restent finis; mais elle n'atteint ni l'infini, limite des infiniment grands, ni le zéro, limite des infiniment petits: ces deux états extrêmes de la grandeur sont de pures idées, accessibles à la seule raison" (L. Couturat, De l'infini mathématique [Paris, 1896], p. 562).

10. Suppose we want to find out the number of things in a given collection,[8] presumably identified by some description. Unless the things are mathematical or logical entities it will be impossible to deduce the size of the collection from the description alone; and somebody will have to do the work of taking a census. Of course he can do this without having any idea of how large the collection will turn out to be: his instructions may simply take the form, "Start counting and keep on until there is nothing left in the collection to count." This implies that there will be a point at which there will be "nothing left to count," so that the census-taker will then know his task to have been completed.

Now suppose we can know that the collection is infinite. If, knowing this, we were to say, "Start counting, and continue until there is nothing left to count" we should be practicing a deception. For our census-taker would be led to suppose that sooner or later there would be nothing left to count, while all the time we would know this supposition to be false. An old recipe for catching guinea pigs is to put salt on their tails. Since they have no tails, this is no recipe at all. To avoid deception we should have said, in the case of the infinite collection, "Start counting and *never* stop." This should be enough to tell an intelligent census-taker that the collection is infinite, so that there is no sense in trying to count it.

If somebody says to me, "Count all the blades of grass in Hyde Park," I might retort, "It's too difficult; I haven't enough time." But if some cosmic bully were to say, "Here is an infinite collection; go ahead and count it," only logical confusion could lead me to mutter, "Too difficult; not enough time." The trouble is that, no matter what I do, the result of all my work will not and cannot count as compliance with the instructions. If somebody commands me to obey a certain "instruction," and is then obliging enough to add that nothing that I can do will count as compliance with that instruction, only confusion could lead me to suppose that any genuine task had been set.

[8] Or class or set or aggregate, etc.

11. However, some writers have said that the difficulty of counting an infinite collection is just a matter of *lack of time*.[9] If only we could count faster and faster, the whole job could be done in a finite time; there would still never be a time at which we were ending, but there would be a time at which we already would have ended the count. It is not necessary to finish counting; it is sufficient that the counting shall have been finished.

Very well. Since the task is too much for human capacity, let us imagine a machine that can do it. Let us suppose that upon our left a narrow tray stretches into the distance as far as the most powerful telescope can follow; and that this tray or slot is full of marbles. Here, at the middle, where the line of marbles begins, there stands a kind of mechanical scoop; and to the right, a second, but empty tray, stretching away into the distance beyond the farthest reach of vision. Now the machine is started. During the first minute of its operation, it seizes a marble from the left and transfers it to the empty tray on the right; then it rests a minute. In the next half-minute the machine seizes a second marble on the left, transfers it, and rests half-a-minute. The third marble is moved in a quarter of a minute, with a corresponding pause; the next in one-eighth of a minute; and so until the movements are so fast that all we can see is a gray blur. But at the end of exactly four minutes the machine comes to a halt, and now the left-hand tray that was full seems to be empty, while the right-hand tray that was empty seems full of marbles.

Let us call this an *infinity machine*. And since it is the first of several to be described let us give it the name "Alpha."

12. I hope nobody will object that the wear and tear on such a machine would be too severe; or that it would be too hard to construct. We are dealing with the logical coherence of ideas, not with the practicability of mechanical devices. If we can conceive of such a machine without contradiction, that

[9] "Quand vous dites qu'une collection infinie ne pourra jamais être numérotée tout entière, il ne s'agit pas là d'une impossibilité intrinsique et logique, mais d'une impossibilité pratique et matérielle: c'est tout simplement une question de temps" (L. Couturat, *op. cit.*, p. 462).

will be enough; and believers in the "actual infinite" will have been vindicated.

13. An obvious difficulty in conceiving of an infinity machine is this. How are we supposed to know that there are infinitely many marbles in the left-hand tray at the outset? Or, for that matter, that there are infinitely many on the right when the machine has stopped? Everything we can observe of Alpha's operations (and no matter how much we slow it down) is consistent with there having been involved only a very large, though still finite, number of marbles.

14. Now there is a simple and instructive way of making certain that the machine shall have infinitely many marbles to count. Imagine the arrangements modified as follows. Let there be only *one* marble in the left-hand tray to begin with, and let some device always return *that same marble* during the time at which the machine is resting. Let us give the name "Beta" to a machine that works in this way. From the standpoint of the machine, as it were, the task has not changed. The difficulty of performance remains exactly the same whether the task, as in Alpha's case, is to transfer an infinite series of qualitatively similar but different marbles; or whether the task, as in Beta's case, is constantly to transfer the *same* marble —a marble that is immediately returned to its original position. Imagine Alpha and Beta set to work side by side on their respective tasks: every time the one moves, so does the other; if one succeeds in its task, so must the other; and if it is impossible for either to succeed, it is impossible for *each*.

15. The introduction of our second machine, Beta, shows clearly that the infinite count really is impossible. For the single marble is always returned, and each move of the machine accomplishes nothing. A man given the task of filling three holes by means of two pegs can always fill the third hole by transferring one of the pegs; but this automatically creates another empty place, and it won't help in the least to "keep on trying" or to run through this futile series of operations faster and faster. (We don't get any nearer to the end of the rainbow by running faster.) Now our machine, Beta, is in just

this predicament: the very act of transferring the marble from left to right immediately causes it to be returned again; the operation is self-defeating and it is logically impossible for its end to be achieved. Now if this is true for Beta, it must be true also for Alpha, as we have already seen.

16. When Hercules tried to cut off the heads of Hydra, two heads immediately grew where one had been removed. It is rumored that the affair has been incorrectly reported: Zeus, the all powerful, took pity on Hercules and eased his labor. It was decreed that only *one* head should replace the head that had been cut off and that Hercules should have the magical power to slash faster and faster in geometrical progression. If this is what really happened, had Hercules any cause to be grateful? Not a bit. Since the head that was sliced off immediately grew back again, Hercules was getting nowhere, and might just as well have kept his sword in its scabbard.

17. Somebody may still be inclined to say that nevertheless when the machine Beta finally comes to rest (at the end of the four minutes of its operation) the single marble might after all be found in the right-hand tray, and this, if it happened, would *prove* that the machine's task had been accomplished. However, it is easy to show that this suggestion will not work.

I said, before, that "some device" always restored the marble to its original position in the left-hand tray. Now the most natural device to use for this purpose is another machine— Gamma, say—working like Beta but *from right to left*. Let it be arranged that no sooner does Beta move the marble from left to right than Gamma moves it back again. The successive working periods and pauses of Gamma are then equal in length to those of Beta, except that Gamma is working while Beta is resting, and vice versa. The task of Gamma, moreover, is exactly parallel to that of Beta, that is, to transfer the marble an infinite number of times from one side to the other. If the result of the whole four minutes' operation by the first machine is to transfer the marble from left to right, the result of the whole four minutes' operation by the second machine must be to transfer the marble from right to left. But there is only one marble and it must end somewhere. If it ought to be found on the right, then by the same reasoning it ought to be found on the left. But it cannot be both on the right and on the left. Hence neither machine can accomplish its task, and our description of the infinity machines involves a contradiction.

18. These considerations show, if I am not mistaken, that the outcome of the infinity machine's work is independent of what the machine is supposed to have done antecedently. The marble might end up on the right, on the left, or nowhere. When Hercules ended his slashing, Zeus had to decide whether the head should still be in position or whether, after all, Hercules' strenuous efforts to do the impossible should be rewarded.

Hercules might have argued that every time a head appeared, he had cut it off, so no head ought to remain; but the Hydra could have retorted, with equal force, that after a head had been removed another had always appeared in its place, so a head ought to remain in position. The two contentions cancel one another and neither would provide a ground for Zeus' decision.

Even Zeus, however, could not abrogate the continuity of space and motion; and this, if I am not mistaken, is the source of the contradiction in our description of the machine Beta. The motion of the marble is represented, graphically, by a curve with an infinite number of oscillations, the rapidity of the oscillations increasing constantly as approach is made to the time at which the machine comes to rest.[10] Now to say that motion is continuous is to deny that any real motion can be represented by a curve of this character. Yet every machine that performed an infinite series of acts in a finite time would have to include a part that oscillated "infinitely fast," as it were, in this impossible fashion. For the beginning of every spatio-temporal act is marked by a change in the velocity or in some other magnitude characterizing the agent.

19. It might be thought that the waiting intervals in the operations of the three infinity machines so far described have

[10] For further discussion, see the next essay.

been essential to the argument. And it might be objected that the steps Achilles takes are performed consecutively and without intervening pauses. I will now show that the pauses or "resting periods" are not essential to the argument.

Consider for this purpose two machines, Delta and Epsilon, say, that begin to work with a single marble each, but in opposite directions. Let Delta start with the marble a and Epsilon with the marble b. Now suppose the following sequence of operations: while Delta transfers marble a from left to right in one minute, Epsilon transfers marble b from right to left; then Delta moves b from left to right in half a minute while Epsilon returns a from right to left during the same time; and so on, indefinitely, with each operation taking half the time of its predecessor. During the time that either machine is transporting a marble, its partner is placing the other marble in position for the next move.[11] Once again, the total tasks of Delta and Epsilon are exactly parallel: if the first is to succeed, both marbles must end on the right, but if the second is to succeed, both must end on the left. Hence neither can succeed, and there is a contradiction in our description of the machines.

20. Nor will it help to have a machine—Phi, say—transferring marbles that become progressively smaller in geometrical progression.[12] For, by an argument already used, we can suppose that while Phi is performing its operations, one of the machines already described is going through its paces at the same rates and at the same times. If Phi could complete its task, Alpha, Beta, Gamma, Delta and Epsilon would have to be able to complete their respective tasks. And we have already seen that this is not possible. The sizes of the successive tasks have nothing to do with the logical impossibility of completing an infinite series of operations. Indeed it should be clear by this time that the logical possibility of the existence of any one of the machines depends upon the logical possibility

[11] An alternative arrangement would be to have three similar machines constantly circulating three marbles.

[12] Somebody might say that if the marble moved by Beta eventually shrunk to nothing there would be no problem about its final location.

of the existence of all of them or, indeed, of any machine that could count an infinite number of objects. If the idea of the existence of any one of them is self-contradictory, the same must be true for each of them. The various descriptions of these different hypothetical devices simply make it easier for us to see that one and all are logically impossible. And though a good deal more might be said about this, I hope I have said enough to show why I think this notion of counting an infinite collection is self-contradictory.

21. If we now reconsider for a moment the arguments that have been used in connection with our six infinity machines, we can easily see that no use was made of the respects in which counting differs from any other series of acts. Counting differs from other series of acts by the conventional assignment of numerals to each stage of the count, and in other respects, too. But every series of acts is like counting in requiring the successive doing of things, each having a beginning and end in space or time. And this is all that was used or needed in our arguments. Since our arguments in no way depended upon the specific peculiarities of counting they would apply, as I said at the outset, to any infinite series of acts.

22. And now let us return to Achilles. If it really were necessary for him to perform an infinite number of *acts* or, as Aristotle says "to pass over or severally to come in contact with infinite things" (*Physics*, 233a), it would indeed be logically impossible for him to pass the tortoise. But all the things he really does are finite in number; a finite number of steps, heart beats, deep breaths, cries of defiance, and so on. The track on which he runs has a finite number of pebbles, grains of earth, and blades of grass,[13] each of which in turn has a finite, though enormous, number of atoms. For all of these are things that have a beginning and end in space or time. But if

[13] Cf. Peirce: "I do not think that if each pebble were broken into a million pieces the difficulty of getting over the road would necessarily have been increased; and I don't see why it should if one of these millions—or all of them—had been multiplied into an infinity" (*op. cit.*, 6.182).

[107]

anybody says we must imagine that the atoms themselves occupy space and so are divisible "in thought," he is no longer talking about spatio-temporal things. To divide a thing "in thought" is merely to halve the numerical interval which we have assigned to it. Or else it is to suppose—what is in fact physically impossible beyond a certain point—the actual separation of the physical thing into discrete parts. We can of course choose to say that we shall represent a distance by a numerical interval, and that every part of that numerical interval shall also count as representing a distance; then it will be true a priori that there are infinitely many "distances." But the class of what will then be called "distances" will be a series of pairs of numbers, not an infinite series of spatio-temporal things. The infinity of this series is then a feature of one way in which we find it useful to *represent* the physical reality; to suppose that therefore Achilles has to *do* an infinite number of things would be as absurd as to suppose that because I can attach two numbers to an egg I must make some special effort to hold its halves together.

23. To summarize: I have tried to show that the popular mathematical refutation of Zeno's paradoxes will not do, because it simply assumes that Achilles can perform an infinite series of acts. By using the illustration of what would be involved in counting an infinite number of marbles, I have tried to show that the notion of an infinite series of acts is self-contradictory. For any material thing, whether machine or person, that set out to do an infinite number of acts would be committed to performing a motion that was discontinuous and therefore impossible. But Achilles is not called upon to do the logically impossible; the illusion that he must do so is created by our failure to hold separate the finite number of real things that the runner has to accomplish and the infinite series of numbers by which we describe what he actually does. We create the illusion of the infinite tasks by the kind of mathematics that we use to describe space, time, and motion.

VII

Is Achilles Still Running?

I SHALL here try to answer some objections that have been made to the foregoing analysis of the Achilles paradox.[1] To judge by the reiterated interest in Zeno's paradoxes shown by each successive generation of philosophers, it is unlikely that any new solution will achieve immediate or widespread support. I suspect that part of the fascination of these puzzles is due to their versatility: the Achilles, for instance can plausibly be regarded as concerned with the possibility of motion —or, as directed against the reality of any physical continuum —or even as an argument against the consistency of pure mathematics. Unless all plausible interpretations are discussed together (a task too tedious for anybody but a Ph.D. Candidate) any "solution" will seem to *some* readers to miss the point. So, without extravagant hopes of converting my critics, I shall merely try to make plainer to a forbearing reader the structure of the argument expounded in the previous essay.[2]

[1] I am fortunate in being able to refer to six able discussions of the original paper. These appeared in *Analysis* during 1951 and 1952. Their authors and titles were: (1) Richard Taylor, "Mr. Black on Temporal Paradoxes" (12: 38–44); (2) J. O. Wisdom, "Achilles on a Physical Racecourse" (12: 67–72); (3) L. E. Thomas, "Achilles and the Tortoise" (12: 92–94); (4) Adolf Grünbaum, "Messrs. Black and Taylor on Temporal Paradoxes" (12: 144–158); (5) Richard Taylor, "Mr. Wisdom on Temporal Paradoxes" (13: 15–17); (6) J. Watling, "The Sum of an Infinite Series" (13: 39–46). (I shall refer to these papers by citing the author's name and the page.) Since I shall be concentrating upon points of disagreement between myself and these critics, I take this chance of saying how much I have profited from their remarks.

[2] Are these puzzles worth so much attention? I think so. Richard Taylor calls the Achilles a "very old . . . and very silly problem" (p. 17). Peirce said "this ridiculous little catch presents no difficulty at all to a mind adequately trained in mathematics and logic, but is one of these which is very apt to excite minds of a certain class to an obstinate determination

The first objection to be answered is that in the description of "infinity machines" and specifically the machine "Beta" the mistake was made of ascribing to infinite collections properties that necessarily belong only to finite collections. The notions of the infinity machines, Taylor says, "all tacitly rest upon a self-inconsistent notion of 'an infinite collection,' viz., that of a collection which . . . both has and has not a last member" (p. 39). He goes on to explain that the puzzle of the final whereabouts of the marble that is shifted by Beta an infinite number of times arises only as a result of "the gratuitous assumption that a discrete infinite series ought to have both a first and a last member, which by definition it cannot" (p. 43).[3]

Considering the machine Alpha, Taylor says, "If, as supposed, the supply of marbles is infinitely large, and there is a first one, there cannot be a last one" (p. 39). Similarly, according to him, there cannot be, in the situation described, any *last* operation for Beta to perform, and hence there is no problem about the marble's final position. He adds that although the machine cannot *end* its task—if this means per-

---

to believe a given proposition" (*Collected Papers* [Cambridge, Mass., 1935], 6.177). This is enough to make one cringe. However, Hegel said, "Zeno's dialectic of matter has not been refuted to the present day; even now we have not got beyond it, and the matter is left in uncertainty" (E. S. Haldane's ed. of the *Works,* 1 [London, 1892]: 265), and Russell called Zeno's argument "immeasurably subtle and profound" (*Principles of Mathematics* [Cambridge, 1903], p. 347). It is pleasant to find Hegel and Russell agreeing for once.

[3] Grünbaum also thinks I assumed the existence of a *last* operation in the series of operations performed by each machine and adds that this is a "synthetic assertion" (p. 146) that has to be shown "either *physically* false or gratuitous" (p. 147). Watling, on the other hand, says that my "proof that the machine cannot finish rests, not on the false assumption that an infinity of acts has a last act, but on the true assumption that it has no last act." However, he thinks the false assumption is needed: "the proof is only valid if finishing does require performing a last act" (p. 39).

forming a *last* operation—it certainly can "end" or "finish" its (infinite) task, in the sense of counting all the marbles assigned to it. The machines can all finish their tasks in "the sense in which to finish a number of tasks is to do them all" (Watling, p. 39).

It seems I must have failed to make sufficiently clear the respect in which it was claimed "the expression 'infinite series of acts' is self-contradictory." I did not want to deny that there is a good sense of "finish" in which Alpha might be said to have finished its infinite task if it were found to have moved all the marbles, nor that Beta would have "finished" its work if found to have moved the single marble an infinite number of times. Far from denying this, I took explicit account of this sense of "finish" at the end of section 11 by considering the possibility that "it is not necessary to finish counting; it is sufficient that the counting shall have been finished." In the sense in question, the verb "to finish," when applied to an infinite series of tasks, can be conjugated in the past perfect, the pluperfect, and the present imperfect, but not in other tenses: one can say, "I have finished," "I shall have finished," "I am finishing," but not "I finished *at* such and such a time." It cannot be denied that there are certainly *some* tasks that can be finished without the performance of a terminal act. (The task of falling asleep might be an example.)

Yet this concession leaves the question of the ultimate fate and location of the single marble (shifted infinitely often during a finite period of time) unanswered. You may say Beta will have done all that is demanded if it moves the marble an infinite number of times. Well and good; but if the series of operations is to be conceivable you must be prepared to tell me where the marble will be found after the machine has stopped—and how it is to get there. The machine was supposed to be performing an infinite number of finite oscillations in a finite period of time: the claim that such a motion is incompatible with the marble being *anywhere* at the end of the work period still remains unanswered.

[111]

The line of argument did indeed rest upon a postulate, though not the one imputed by the critics. It may be as well to state it explicitly:

If a body is at a point P and at rest there at an instant t, then for each ϵ, however small, there must be a corresponding distance, $\delta(\epsilon)$, such that the body was no further from P than ϵ throughout the interval of time $(t - \delta, t)$.

Or, more briefly:

In order to be instantaneously at rest at a certain position, a body must necessarily be wholly within an arbitrarily small neighborhood of that position for some time preceding the instant in question.[4]

These are ways of saying that a body cannot be at rest at a point without approaching and *staying* near to that point, i.e., that its motion must be continuous. Now this postulate of continuity of motion is violated by the supposed behavior of the marble when shifted by the infinity machine Beta. The marble is moved the *same* finite distance at each operation; since the postulate is true, we must infer that the marble cannot come to rest; and hence the machine cannot stop working. (Similarly, a pendulum that swings always with constant amplitude, once set in motion, could never again be at rest.) On the other hand, if the machine does finally come to rest (in order to *"have* finished" its task) the postulate will have been violated, because the marble cannot still be in motion and cannot come to rest at one point of its path rather than another.

The postulate stated above and the more general postulates of continuity of which it is a special case are *necessary truths*. Indeed, if we ignore possible complications in quantum mechanics, we can say, roughly, that velocity, acceleration, and the other variable magnitudes relevant to our discussion are all necessarily continuous.[5] Now because the "postulate" of

---

[4] Cf. the discussion of "rest at an instant," below.

[5] Cf. also the examples of necessary truths about space and motion discussed in the next essay.

continuity of motion is a necessary truth, it partly determines what we shall count as a "real" or "physically possible" motion. If there were evidence that seemed to show that a body was at P at some instant, and at Q at a later instant, without having passed through any point of the sphere of radius PQ having its center at P, we should refuse to believe the alleged evidence. We should refuse to believe that a real body could "jump" from P to Q across the intervening space. Conversely, willingness to take such evidence seriously would require a change in our present concepts of space, time, and motion.

The "contradiction" in the previous description of Beta therefore arose from a clash between the description of the machine and postulates of continuity that partially define the meanings of "motion" and related terms. When there is such a clash, we may properly speak of the description being "self-contradictory," even though that description does not have the form of an explicit contradiction like *A-and-not-A*.

The following is a simpler analogue that may help to make the point clearer. Suppose a "description" of a device were offered of such a character that in order for that device to be exemplified it would be necessary that some day of the week should be both Monday and Friday. Then that description could properly be called "self-contradictory." For the words "Monday" and "Friday" belong to a constellation of related terms (names of days of the week) such that "no day of the week can be both Monday and Friday" is a necessary statement. But this is to say that an expression of the form "X is both Monday and Friday" is outlawed as violating the rules of the linguistic subsystem in question. If anybody prefers to say that the description of the device must therefore be senseless (or even "a priori false but synthetic"), I need not disagree with him. I shall be satisfied if it is granted that the "description" of the device could not possibly describe a real thing. And I shall be equally satisfied if it is conceded that the "description" of Beta *cannot* describe a real machine.

[113]

When I published the original essay, I thought that *any* infinite series of "acts" performed in a finite period of time would necessarily involve abrogation of some postulate of continuity. The plausibility of this idea depended upon the definition of an "act" as "something marked off from its surroundings by having a definite beginning and end" (section 9 of the last essay). This now needs to be made more precise.

Suppose the condition of a body throughout a period of time (t_1, t_2) is partially represented by means of a variable magnitude, m, which is such that (a) m changes during (t_1, t_2), i.e., does not preserve the same value throughout the period, (b) m has "turning points" at both t_1 and t_2, i.e., has either a maximum or minimum at t_1 and either a maximum or minimum at t_2. When these conditions are fulfilled, I propose to say the body in question undergoes a *well-bounded change.*[6] Now a well-bounded change, when caused by the body itself, is just what was called an "act" in the preceding essay.

A simple example is provided by a ball bouncing on a horizontal surface. In each interval of time from one instant of maximum contact with the ground to the next, the ball passes through a well-bounded change. For the variable *"m,"* to which reference was made in our definition, can here be taken to be the height of the ball's center of gravity from the ground. We notice that m and its successive derivatives must all be *continuous* functions of the time variable during any motion of the ball that we judge to be "physically possible." When a *man* is jumping up and down, the well-bounded changes through which he is passing are due to his own efforts, so we say he is performing a series of *acts.*

The argument of the earlier essay took for granted that it was physically impossible for any body to perform an infinite series of successive "acts" in a finite period of time (or, more generally, to pass through an infinite series of well-bounded

---

[6] This is a nonce-expression. I forbear to consider complications that will suggest themselves to the mathematical reader, e.g., those resulting from substitution of more general terms in place of "maximum" and "minimum" in the definition.

changes in such a time). Partly as a result of my critics' comments, I am now no longer confident that any breach of continuity of motion need be involved. The following example will help to make the matter clearer.

Suppose Achilles chases the tortoise in a series of leaps, instead of in a smooth motion, and suppose, in order to simplify the discussion, that the tortoise remains at rest while this is going on.

If Achilles' initial distance from the tortoise is d, I thought that an infinite series of jumps $\frac{1}{2}d$, $\frac{1}{4}d$, $\frac{1}{8}d$, . . . successively performed in the times $\frac{1}{2}t$, $\frac{1}{4}t$, $\frac{1}{8}t$, . . . would necessarily involve some breach of continuity at the end point. This is certainly true if Achilles jumps the same height, h, every time. For he is then performing an infinite series of finite vertical oscillations. But suppose the successive heights of the jumps are h, $\frac{1}{2}h$, $\frac{1}{4}h$, etc., so that these heights converge to zero, and let us say for short that the acts performed by him then constitute a *convergent series of acts*. It is no longer clear that it is physically impossible to perform an infinite convergent series of acts in a finite time. Indeed, if *every* physical magnitude connected with the hypothetical motion (e.g., the velocities concerned, the forces exerted, etc.) were to define an infinite *convergent* series of acts, I would have to concede that the motion would not involve abrogation of continuity at the end point. And then I would also have to concede that the illustration of the "infinity machines" did not establish what it was intended to establish, since all of them involved at least one *non*convergent series of acts (e.g., the one associated with the distances covered by the marble dispenser).

A further reason for believing I was wrong is that if I was right it must be physically impossible for a bouncing ball ever to come to rest in a finite time! For consider the traditional analysis of what happens when an imperfectly elastic ball bounces on a horizontal plane. The analysis assumes that after an infinite series of bounces (i.e., "well-bounded changes") performed in a finite period of time, the ball will be at rest. If such a description is incompatible with continuity of all the physical magnitudes concerned, either the elementary physics involved is defective (which I can hardly believe) or else I made a mistake. I must grant that my attempt to show the senselessness of the expression "an infinite series of acts" miscarried.[7]

I must also plead guilty to having insufficiently distinguished two questions, (a) whether the notion of "infinite series of successive acts" is logically absurd *per se,* and (b) whether the notion of "infinite series of successive acts *performed in a finite time"* is logically absurd. At best I would have succeeded in giving an affirmative answer to the latter but not the former question. For instance, nothing in the original essay could show that there is anything absurd in the notion of an immortal (with all time at his disposal) continuing to shift marbles *ad infinitum.* (For now there is no end to the series of acts and so no question about the final location of the marble.)

There remains, however, another ground that still leads me to suppose that talk of an infinite series of acts performed in a finite time is illegitimate. I want to argue that it is part of the "grammar" of a word like "jump" that it shall be inadmissible to speak of "jumps" that are *indefinitely* small or *indefinitely* brief.

Whenever we are told that Achilles made a certain jump, we are entitled to ask, "How far did he jump?" and "How long did the jump take?" Suppose the answers to the questions were to be, respectively, "One-thousandth of an inch" and "One-millionth of a second." We should certainly refuse to take such answers seriously. Some people would say the reason for this is simply that what is alleged to have happened is too in-

---

[7] The point is well brought out in Watling's penetrating discussion of my Hydra example. Cf. his statements that Achilles "has places to be in besides those between him and the tortoise, and so he can catch the tortoise" (p. 41), and again, "It is logically possible for Achilles to have no more tasks to perform, which was not logically possible for Hercules [when the head he cut off immediately reappeared]" (p. 42).

credible to be accepted. But I want to urge that there is a *logical absurdity* in saying that a man jumps a thousandth of an inch, if the word "jump" is understood in any of its ordinary, everyday, uses. When we normally speak or think of a jump made by a man, we have in mind primarily the kind of change of position that can be observed with the unaided senses. The use of the term presupposes the truth of certain generalizations that set limits upon the distances jumped and the times taken for such jumps. When the limits are violated, as in the statement, "Achilles jumped a thousandth of an inch in a millionth of a second," the sentence fails to express a genuine statement.[8]

It is easy enough to imagine meanings that might plausibly be attached to the sentence "Achilles jumped one-thousandth of an inch in a millionth of a second," e.g., if we applied an electric shock to the sole of his foot and measured the shift in his position by some very precise instrument. But to say that we should still mean the same by "jump" in this connection is like saying that "temperature" means the same as "warmth." Such a use of "jump" might count as a plausible extrapolation from everyday uses. But try now to imagine a jump of atomic dimensions! We no longer have any plausible way of connecting a means of verification with the sentence "Achilles jumped a distance equal to the diameter of a hydrogen atom"—the sentence does not have and cannot plausibly be given a use. In order for the sentence "Achilles jumped a distance d" to have a use, d must not be too small—though it is of course impossible to say exactly how large d must be for the sentence to be significant. Let us say that there is a *limitation of scale* upon the applicability of the word "jump."

I believe limitation of scale characterizes the use of a vast number of words applicable to material objects and spatio-temporal events. For example, we can speak sensibly of the color of a tennis ball, but not of the color of an electron. As a special case of limitation of scale, I believe we cannot prop-

---

[8] Cf. the discussion of presuppositions in the second essay of this book, and especially the example, "I am two feet tall."

erly speak of indefinitely brief *acts*. For this reason I want to reaffirm my original contention (which was central to my discussion of the Achilles paradox) that all the things Achilles "really does are finite in number" (section 22 of the previous essay). This is to be regarded as a *necessary statement,* not an empirical affirmation of Achilles' contingent physical limitations. We cannot even imagine what a world would be like in which a person could do infinitely many things in succession in a finite period of time. For that matter, I must now say, we cannot even conceive what it would be like for a man to perform a sufficiently large *finite* number of acts of a given kind in a finite time. The present objection is to the indefinitely small—not the infinitely large (though there are other objections to the latter).

These remarks would not be acceptable to those of my critics who continue to hold that the impossibility of performing infinitely many acts in a finite time is an empirical impossibility—a mere "medical impossibility," to use Russell's striking phrase.[9] They want to say, for instance, that the "infinite divisibility of matter" is *logically* possible even though in fact false. Taylor says that each material body "is divisible without end; however far a stone, for instance, might be divided, so long as any part remains, that part can be thought of as sundered" (p. 41). And he adds:

So also one can think of any object or magnitude whatever as capable of diminution, or as separable into parts, without at all utilizing numbers. If, moreover, we can *think* of an object without actual contradiction (however difficult it may be to the imaginations of some), what proof can be given that an object is not such, in fact? What reason can be given for saying that a stone, for instance, cannot consist of infinitely many parts [10] [p. 42]?

[9] *Aristotelian Society Proceedings,* 36 [1935–1936]: 143.

[10] Contrast Aristotle's argument against any belief in the existence of the infinite that is based on the reason that mathematical magnitudes are "infinite because they never give out in our thought" (*Physics,* 203b 24). Aristotle says, "To rely on mere thinking is absurd, for then the excess or

What exactly are we supposed to imagine here? In order to "sunder a thing in thought, i.e. . . . simply imagine it as separated" (Taylor, p. 42) we must at least be able to imagine that the thing in question has two distinct parts—and this is indeed all that is required for imagining "divisibility." (For it makes no sense to imagine a time or a continuous motion actually "sundered.") Whether or not we can imagine the parts actually separated, so long as we feel constrained to grant that each part of the thing *has* at least two distinct parts, we shall be committed to "infinite divisibility." Indeed, instead of saying that the parts are "separable" we should do better to talk of their being "distinguishable."

There is no great mystery about the mental picture that accompanies the notion of infinite divisibility and renders it congenial to the "imagination." We think of the original body as having *extension* and we abstract from all its other properties, i.e., we think of it as a "geometrical solid" (transparent, invisible, intangible, but still occupying space). Then we imagine a plane (or other boundary) bisecting this geometrical solid and thus determining two distinct parts exactly like the original body *in respect of having extension*. And then it is almost inevitable to imagine the process repeated *ad infinitum*.

However, a picture (whether an "image" or an actual diagram) proves nothing. Nor do we need the picture, since the line of thought can be expressed formally. It is simply this: (a) A material body has extension. Therefore, (b) a body must have at least two distinct parts. (c) Each such part must be extended. And thus by repetition of the previous argument, (d) the body has infinitely many distinct parts.[11]

---

the defect is not in the thing but in the thought. One might think that one of us is bigger than he is and magnify him *ad infinitum*. But it does not follow that he is bigger than the size we are, just because some one thinks he is, but only because he *is* the size he is. The thought is an accident" (208a 15–20).

[11] To make the argument strict, further premises would be necessary, e.g., to ensure that the parts referred to at each stage are *new*. The reader can supply such detail for himself if he thinks fit.

But what reason have we for believing that every extended body must consist of at least two extended parts? Certainly, experience cannot establish it. If true at all, it must be necessarily true, and the strength or weakness of our imaginations has nothing to do with the matter.

Belief in the infinite divisibility of matter is linked to belief in the infinite divisibility of space. If you admit that a body contains infinitely many extended parts, you commit yourself to holding that the space occupied by the body has infinitely many parts—one for each of the parts that compose the original body. Or concede that space is infinitely divisible: you seem then compelled to say that a body might have infinitely many material parts, one for each portion of space. It is only in respect of its *extension* that we are tempted to think of a piece of matter as "infinitely divisible." We think it logically possible for continual subdivision of a piece of copper to continue to yield nothing but copper (and no holes!) because we have the stubborn notion that there would always be a corresponding *space,* which might possibly be entirely filled with copper. The same considerations that favor the infinite divisibility of space favor the infinite divisibility of matter: the mental picture that recommends the one serves equally well for the other.

Now with regard to the infinite divisibility of space,[12] I must repeat what I have already said about the supposed infinite divisibility of matter. No mental picture that we form of space (a lattice of intangible and transparent cubes?) can have any tendency to support the principle of infinite divisibility; nor can it be established by experience.

There are, however, a number of considerations that make the principle of the infinite divisibility of space (and, consequently, the infinite divisibility of matter) almost irresistibly attractive. These considerations arise as natural extensions of certain commonplace truths about space, time, matter, and

[12] Cf. L. E. Thomas: "We know that space and time are infinitely divisible" (p. 92). Do we really know it?

motion that form part of the "common-sense view of the world." [13] By the common-sense view of the world I mean what every layman takes for granted about the physical world before he is exposed to the sophisticated views of geometry, physics, and epistemology. The common-sense view of the world is characterized by taking for granted the truth of such assertions as the following: (a) There exist many bodies of which my own body is an exemplary instance. (b) Every such body resists penetration by other bodies (has inertia), (c) has a recognizable outline and shape (which may, however, change from time to time), (d) usually has a distinctive color, taste, and smell (though some of these may be lacking), (e) persists as recognizably the same in spite of changes, (f) produces and suffers causal effects, (g) is either in motion or at rest, (h) is either in contact with or at a distance from my own body (and similarly for its relation to other bodies), (i) has *concealed* parts with regard to which similar statements may be made, (j) and has, more generally, concealed *properties* that are not evident to direct inspection but are progressively revealed by other means (e.g., by dissolving it in a liquid). Furthermore, all such assertions as the foregoing are taken without question to be confirmable by all other men suitably placed.[14]

Now the generalizations about material bodies that go to make up the common-sense view of the world are derived from limited experience of relatively few macroscopic bodies. But the character of these observations powerfully invites extrapolation: there is a kind of "open horizon" about primitive experience of the spatio-temporal environment. We learn in infancy of the power of certain bodies to interfere with the motion of our own body and find it very natural to suppose that all *bodies* have the same property of inertia (though we

[13] Cf. G. E. Moore's list of "truisms" in his "A Defence of Common Sense," *Contemporary British Philosophy*, ed. J. H. Muirhead, Second Series (London, 1925), p. 194.

[14] Do these contentions define what is sometimes called "naïve realism"? If so, we all start life as naïve realists, and remain so, in spite of everything that science and philosophy teach us.

[121]

may not know that learned label). Direct inspection shows that a vast variety of bodies contain distinguishable and often separable parts (the wheel inside the clock): how natural, how tempting to say that the same is necessarily true of all bodies, even those so small that direct observation is physically impossible.[15]

One thing that makes such extrapolation almost inevitable is the conviction, soon forced upon us by experience, of the presence in bodies of innumerable "concealed" properties—properties revealed by dissection or by still more drastic operations like solution in liquids. Simple optical instruments help to broaden the common-sense view from which all of us start. Magnifying glasses and telescopes promote belief in the existence of innumerable "concealed" properties that are not accessible to unaided observation.

Eventually we reach a stage in which it is difficult if not impossible to distinguish experiential generalizations from geometrical truths that are powerfully *suggested* by experience. Consider such not uncommon experiences as the following (which we can *imagine*, even if we do not have them):

(i) A bar A seems to be exactly the same length as B, and B agrees exactly in length with C, yet C is perceptibly shorter than A.[16]

(ii) A number of red bricks appear to be congruent with one another, and equally so with a number of blue bricks, yet a line of a hundred red bricks is the same length as a line of ninety-nine blue ones.

(iii) If we draw a line AB in a plane and construct on each

[15] Cf. children's riddles: "What's smaller than a fly's mouth?" "What goes into it." "What's smaller than something you can't see?" "Something *it* can't see."

[16] "You may find that, by the most delicate tests you can apply, A is equal to B, and B to C, but A is noticeably unequal to C. When this happens, we say that A is not really equal to B or B to C. Oddly enough, this tends to be confirmed when the technique of measurement is improved. But the real basis of our relief in the axiom is not empirical" (Russell, *Human Knowledge* [London, 1948], p. 302).

side of it equilateral triangles, ACB, ADB, the join of C and D bisects the original line.

Observations such as (i) suggest strongly the existence of lengths *not directly perceptible*. (ii) suggests an indirect way of detecting such small distances; and also suggests that the differences in length involved might be as small as we please (by replacing the number 100 by 1,000, 10,000, and so on). (iii) reinforces the notion of the indefinitely small by showing how *any* length might (theoretically!) be halved. Now (i), (ii), and (iii) together—not to speak of a multitude of supporting considerations that might be cited—strongly recommend the idea of the infinite divisibility of length.

If we yield to these inducements and allow ourselves to speak of indefinitely small lengths, we are then transforming the "common-sense view of the world" by introducing a *change in language*. At the most unsophisticated level, length is something that we can directly perceive; then it becomes a similar property of concealed bodies (bodies outside the range of normal observation); and then eventually something that we have no direct way of observing at all. The procedures for establishing that the length of A differs from the length of B by one part in a million are more indirect than the procedure we use to show that the one is three times the length of the other. By the time we begin to speak of a length the billionth part of a pinhead, we have *no* idea of how to test assertions in which such a phrase might occur. The use of references to indefinitely small lengths is proleptic: at best we anticipate that methods of observation and measurement yet to be invented will eventually provide an empirical meaning for statements about exceedingly small lengths. Meanwhile we calculate with such small numbers just as happily as if they were large ones without worrying about lack of empirical content. (In any practical situation, there is always a lower limit to the lengths that concern us: it is in *philosophical* discussions that one feels the need to say that lengths are indefinitely divisible.)

There is no logical necessity, however, for these proleptic

[123]

drafts upon meaning to be honored. We may be powerfully inclined to think that small spaces (no matter how small) must have the same geometric properties as large spaces (no matter how large), i.e., that geometrical properties are invariant with respect to changes of scale. But the elaboration of non-Euclidean geometries has taught us that what is true of small regions of space need not therefore be true of large regions (e.g., in elliptic geometry there is a *maximum* triangle, so, spatial intuition to the contrary, it is not possible indefinitely to *enlarge* bodies). And the same may be said even of divisibility.[17]

From the standpoint here outlined, the axiom of infinite divisibility, like the other axioms of any geometry, may be regarded as a *convention*. It is a very natural convention, strongly suggested by certain features of macroscopic experience of space and one that a mathematician can hardly avoid making without immeasurably complicating his task. Yet it remains a convention for all that: to say space is infinitely divisible is to say something important about the mode of representation we choose to adopt in speaking about bodies and their relations—it is not, as it seems to some of my critics, an assertion about the character (the necessary character?) of Space.

Such reflections as these are by no means original. Any number of able writers have pointed out in detail the extent of the elaboration involved in passing from the naïve common-sense view of the world to the standpoint of even the crudest geometry. But it is easy to forget the magnitude of the intellectual construction involved and to suppose the links between geometry and experience to be as direct as those between the commonplaces of naïve realism and the world. (The mistake of imagining an electron as a billiard ball—only smaller.)

Taylor falls into this error when he represents Zeno as saying, "Do not confuse me, finally, with distinctions between various kinds of distance; I know of only one kind, and we can

[17] It is worth noting that the axioms of geometry remain true if the "points" are taken to be a selected class of *extended* bodies.

talk about that." [18] But I am afraid such distinctions are necessary if we are not to indulge in altogether oversimplified notions of the relations between geometry and experience. Failure to observe distinctions may, in the long run, produce as much confusion as the attempt to heed them.

So I return, unrepentant, to my assertion in the earlier essay that the infinity of the series into which Zeno's argument divides Achilles' path is "a feature of one way in which we find it useful to *represent* physical reality" (section 22 of the last chapter). To suppose that he must therefore do infinitely many things—or even that he must therefore "pass over" infinitely many spaces in any sense which gives rise to paradox is quite gratuitous.

To summarize: In these supplementary remarks, I have been trying to elaborate and render clearer the underlying thought of my analysis of the Achilles paradox, viz., that the plausibility of the argument rests upon subtle confusions between two ways of talking about space, time, and motion. The notion of an "act" or a "task" is indigenous to "common-sense language." Among the rules that determine the correct use of the interconnected constellations of words belonging to this language are certain "postulates of continuity" whose character I have tried to explain. Originally, I thought that the expression "an infinite series of acts performed in a finite period of time" involved a breach of such continuity postu-

[18] Taylor, p. 16. Zeno's retort is supposed to be in answer to Wisdom's attempt (passim) to distinguish between "mathematical" and "physical" distance. I agree with Wisdom's intent when he says that ' we must deny that the mathematical description is a correct descriptio of pl ysical distance" (p. 69), but his statement invites misconstruction. Ther(is no reason why we should not say, if we please, that the mathematical d :rip-tion *is* correct: the mistake to be avoided is that of assuming that each distinguishable item of the mathematical description must be in one-to-one correspondence with a distinguishable item of physical reality— that because we have a *mathematical use* for the expression "distance ϵ" (no matter how small ϵ may be) there must be corresponding physical distances as small as we like.

lates and thus committed their user to sinning against the grammar of common-sense language. This conclusion may have been mistaken. So I have fallen back upon the defense that common-sense language does not permit of reference to the *indefinitely* small. I have tried to show that any belief to the contrary cannot be defended by appeals to the "imagination." The "infinite divisibility of space" is a *convention* that helps to determine the character of a language (the language of geometry) that replaces common-sense language when we turn from the problems of everyday life to the more exacting tasks of technology and pure science. But if we do not expect this more precise language to display a one-to-one correspondence between its terms and the distinguishable items of everyday experience, we shall avoid the error for supposing that Achilles is condemned to performing infinitely many *tasks*. We can *say* that Achilles has to run ten yards, then one yard, then a tenth of a yard, and so on, and continue so long as paper and ink are available. But this in no way complicates Achilles' task: he may cheerfully catch the tortoise in blissful ignorance of the mathematician's readiness to represent the immortal race by formulas of indefinitely increasing complexity.

VIII

The Paradox of the Flying Arrow

1. *Introduction.* It is generally agreed that Zeno's four arguments, the "Achilles," the "Dichotomy," the "Arrow," and
the "Stadium," were intended to complement one another.
The first two try to deduce absurdities from assumptions of
infinite divisibility (whether of space, time, or motion); the
others take for granted that space, time, or motion consist of
indivisible parts. "They [i.e., the four arguments] form a
dilemma in which the possibility of motion is denied both
on the assumption of infinite divisibility and on the assumption of indivisibles" (H. D. P. Lee, *Zeno of Elea* [Cambridge,
1936], p. 103).

Having already discussed the arguments against infinite
divisibility in the last two essays, I shall now, for the sake of
completeness, offer some analysis of Zeno's remaining arguments. The paradox of the flying arrow is as puzzling as the
Achilles, and I do not think the able commentators whom it
has fascinated have thrown sufficient light upon the nature of
the mistakes committed.

2. *The classical statement of the paradox.* Our primary source,
as in the case of Zeno's other arguments against motion, is
Aristotle. He states the argument thus:

Zeno's reasoning, however,[1] is fallacious, when he says that if
everything when it occupies an equal space is at rest and if that
which is in locomotion is always occupying such a space at any
moment, the flying arrow is therefore motionless [*Physics* 239b 5,
Oxford translation].

[1] Aristotle has just been arguing (in an interesting but difficult section) that although at "any moment" a moving body "is always against
something stationary" (i.e., would be exactly opposite a suitably placed
stationary body of the same dimensions), this does not prove that the
body is at *rest* at every given moment.

[127]

This is said so tersely that it is hard to understand, and the argument must be slowed down if it is to have any power to puzzle us. As we try to make out its meaning, much will depend on how we read the expression "at the *moment*." For "moment" can mean a very brief *period* or interval of time (as in "wait a moment") or again an unextended *boundary* between periods of time, a "point-instant" (cf. such expressions as "at the moment of impact"). To avoid confusion I shall always use "moment" to mean an *interval* of time; whenever it is necessary to speak of the extremity of a time-interval or a boundary between intervals, I shall use the word "instant." According to this stipulation, it will be correct to speak of what happens *"during* a moment" but incorrect to say anything happens "during an instant"; the expression *"at* an instant" will make sense, but there will be no sense attached to the expression "at a moment." (This involves a deviation from the ordinary usage in which "moment" and "instant" are approximate synonyms.)

I do not know whether, in reporting Zeno's argument about the arrow, Aristotle intended to refer to "moments" having duration or to durationless *instants*. At any rate, there are these two possible interpretations of what he said, and two different versions of the paradox of the arrow that result. I am inclined to think that the original form of Zeno's argument referred to moments, not instants, and I shall examine this version first.

Aristotle says the argument is directed against the assumption that there are indivisible moments. So, if we take moments to have duration and yet to be indivisible, a colloquial paraphrase of the argument might run as follows:

3. *An informal paraphrase.*

You hold that there are indivisible "moments," i.e., miminal or atomic time intervals. Anything that happens, you say, must take at least a "moment."

Consider, then, what happens when an archer releases an arrow from the bow, expecting it will fly to the target. Throughout the first "moment" after the archer "lets go," the arrow must occupy a space into which it fits exactly (an "equal space," as Aristotle said)—or, to put the matter in another way, the arrow must be in one and the same space throughout that moment. For in order to be in two or more places, it would have to be in one place during part of the moment and in another during another part of the moment. But you maintain (and I agree for the sake of argument) that a moment is indivisible, i.e., that there cannot be such a thing as a part of a moment. Hence, as I said before, the arrow cannot be in two places (or more) during the first moment (or, for that matter, during *any* moment).

Now if the arrow is occupying one and the same place throughout the first moment, it must be at rest during that moment. (For to move during a period of time is to *change* position during that time.) [2] But if the arrow is at rest throughout the first moment after it has been released, there is no reason why it should ever move to a different place. It follows that the arrow never leaves the bow and can never reach the target.

Perhaps this elaboration of the argument (which turns upon treating a "moment" as having duration) leaves the reader cold, because he cannot take seriously the assumption that time consists of extended but indivisible periods. If so, I must ask him to wait for the alternative version in terms of instants that is discussed later.

4. *Aristotle's solution.* After stating Zeno's argument (as reported above) Aristotle dismisses it succinctly in the following words: "This is false, for time is not composed of indivisible moments any more than any other magnitude is composed of indivisibles" (loc. cit.). A few lines later he says, still more explicitly, "[Zeno's] conclusion follows from the assumption that time is composed of moments: if this assumption is not granted, the conclusion will not follow" (239b 30).

---

[2] "For if a thing—itself and each of its parts—occupies the same space for a definite period of time, it is at rest: for it is in just these circumstances that we use the term 'being at rest'—when at one moment after another it can be said with truth that a thing, itself and its parts, occupies the same space" (*Physics* 239a 26).

What reasons does Aristotle have for saying that a continuous magnitude cannot be composed of indivisible parts? In the first place, he regards a thing as "continuous" when its parts have identical boundaries.[3] Applied to our special case, this would mean: If a continous period of time is composed of moments, two consecutive moments must have an identical boundary (i.e., the instant at which one ends must be the very same instant at which the next moment begins).

But according to Aristotle, anything that has a boundary must have *parts* (for can we not distinguish between the boundary and that of which it is the boundary?).[4] Now to call something indivisible is to say it has no parts: hence indivisible things have no boundaries; and hence also a continuous thing cannot have indivisible parts. Or, applied specifically to moments: Moments cannot have boundaries because they are indivisible. Hence two moments cannot be contiguous, and so time cannot be composed of indivisible moments. It will be noticed that Aristotle simply denies the truth of one of Zeno's premises. He seems to hold that the argument is formally valid and that motion would be impossible if time were composed of "moments."

5. *Criticism of Aristotle's solution.* It seems to me that this argument of Aristotle's miscarries through an important ambiguity in the notion of "indivisible" and the related notions of "part" and "composition."

There are two senses of "part" (and two corresponding

---

[3] "The 'continuous' is a subdivision of the contiguous: things are called continuous when the touching limits of each become one and the same and are, as the word implies, contained in each other: continuity is impossible if these extremities are two" (227a 10–13).

[4] Cf. Aristotle's argument to prove that a line is not composed of points: "A line cannot be composed of points, the line being continuous and the point indivisible. For the extremities of two points can neither be *one* (since of an indivisible there can be no extremity as distinct from some other part) nor *together* (since that which has no parts can have no extremity, the extremity and the thing of which it is the extremity being distinct)" (231a 25). Note especially the statements in parentheses.

senses of "composed" and "divisible") that we need to distinguish. (a) A finger is properly said to be a part of a hand, a day part of a week, and the class of prime integers a part of the class of integers. Here, the part and the whole are of the *same logical type*—physical objects, periods of time, and classes of integers, respectively. In such cases let us follow Broad [5] in saying that the parts are *components* of the whole. (b) It is also quite proper, however, to say that a man is part of a family, a sentence part of a poem, and courage part of somebody's character. In such cases, where the part and whole are of *different logical types,* let us call the part a *constituent* of the whole. (Thus a component is a homogeneous part, while a constituent is a heterogeneous part of a complex.)

Now Zeno's argument, as we have interpreted it, assumes that moments have no homogeneous parts or *components,* i.e., that there are no intervals of time of shorter duration than moments; but this does not prevent us from holding that moments are complexes having *constituents:* Minimal or atomic intervals might well be bounded by distinct *instants.* It would be quite proper to call time intervals having no components "indivisibles" (in one important sense of that word) and Aristotle has not proved (even on his own premises about continuity) that time cannot be composed of moments indivisible in *this* sense. In order for his argument to count as sound, we must suppose he would not call anything indivisible unless it contained neither constituents nor components. In the case of the "moments" mentioned in Zeno's argument, this would mean that Aristotle insists that they have no extremities, i.e., that they be taken to be *instants.* Aristotle cannot al-

---

[5] "We must distinguish between two senses at least of part and whole, viz., the sense in which a point is part of a line and the sense in which a little line is part of a bigger one. In the first sense we mean by 'part' a term or constituent in a related complex which is of a different nature from its terms. A point is part of a line in the sense in which McTaggart is part of Trinity. In the second sense we mean by 'part' something which is of the same nature as the whole" (C. D. Broad, *Mind,* 30 [1921]: 323). Cf. also the same author's *Examination of McTaggart's Philosophy,* 1 (Cambridge, 1933): 331.

low time to consist of such instants; for his definition of continuity would then require that each instant be "contiguous" to a consecutive instant, which is clearly impossible.[6] Nowadays, however, a mathematician would say this simply shows Aristotle's conception of continuity to be defective; and he would be ready to give an alternative definition that would allow a set of instants (or a set of points) to count as "continuous."[7] But Aristotle can hardly be blamed for not having provided arguments to anticipate objections of this degree of sophistication.

To sum up this discussion on Aristotle's treatment of the argument: Aristotle's refutation requires us to suppose that Zeno was referring to durationless instants: it does not succeed against the supposition that time is composed of extended but indivisible moments, nor will it stand if Aristotle's conception of continuity is rejected, as it commonly would be today. On the whole, then, some further discussion of the paradox seems to be required.

Although Aristotle's attempt at solution fails, as I think it does, there are many passages in the *Physics* where he points the way to a correct answer, and I shall cite these when I explain my own solution.[8]

---

[6] Cf. the passage cited in footnote 4 above.

[7] "Mathematicians have distinguished different degrees of continuity and have confined the word 'continuous,' for technical purposes, to series having a certain high degree of continuity. But for philosophical purposes, all that is important in continuity is introduced by the lowest degree of continuity, which is called 'compactness.' A series is called 'compact' when no two terms are consecutive, but between any two there are others" (Russell, *Our Knowledge of the External World* [London, 1926], p. 138). See also footnote 10 below.

[8] Aristotle's position is further complicated by his doctrine that the indivisibles belonging to continuous magnitude have merely *potential* existence until actualized by a division of the continuous magnitude. ". . . any one of the points lying between the two extremes is potentially a middle-point: but it is not actually so unless that which is in motion divides the line by coming to a stand at that point and beginning its motion again" (262a 23–25). ". . . though what is continuous contains an infinite number of halves, they are not actual but potential halves.

6. *A modern version of the paradox.* I first supposed Zeno's original argument to use the assumption that time is composed of extended but indivisible *moments*.[9] Although the modern writer is likely to find this assumption uncongenial, he is quite likely to say (as we shall find Russell does) that a period of time is nothing but a class of indivisible and unextended *instants*. Given this alternative assumption, however, it is possible to frame an argument that is suggested by, but is not identical with, Aristotle's original version. This more sophisticated version is even harder to refute. I shall first state it in colloquial language, using such words as might naturally arise in discussion and aiming initially at persuasion rather than precise formulation. In this way, I hope to make it easier to see the underlying pattern of thought.

Consider an arrow that is shot from a bow to a target. During its flight, the arrow changes its position (if you will allow me to state the obvious) for it starts in one place, ends in another, and passes through an enormous number of others on the way. Consider any one of these places, say the one exactly midway between the bow and the target. The arrow cannot *stay* in that place for any length of time, no matter how small; for the arrow is constantly moving during the flight, and therefore *changes* its position during every interval of time. The arrow must, therefore, be at that place (the halfway mark) only for an *instant*.

At this instant, the arrow is at a perfectly definite place, for a body cannot be in two places at once. And that place is exactly filled by the arrow at that instant or, to put the matter in another

---

If the halves are made actual, we shall get not a continuous but an intermittent motion" (263a 27–30). So perhaps Aristotle would have said that the "instants" of the arrow's flight do not *actually* exist if the arrow is in continuous motion. Each of them *could* exist and *would* exist—if the motion had stopped at that instant—and then the arrow really would have been at rest at that instant! I think this involves a meaning of "instant" which is not the one we shall be concerned with, viz., the meaning in which there *actually* are "instants" only at the commencements and the terminations of motions. But the topic is difficult and I shall not pursue it further.

[9] This assumption is attacked in the argument about the stadium, discussed in the next essay.

way, the space occupied at the instant is of exactly the same dimensions as the arrow itself. But doesn't this mean that the arrow must be *at rest* at that instant? For, at that instant, it is confined to a space exactly equal to it—at that time, it has *no room* in which to be moving. And (as we have seen) the arrow is not in that position for any length of time—it has, at that instant, *no time* in which to be moving.

If this seems strange, consider the following comparison. After the arrow has reached the target, I pick it up, and hold it, once again, at the halfway mark. This time, there is no doubt that the arrow is motionless. But the first time the arrow was in *exactly the same condition* at the instant it was passing through the halfway mark. Both times, the arrow *exactly fits* the place in question. So the arrow must have been at rest the first time, just as it is the second time.

You still think motion is something more than being *at* different places at different times? Then consider the following comparison, First, I shoot the arrow from bow to target in the normal way. During the flight, the arrow passes through each definite position in the path at some definite instant. Next, suppose that after the arrow has been retrieved, some contrivance (a machine, if you like) now makes the arrow occupy again each of the places previously occupied—and *exactly one minute later* than the corresponding instant. (So that if it was at *P* at *t* minutes after noon, the first time, it is brought to *P* again at *t* + 1 minutes after noon the second time.) I suggest that there would be no conceivable way of distinguishing the second episode from a real "flight." No observation that could possibly be made the second time could show that the arrow was not behaving in exactly the same way as it did the first time. Hence, it was at rest at each instant both the first time and the second.

I began by talking about the place at the halfway mark. But what I have said clearly applies to every place passed during the flight. The arrow is at rest at *every* instant of the flight; so, although it is at different places at different times, it is always motionless.

In this version, there is no talk of extended moments, but I have spoken freely of unextended instants. I have tried to reinforce the picture of the arrow *frozen,* as it were, at each place and each instant. To be even half persuaded, we have to think of motion as an infinite series of instantaneous *states* —a series of still lifes—tableaux of "arrested motion." These might be compared to the static pictures of which a cinematograph reel is composed.[10]

7. *Some alternative versions.* The reader may wish to compare my exposition of the argument with the briefer paraphrases made by other commentators. The following are typical:

The arrow, which is supposed to be flying, is never really doing so, because at every moment it is not moving but simply occupying a certain space [D. Ross, *Aristotle's Physics* (Oxford, 1936), p. 79].

. . . the arrow in motion which cannot move because at any time in its course it is in an indivisible instant in which there cannot be any motion . . . [H. Cherniss, *Aristotle's Criticism of Presocratic Philosophy* (Baltimore, 1935), p. 155].

[Zeno] points out that at each instant the arrow simply is where it is, just as it would be if it were at rest. Hence he concludes that there can be no such thing as a *state* of motion, and, therefore, adhering to the view that a state of motion is essential to motion, he infers that there can be no motion and that the arrow is always at rest [Russell, *History of Western Philosophy* (New York, 1945), p. 805].

The argument is this. It is impossible that the arrow can move in the instant, supposed indivisible, for, if it changed its position, the instant would at once be divided. Now the moving body is, in the instant, either at rest or in motion; but as it is not in motion it must be at rest; hence, as by hypothesis time is composed of nothing but instants, the moving body is always at rest [T. Heath, *Mathematics in Aristotle* (Oxford, 1949), p. 127].

[10] "A cinematograph in which there are an infinite number of pictures, and in which there is never a *next* picture because an infinite number come between any two, will perfectly represent a continuous motion" (Bertrand Russell, *History of Western Philosophy* [New York, 1945], p. 805).

It will be noticed that these writers do not make the distinction between "moment" and "instant" that I have thought to be relevant in understanding Aristotle's original form of the paradox. Nearly all the modern commentators have assumed that the paradox dealt with *unextended* instants, and it is this form of the argument that will concern us for the rest of the discussion.

8. *Russell's solution.* Russell, who has discussed the paradox on several occasions,[11] takes the heroic course of accepting the conclusion that the arrow is always at rest. In his earliest discussion he states Zeno's conclusion in the words, "The arrow in its flight is immovable," and then adds the comment, "This has usually been thought so monstrous a paradox as scarcely to deserve serious discussion. To my mind, I must confess, it seems a very plain statement of a very elementary fact." [12] And in another striking passage he says, "Weierstrass, by strictly banishing all infinitesimals, has at last shown that *we live in an unchanging world,* and that *the arrow, at every moment of its flight, is truly at rest.*" [13]

This sounds as if Weierstrass (or Russell?) had made an extraordinary and shocking discovery about the world. We

[11] See his *Principles of Mathematics* (Cambridge, 1903), p. 347, 350–353, *Our Knowledge of the External World* (rev. ed.; London, 1926), pp. 178–180, *History of Western Philosophy* (New York, 1945), pp. 804–806.

[12] *Principles,* p. 350. The "very elementary fact" is that "Every possible value of a variable is a constant" (p. 351)—or, rather, the special form of this applicable to the case in which the variable in question is a variable position.

[13] *Principles,* p. 347. Russell adds, "The only point where Zeno probably erred was in inferring (if he did infer) that, because there is no change, therefore the world must be in the same state at one time as another. This consequence by no means follows . . ." I see no evidence that Zeno did make this inference. My guess is that he would have been content, and perhaps more than a little surprised, to find a great logician judging that the world had been proved to be unchanging. And I think he would have been interested to know how Russell proposed to explain the different conditions of the world at different times.

seem to be told that nothing changes and nothing moves, and that every time we say men grow old or the moon rises, we are making a *mistake*. And it is not a mistake of fact: the arguments that Russell accepts prove, if they prove anything, that everything is *necessarily* unchanging and at rest. So the supposition that anything might be in motion has to be as absurd as the supposition that matter does not occupy space or that numbers can change. There is a logical absurdity on this view in seeking to apply the term "motion" to anything. Or to put the point in another way, anybody who fancies that he has a *conception* of "motion" must be deceiving himself—the word "motion" has no use whatever.

In this case, "rest" cannot mean "the absence of motion" and it is difficult to see what else it can mean, or what it can mean to say that a body is necessarily at rest at every instant.

But this is an unsympathetic way of presenting Russell's position. A more plausible interpretation would be the following: "There is no reason to deny that motion does occur, as our senses constantly testify; and hence the word 'motion' does have a good use. But what we *mean* by 'motion' is simply *being at* different places at different times. To 'be at' a definite place is simply to occupy that place—call this 'being at rest' or not as you please. Thus 'motion' simply means 'occupation of different places at different instants.' "

So construed, Russell's solution is not a denial of the reality of motion, but an analysis of what the word "motion" *means*. And the proposal no longer has quite the paradoxical appearance it had at the outset. The chief objection to it, so far as I can see, is that it is an *incorrect* analysis. "Occupation of a space at an instant" has to be defined in terms of "motion during an interval" and not vice versa, as I shall try to show below.

9. *What remains to be done.* Aristotle, Russell, and the other philosophers who have discussed the paradox have failed to make one point (or, perhaps have failed to emphasize it sufficiently) which, if sound, will enable the sophistry concealed in the original argument to be shown much more directly.

In the versions of the paradox presented above (sections 6 and 7), there occur the following phrases: "The arrow is at rest at that instant" (my version), "at every moment it [the arrow] is not moving" (Ross), "the moving body is, in the instant, either at rest or in motion" (Heath). Aristotle's own version does not contain explicit reference either to "rest at an instant" or "motion at an instant." But we cannot draw the conclusion offered unless we may infer from "What is in flight is always occupying an equal space *at any given instant*" (a given premise) and "Nothing is in motion when occupying a space equal to itself" (another given premise) to "Whatever is in flight is motionless *at a given instant*" (an unstated intermediate conclusion). I wish to consider the propriety of using the phrases, "motion at an instant" and "rest at an instant."

There are familiar uses of the words "motion" and "rest" that can be identified by the following necessary statements: (a) What is in motion is a body. (b) Every motion *lasts* a certain length of time. (c) A body is at rest if and only if it is not in motion. Now in *this* sense of "motion" it is logically absurd to say that a body is in motion *at an instant*. For the question "How *long* did the motion in question last?" becomes senseless and criterion (b) above is violated. The question is as absurd as the question, "How heavy is empty space?" We can sensibly speak of weight only in connection with matter and we can sensibly speak of the duration of motion only if we are asked about motion during some interval of time. Now if it is absurd to speak of motion at an instant (in this sense), it is equally absurd to speak of rest at an instant (in the corresponding sense).[14] For rest is the absence of motion (cf. (c) above) and where it is absurd to speak of "motion" it is also absurd to speak of "no motion." (It is just as absurd to say numbers are at rest as it is to say that they are in motion.)

If this sense of "motion" were the *only* sense of the word,

[14] Cf. Aristotle: "Nothing can be in motion in a present" (234a 24) and "Nor can anything be at rest in a present" (234a 32). And "at a moment it is not possible for anything to be either in motion or at rest" (239b 1).

[138]

the argument about the flying arrow could be punctured very simply. It would be sufficient to say that it is nonsensical to speak either of motion or of rest *at an instant,* and a crucial premise of the argument would have to be rejected as involving a violation of language. Unfortunately, the matter is not so simple. There happen to be good senses in which we *can* speak of "motion at an instant" or "instantaneous motion" and "rest at an instant" or "instantaneous rest." So it is necessary to show (or, rather to remind ourselves, since everything that needs to be said is familiar) that the sense in which we can speak of a body moving *during* a period of time is other than the sense in which we can speak of its being in motion *at* an instant; and the sense in which we can speak of a body being at rest during a period is other than the sense in which we can speak of its being instantaneously at rest. For then it will be clear that the arrow is not at rest at any points of its path except the first and the last, and the argument will collapse. The temptation to say the arrow must be at rest at every instant arises from confusion between the two senses. We are inclined to say, "The arrow is at rest at each instant," when all we are entitled to say is, "It is senseless to speak of a body 'moving *at* an instant' in the sense in which it is 'moving *during* an interval of time.' " Similar confusions arise in connection with the expression "space occupied" that plays an important part in the argument.

I shall try now to make prominent the difference in meaning between "motion during an interval" and "motion at an instant." Each of these expressions belongs to a constellation of related expressions, whose linguistic connections will need to be explored.

10. *Some simplifying assumptions.* In order to avoid irrelevant complications, let us agree to speak exclusively of *linear* motions and *perfectly rigid* bodies. When any reference is made to "a body moving" we are to understand, accordingly, that the motion is along a straight line and that in the course of that motion the body's size and shape remain unchanged.

[139]

The notion of space with which we work might as well be that of "absolute Space," i.e., a single and unique reference system for the determination of positions. And if this is uncomfortably abstract, no harm will be done to our analysis by thinking of this "Space," quite crudely, as an immense cavity (an enormous room, sans walls, sans floor, and sans ceiling!). In other words, we can adhere to "the common practical view of Space as a single box 'with no sides to it,' in which the things and events of the physical world move and have their beings." [15] Accordingly, "*a* space" (without the capital letter) will, for us, always mean some bounded and identifiable portion of this single and unique container.

I shall also take for granted that no mischief will result from thinking of a single absolute Time, "like a simple Space consisting of a single straight line," [16] of which particular periods of time are bounded and identifiable portions. All the "times" we shall be talking about for the present will be "stretches" or "intervals" or "periods" of time. For it is with these that all temporal observations are primarily concerned.

11. *Three meanings of "space occupied."* It would be generally agreed that any body, whether in motion or at rest, must "occupy space" or "take up room." This is a necessary truth that plays an important part in Zeno's argument. Upon examination, however, we can detect three different senses in which a body can be said to "take up room" and, correspondingly, three different senses of the sentence expressing the necessary truth.

(i) Whether a body is moving throughout a given period of time or is at rest during part or all of that time, there exists what I shall call *the least space to which it is confined during that time.* Suppose the body moves only in a straight line, as we are assuming for simplicity, let its length be l, and the total advance made by the tip of the body during the time in question be d; then the least space to which the body was

[15] C. D. Broad, *Scientific Thought* (London, 1923), p. 27.

[16] Broad, *ibid.*, p. 54.

confined during the time will be a cylinder of length $l + d$. Imagine a skin of cellophane stretched around the body, sufficiently far from it not to impede the motion, and sufficiently close for further contraction to be impossible without penetration by the moving body. Then the cellophane skin outlines the boundary of "the least space to which the body is confined" during the time in question. Let us say, for short, that a body, whether in motion or at rest during a period of time, *reserves* a space during that period. (Unfortunately, there is no exact colloquial equivalent for "space reserved" and the use of "space occupied" encourages the very ambiguities we want to avoid.) If a body is in motion during a period of time, it must, of course reserve (or "sweep out") *different* spaces during different parts of that time.

(ii) When and only when a body is at rest *throughout* a period of time, it may be said to *"hold"* one and the same space throughout that time. When the body is moving, however, it is changing position, and it is then nonsensical to speak of "the space held by it."

(iii) Finally, there is another, and more elusive sense, in which we commonly say that a body must "occupy space" or "take up room." No matter whether the body is at rest or in motion, its parts are at various distances from one another (and, so long as it is rigid, the same distances); and it constantly retains the power to resist penetration and to interfere with the motion of other bodies that impinge upon it. This is commonly described by saying the body "has extension" (and if it is rigid the same extension). Here we are thinking either of "instantaneous occupation of a space" (for which see below) or else of the "extension" of the material body. There is one sense, at least, in which to say that a body always "takes up room" is to say that it has spatial dimensions (and, if it is rigid, always the same dimensions). It is easy to imagine the body's "extension" as a kind of ghost that constantly accompanies the body—a perfectly, transparent, and intangible "body" of the same shape and size—an unsubstantial and inseparable twin that is always in the same place as its corporeal brother.

[141]

The following relations between the above notions are important for our purpose: (a) The space *reserved* by a body is necessarily greater than or equal to that body, i.e., the body is either congruent with that space or congruent with some proper part of it. (b) The space *held* by a body is necessarily congruent with it, i.e., the body "exactly fits" it. (c) If the space reserved is "equal" to the body, that body is necessarily at rest throughout the period of time in question, and the space reserved then coincides with the space held. (d) The extension of a body is always congruent with that body.

Consider now what happens when the body is at rest. In the general case, "space reserved," "space held," and "extension" refer to three different things. But when the body is at rest, there is a single and unique space which is both the space reserved and the space held, and this, too, is easily confused also with the extension of the body. The three notions are then hard to distinguish, and especially so when all three are expressed by the vague words "space occupied."

12. *The meaning of "space occupied at an instant."* So far I have been confining myself exclusively to periods (or intervals or stretches) of time, and for the excellent reason that our primary information about bodies is always of their behavior during periods of time. There are, however, derivative senses in which we can speak also of *instants* of time, and notions connected with such instants.

An example or two may help to explain what I mean by "primary" and "derivative" meanings. Every tree necessarily has a trunk, but we can identify trees and make all manner of assertions about them without ever referring to their trunks. On the other hand, the trunk must be the trunk *of* some tree; so we cannot speak of "trunks" unless we have previously introduced the term "tree." I say the meaning of "trunk" is derivative from (or "tied to") the meaning of "tree." Again, every material body must have a surface, but bodies can be identified and referred to without any mention of their surfaces. But a surface must be the surface *of* a body. We can imagine a language for talking about bodies that does not contain the word "surface" or some synonym; but we can frame no conception of a language of surfaces that does not contain the word "body" or some synonym.

Similarly an "instant" is most conveniently defined as a boundary *of* a period—*"where"* some period ends or begins.[17] The following necessary statements help further to determine the uses of "instant." (a) Every instant is the end of indefinitely many periods and the beginning of indefinitely many. (b) It makes no sense to ask "how long" an instant "lasts." (c) It makes no sense to talk about anything happening "during" or "throughout" an instant.

It follows that there can be no sense in talking about motion or rest *during* an instant; and hence that the notions of "space reserved" and "space held," discussed above, have no application to instants. (For in defining them we were compelled to talk about motion and rest *during* periods of time.)

Nevertheless, we can easily define a *derivative* notion of "space occupied *at an instant*" in the following way. If an instant ends one period and begins another, let us say it "separates" them. For any given body, there will be a unique space reserved for each of those two periods (as we saw above), and it follows from our ideas about the continuity of motion that those two spaces *must have a common part*. It is this common part that we can choose to call "the space instantaneously occupied at the instant in question." An important consequence of this definition is that the space instantaneously occupied must be "equal" to (congruent with) the body in question.

[17] Cf. Aristotle: "The 'now' . . . is a limit of time for it is the beginning of the one and the end of the other" (222a 10). "In so far then as the 'now' is a boundary, it is not time, but an attribute of it" (220a 21). Ross paraphrases this: "In so far, then, as the now is a limit, it is not time but is merely something involved in the nature of time" (*op. cit.*, p. 603).

13. *The meaning of "instantaneous rest" and "instantaneous motion."* We shall need some preliminary definitions. Suppose an instant i separates the periods P_1 and P_2: let us say that i *belongs* to the combined period P, consisting of P_1 succeeded by P_2. Suppose during P (of duration t), a body changes its position by a distance d: let us call the quantity d/t the *average velocity* of the body during P. (The reader is reminded that we are dealing with linear motions exclusively.)

A body may be said to be *instantaneously at rest at an instant i* when and only when any of the following conditions is satisfied:

A: i ends a period throughout which the body is at rest.
B: i begins a period throughout which the body is at rest.
C: i belongs to periods during which the average velocity of the body in question is as small as we please (i.e., no matter how small a positive quantity ϵ be assigned, it is possible to find at least one period to which i belongs for which the average velocity of the body is smaller than ϵ).

A body may be said to be *instantaneously in motion* at an instant if and only if it is not instantaneously at rest at that instant.

From these definitions it follows that in order to determine whether a body is at rest or in motion *at an instant* we *must* use the notions of rest and motion during periods (i.e., the notion of instantaneous motion is "derivative" from the notion of motion during an interval). If this is what Russell intended to say when he asserted that there was no such thing as a *state* of motion at an instant, we can certainly agree with him.

14. *Applications to the paradox.* My basic idea is that there is a constant temptation to slide from one of the notions we have been discussing to another, and in so doing to misapply the necessary statements that characterize some of these notions but not others. A body that "occupies an equal space" in the sense of "holding" it throughout a *period* of time is neces-

sarily at rest throughout the period. Now a body *instantaneously* occupies a space equal to itself, and hence we have some temptation to say that it is necessarily at rest *at that instant*. But in the sense of "rest" that applies to periods it is nonsensical to speak of a body being either at rest or in motion at an instant. And in the sense in which it does make sense to ask whether a body is instantaneously at rest or in motion, it is not the case that the contingent statement "The body is instantaneously at rest" follows from the necessary statement "The body is instantaneously occupying a space equal to itself." For in order to discover whether the body is really at rest (instantaneously) at the instant in question, we must investigate its behavior during intervals to which that instant belongs.

Let us try to clinch the case, by reproducing Zeno's premises with an appropriate comment in each case.

A: Nothing is in motion when it occupies a space equal to itself.

Comment: It all depends upon what you mean by "when" and "occupies a space equal to itself." It is true that if the space *reserved* by a body during a period of time is congruent with that body, the body must have been at rest throughout that time. Or, to put the matter in another way, if the body *holds* a space during that time, that space is necessarily congruent with that body and that body is at rest throughout the time. But if you mean that a body which "occupies the same space" in the sense of preserving the same shape and size is necessarily at rest, what you say is plainly false. And if "when" refers to an instant, what you say is again plainly false. A body necessarily occupies a space "equal to itself" at an instant; but, as our explanations show, it is not then necessarily at rest.

To summarize: The only sense in which the premise expresses a truth is:

A': Nothing is in motion during a period of time if it occupies one and the same place (necessarily equal to itself) throughout that time.

[145]

The second premise is:

B: What is in flight is always at any given instant occupying a space equal to itself.

Comment: In the only sense of "occupying a space" that can be used, viz. "occupying a space instantaneously," this is a truth and a necessary truth.

We need an intermediate conclusion, not stated in the original argument. Let us try:

C: Hence, what is in flight is at any given instant not in motion.

Comment: This is supposed to follow from A and B. But it will seem to do so only so long as we allow ourselves to be misled by the ambiguity in formulation A. As soon as we replace A by A', which is the only version of A that we can admit to be true, it becomes plain that C does not follow. That occupation of the same space throughout a *period* of time is a necessary and sufficient condition for rest throughout that period of time by no means entails that *instantaneous* occupation of a unique place is a necessary and sufficient condition for *instantaneous* rest. So we cannot prove that the arrow is at rest at any instant, and a fortiori we cannot prove that the arrow is always at rest.

15. *Retrospect.* In this discussion I have tried to give Zeno his head, as it were, by elaborating upon the train of thought that makes his argument plausible, however sure we may be that the conclusion is absurd. We are to be captivated by a picture of the flying arrow frozen in every instant—with neither space nor time in which to move. Neither Aristotle's answer nor Russell's seems quite satisfactory—the first because it amounts only to denying that instants are parts of time in the sense in which periods are, and the second because it *accepts* (or makes a show of accepting) Zeno's conclusion. My idea has been that the paradox rests upon confusion between related but distinct senses of "motion," "rest," and "occupation of

a space." A review of some of the differences in the uses of these words when applicable to periods and instants respectively can help us to remember that in the sense in which a body may properly be said to move during a stretch of time it is nonsensical to speak of its being in motion at an instant, though there is a derivative sense in which we can properly speak of instantaneous motion too. To allow ourselves to forget the difference in logical type between "period" and "instant" is to expose ourselves to the error of thinking of the instant as an extremely small (an infinitely small) period of time—or of the period of time as an aggregate (nothing more than an aggregate) of instants. But if we can hold the different though related notions that apply to periods and instants sufficiently distinct, there is no reason why this ancient conundrum should have any further power to tease us.

IX

The Paradox of the Stadium

1. "THE PARADOX of the stadium" or the "racecourse" is the last of the famous four arguments of Zeno that have been handed down to us. It seems to me the least interesting of the four, and I shall deal with it less elaborately.

2. Aristotle's account of the argument (in Heath's translation) is as follows: [1]

The fourth is the argument about a set of bodies moving in a race-course and passing another set of bodies equal in number and moving in the opposite direction, the one starting from the end, the other from the middle [of the race course], and both moving at equal speed; and the argument leads, he thinks, to the conclusion that the half-time is equal to its double [i.e., to the whole time].

The fallacy in the reasoning lies in the assumption that two bodies moving at equal speeds take equal times in passing, the one a body which is in motion, and the other a body of equal size which is at rest: an assumption which is false.

Suppose, let us say, that the bodies of equal size which are stationary are AA . . . Let BB . . . be the bodies which start from the middle, being equal in number and size to the A's; and let CC . . . be the bodies which start from the end [of the race-course], being equal in number and size to the A's and moving at equal speed with the B's. The effect will be as follows.

In the course of the movements of the B's and C's past one another, the first B will reach the last $[C]$ at the same time as the first C reaches the last $[B]$. It is then found that the first C has passed all the B's while the first B passed half that number [of bodies] [namely, half of the A's]; consequently the time [taken by the first B] is half [that taken by the first C], since each of the

[1] *Physics* VI. 239b 33–240a 18 (Heath, *Mathematics in Aristotle* [Oxford, 1949], pp. 137–138). There has been much scholarly debate about the correct interpretation of the Greek text.

[148]

bodies takes the same time to pass each body. At the same time the first *B* is found to have passed all the *C*'s: for the first *C* and the first *B* will be at the opposite ends [of the *A*'s] at the same moment, because both the first *B* and the first *C* are for an equal time alongside the *A*'s [i.e., each *A*].

The argument then is as above, but it depends on the fallacy aforesaid.

3. The traditional diagrams for illustrating the motions envisaged are as follows. At the outset of the motion discussed the state of affairs is:

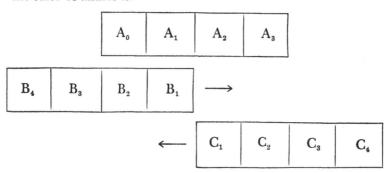

Here all the *A*'s, *B*'s and *C*'s are supposed to be bodies of the same shape and size. The *A*'s are at rest, the *B*'s move to the right with some uniform velocity *v*, and the *C*'s move to the left with the same uniform velocity *v*. (I have added subscripts to the diagram, to help in identifying particular bodies.)

At the end of the motion considered in the argument, the state of affairs is:

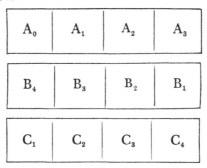

[149]

Each of the C's has now "passed" four of the B's (i.e., has passed *by* three and is now opposite the fourth). For example, C_1 has been opposite B_1, B_2, and B_3, in that order, before reaching its present position opposite B_4. Again, each of the B's has "passed" two of the A's (i.e., has passed by one and is now opposite a second). For example, B_1 has been opposite A_2 before reaching its present position opposite A_3.

4. One way that we might naturally elaborate upon what happened in the course of the motion is as follows: B_1 *gradually* moved into position opposite C_1 and was *exactly* opposite to it at some *instant*—at a time interval, t_1 say, from the beginning of the motion. And then it gradually moved into position opposite C_2, C_3, and C_4, in that order, taking t_1 for each move, so that the total time was $4t_1$. This way of talking, however, takes for granted that it is permissible to speak of instants, and of states of affairs when one of the bodies has partly but not wholly passed another. In what follows, however, we shall be entertaining the hypothesis that the lengths of the bodies cannot be further divided and that the time taken to pass one of them is indivisible. On such assumptions, the motion of B_1 past the C's will consist of four "pulses." Throughout the first of these it is exactly opposite C_1 for a time t_1 and then immediately appears opposite C_2, staying there for the same length of time. By t_1 I wish to refer either to the duration of such a "pulse" (if that is the way the motion is supposed to happen) or the time taken for B_1 to move (continuously) into exact juxtaposition with C_1, if the motion is supposed to be smooth and without "pulses."

Similarly, let t_2 be the time taken for B_1 to "pass" A_2, i.e., either to come gradually into exact juxtaposition, or else to *be* opposite it during a unitary "pulse." Since each B "passes" two A's during the entire motion, and "passes" four C's during that time, we must have

$$4t_1 = 2t_2.$$

5. According to Aristotle, Zeno simply assumes that t_2 equals t_1—"two bodies moving at equal speeds take equal times in

passing, the one a body which is in motion, and the other a body of equal size which is at rest." If this assumption were made, it would at once follow from what has been said above that $4t_1 = 2t_1$, i.e., that "the half-time is equal to the double." On Aristotle's interpretation, then, Zeno would have failed to notice (or deliberately pretended not to notice) that the time taken by two bodies to pass one another is a function of their *relative* velocity. If so, the "argument" would hardly be worth the attention Aristotle gives it.[2]

The modern commentators have agreed that Zeno was probably making a more profound assumption, and that the argument was directed, like the argument about the flying arrow, against the possibility of *indivisibles*.

6. Let us first try to determine the consequences of supposing that space has a "granular" or "atomic" structure. This means there is some length, σ say, which is "indivisible." Hence lengths shorter than σ must be impossible, and all greater lengths must be exact multiples of σ. (We might then call σ the "space-quantum.")

Suppose next that all our A's, B's and C's have this minimal length, σ. Then clearly B_1 cannot move *gradually* into position opposite A_2, for this would involve its moving a distance less than σ to the right: it must *suddenly* appear opposite A_2 and simply *be* there for a length of time t_2, in what I called a "pulse." Now we have seen that this pulse must be made up of two pulses, each of duration t_1, during the first of which B_1 is opposite C_1, and during the second of which it is opposite C_2. Consider the first of these pulses (the one during which B_1 is opposite C_1). B_1 must be *somewhere* in order to be opposite C_1,—but where? Not opposite A_1, for that is where it was at the start of the motion, before it "passed" C_1; nor opposite A_2, for that is where it is after it has passed C_1 in order to be opposite C_2; nor at some point between, for that would mean

[2] "If Aristotle is right in saying that the present argument turns merely on the very obvious fallacy which he here states, Zeno's reasoning in it is merely puerile" (Lee, *Zeno of Elea* [Cambridge, 1936], p. 89).

it had moved less than the minimal distance, σ, to the right.

So the supposition that the lengths of the bodies are indivisible leads to insuperable difficulties.

7. Next let us see what follows if we now assume that *time* is not infinitely divisible. This means there is some minimal duration, τ say, such that no event can last a shorter time than τ, and every event must have a duration that is an integral multiple of τ. (We might call τ a "time-quantum.")

Consider now what would follow if B_1 required exactly τ to "pass" A_2. (This "passing" would, once again, clearly have to take the form of a "pulse," for if not there would be a time, less than τ from the start, at which B_1 would have partly, but not wholly, passed A_2.) We have seen that in order to pass A_2, B_1 must pass C_1. Previously we asked *where* this could happen. Let us now ask *when* it could happen (on the hypothesis now being considered). Not at the outset of the motion, for then B_1 had not yet passed C_1; nor at the end, for then it has already passed C_1 in order to be opposite C_1; nor at any intermediate time, for that would involve the existence of a time shorter than τ, contrary to our hypothesis.

Another way to see this is to consider that upon our hypothesis, t_1 cannot be greater than τ, for this would mean that B_1 is opposite to C_1 *after* it is opposite to A_1; nor *less* than τ, since there are no times shorter than the time-quantum; hence t_1, like t_2, must be exactly equal to τ. Substitution in the equation we derived earlier (see end of section 4 above) gives $4\tau = 2\tau$, or "the half-time equal to the double," as Zeno said.

8. The reader may notice that we have assumed that B_1 passes an A in the minimal time (so that $t_2 = \tau$) and may wonder what would have happened if instead we had assumed that a B passes a C in the minimal time (so that $t_1 = \tau$). In that case, the time taken by B_1 to pass A_2 would be 2τ. In the first half of this time (of duration τ) it would therefore have passed half of A_2. By considering the four A's as made up of eight

bodies, each half the length of an A, we should then be back to the difficulties discussed in the last section. Enough has been said to show that insuperable difficulties follow from any assumption of the atomicity of time, as we already saw them to follow from any hypothesis of the atomicity of space.

9. The arguments used above may help us to see the point of Zeno's introduction of the three sets of bodies. *Between* the "pulse" during which B_1 is opposite to A_2 and the "pulse" during which it is opposite to A_3, there must be another "pulse." For the first is also a pulse during which B_1 is opposite C_2; and the second is a pulse during which B_1 is opposite C_4; and between C_2 and C_4 there comes C_3. Zeno's illustration, therefore, powerfully suggests to us that *events* must be indefinitely divisible—and this, as we have now seen, is incompatible with the indivisibility of space and with the indivisibility of time.[3]

10. I have supposed that the A's, B's, and C's to which reference is made in Zeno's arguments were to be extended bodies. If arguments against indivisibles are to take account of all the possible alternatives, the possibility should be considered that the A's, B's and C's are *un*extended point-masses. Then these can be supposed to be opposite each other only for *instants* (not periods of time), and the argument might be taken to be

---

[3] It is worth noting that the hypothesis of the atomicity of time necessarily commits us to accepting the atomicity of space also. For if during a minimal time, τ, a body covers a distance d, it is impossible that there should be a distance shorter than d. For if there were such a distance, d' say, the body would cover that distance *before* covering the total distance d. But by hypothesis there is no time less than τ for completing the shorter path. Another strange consequence is that there can be only a *single* velocity, viz. σ/τ, where τ is the time quantum and σ the space quantum. (Perhaps this was behind Zeno's assumption that all the bodies in his illustration take the same time to pass one another?)

Similarly we could show that atomicity of space entails atomicity of time.

[153]

directed against the hypothesis of a finite number of such instants, as some commentators have supposed.[4] In view of Aristotle's language, I can hardly think this is right. But if the argument were so intended, then it would merely prove (and quite validly) that between any two instants there must be another instant, and between any two points on a line there must be another point, i.e., that the number of points and instants must be infinite.[5]

11. To summarize: The form of the argument presented by Aristotle is so fragmentary (and the available texts so corrupt) that it is impossible to be sure what Zeno originally had in mind. It is plausible that he was arguing against the absurdity of supposing continuous magnitude to be composed of *extended* indivisibles (and in this way rounding off the considerations brought forward in his other arguments). I have tried to show independently that the hypothesis of atomicity of space and the hypothesis of the atomicity of time produce absurd consequences. We cannot know whether anything like this was in Zeno's mind. But to judge from the subtlety of his other arguments, it is not impossible. In any case, enough has been said to reveal the difficulties faced by anyone who commits himself to asserting the existence of a time-quantum or a space-quantum.

---

[4] Russell says that the argument "is only valid against the assumption that a finite time consists of a finite number of instants" (*Our Knowledge of the External World* [London, 1926], p. 181). Cf. Cherniss: ". . . the stadium which illustrates the argument that a given time is equal to twice itself by showing that two equal series of points . . . must traverse in the same time twice the number of points in each other as in the series at rest" (*Aristotle's Criticism of Pre-Socratic Philosophy* [Baltimore, 1935], p. 156.

[5] For detailed discussion of this way of looking at the argument see Russell, *op. cit.*, pp. 181–183.

3

Induction

X

"Pragmatic"
Justifications of Induction

1. *Abstract.* Ever since Hume asked for the reasons behind inductive reasons, philosophers have been trying, without success, to make induction respectable by treating it as a species of imperfect *deduction*.

Quite recently, a number of writers have found a new approach and, as they hope, a final solution to the ancient "problem of induction." These writers are here called "practicalists," because they try to offer "practical" or "pragmatic" considerations for following inductive policies. Such "practical" reasons are the best we can hope for, they say, because we cannot expect to *know* that the inductive policies will be successful—or even probably successful—in the future. A deductive proof of probable future success is impossible and any inductive arguments from past success must be circular. The only way, to justify induction, we are told, is to show that induction is rational "without reference to the truth or probability of its conclusions." Among the "pragmatic" considerations that have been offered are the following.

(i) Some experts have held that inductive policies are bound to be applicable in all possible worlds. For either inductive arguments will result in the discovery of natural laws (perhaps very complicated ones) or else we shall discover *by induction* the useful information that the universe manifests the maximum amount of "disorder." This argument is plausible only so long as the "inductive policies" are not explicitly formulated. But when this is done, it is found that there can be no question of such policies ever being known to "fail." For they are infinitely adaptable to adverse circumstances; and on practicalist principles all arguments from *experience* of the failure of inductive methods are circular. Thus there is no reason why the inductive policies should ever be abandoned. But if there were, it would be sheer sophistry to regard their abandonment as itself an act of following those policies.

[157]

(ii) Inductive policies have often been praised for being "self-correcting." But what ought properly to be said is that they are so designed as to involve constant *modification* as experience accumulates. That these modifications are progressive and lead us nearer to some *correct* answer, is something that, on practicalist principles, can never be known to be even probable. The inductive policies, accordingly, are no more self-correcting than any number of other policies that also provide for constant *change* in their estimates.

(iii) It has been urged that the inductive policies at any rate satisfy the *necessary* conditions for prediction and generalization; so that anybody following them can be sure of having done everything in his power to discover factual truth, although he can have no guarantee of success. Upon examination, this argument is found to turn upon equivocation concerning the aims of cognitive inquiries. If the aims are defined as those of obtaining true predictions and generalizations *solely by means of the designated inductive policies,* it follows, trivially, that adherence to those policies is a necessary condition for achieving those narrow aims. But if the aims of experimental inquiry are defined less arbitrarily —say, as the acquisition of reliable information about matters of fact by whatever means prove best—it does not follow at all that the orthodox inductive policies are the *only* conceivable ways to obtain such information.

(iv) Sometimes it is conceded that there are methods alternative to induction (which the last argument in effect denied), but it is added that all such methods ("clairvoyance," etc.) must in turn be tested inductively, and are therefore to be regarded as pseudo-inductive methods. This argument, like the others, does not survive close examination. A culture relying exclusively upon the *dicta* of some forecasting oracle would have just as much right as the practicalists to insist that all claims to reliable information about the unobserved must be judged by *their* methods alone.

Arguments such as those given above are supposed to have a "practical" character because intended to be modeled upon arguments used, in everyday life, for making decisions upon insufficient information. Such truly practical decisions are based upon probability estimates, derived from previous experience. The practicalists expressly exclude such judgments (on the score of circularity). It is therefore not surprising that their arguments in support of induction prove to be fallacious. In order to be correct these arguments would have to be deductive, as some of their advocates recognize. But then they would at best help to clarify the *meaning* of "induction" and related terms (a task that is admittedly important) and can be called "justifications" of induction only through confusion. Even as "clarifications," however, the "defenses" prove defective, since they amount in the end to the platitude that there is nothing to stop anybody from *trying* to achieve the aims of induction.

This is cold comfort indeed, and might be enough to return an earnest practicalist to the condition of despairing scepticism in which Hume plunged him. Those who are not satisfied with the traditional formulations of the "problem of induction" need not despair. The supposed "problem" has been so framed as to block at the outset any attempt at solution. But if this is so, to persist in trying to solve it would be like continuing to try to square the circle. The philosophy of induction has many unsolved problems; but the so-called "problem" of justifying induction is not one of them.

2. *Introduction.*

It is certain, that the most ignorant and stupid peasants, nay infants, nay even brute beasts, improve by experience, and learn the qualities of natural objects, by observing the effects which result from them. When a child has felt the sensation of pain from touching the flame of a candle, he will be careful not to put his hand near any candle, but will expect a similar effect from a cause which is similar in its sensible qualities and appearance. If you assert, therefore, that the understanding of the child is led into this conclusion by any process of argument or ratiocination, I may justly require you to produce that argument; nor have you any pretense to refuse so equitable a demand. You cannot say that the argument is abstruse, and may possibly escape your inquiry, since you confess that it is obvious to the capacity of a mere infant. If you hesitate, therefore, a moment, or if, after reflection, you produce an intricate or profound argument, you, in a manner, give up the question, and confess, that it is not reasoning which engages us to suppose the past resembling the future, and to expect similar effects from causes which are to appearance similar [Hume, *Enquiry Concerning the Human Understanding,* Section IV].

The simple argument that Hume desires is a *deductive* argument. For if an inductive argument could satisfy him, it would be sufficient to say that the child and the peasant (and the philosopher too) are arguing from similarity of causes to similarity of effects. *This* is the process of argument obvious to the capacity of a mere infant and equally so to the candid view of any theorist uninfected by sceptical doubts. But for Hume, of course, this process of inductive inference "wants an explanation" and nothing less than an exhibition of the argument in deductive form will satisfy him. It is sad to think of the number of writers led by Hume's example to undertake the self-defeating task of converting induction into a species of deduction.[1]

A number of influential writers have lately tried a substantially new way of solving the problems raised by Hume.[2] They intend to show how induction may be supported by considerations of a "practical" or "pragmatic" [3] order. Hume was right, they say, in holding *demonstration* of the soundness

[1] See Chapter 3 of my *Language and Philosophy* (Ithaca, 1949) for detailed reasons why this approach is futile and why, in my judgment, there is no "problem" of the justification of induction.

[2] The writings to which I shall mainly refer are the following: H. Reichenbach, "Induction" (the concluding chapter of his *Theory of Probability* [Berkeley, 1949]); W. Kneale, "The Probability of Inductive Science" (pt. iv of his *Probability and Induction* [Oxford, 1949]); H. Feigl, "De Principiis non Disputandum . . . ?" (in *Philosophical Analysis*, ed. by M. Black [Ithaca, 1950]); and J. O. Wisdom, *Foundations of Inference in Natural Science* (London, 1953). I shall refer to passages in these writings by page numbers only.

Similar ideas are now popular, and I may have overlooked other writers whose views would deserve equal prominence.

[3] This label is used by Reichenbach (p. 481) and by Feigl (p. 122). See also page 155 of the latter's article for a sharp opposition between "pragmatic" and "cognitive" justification.

of inductive arguments to be impossible; but he did not see that satisfactory considerations of a "practical" sort can be advanced in support of inductive policies. My task in this essay will be to assemble the defenses of inductive argument advanced by these writers, making plain the senses of "practical" (or "pragmatic") that are relevant, and to decide how far these recent investigations have advanced the "problem of induction."

For the sake of easy reference, I shall refer to the writers whose doctrines are to be criticized as *"practicalists."* The next section will make plain what is implied in the application of this label.

3. *The background of "practicalism."* All the writers to be discussed agree with Hume in three crucial points: (a) Induction *needs* justification, (b) strictly speaking, it is impossible to know the conclusion of even the strongest inductive argument to be true or even probable,[4] and (c) attempts to defend inductive procedures by appeal to the past successes of inductive procedures are hopelessly circular.

I shall not argue at this point against the assumption that induction needs justification (but see the concluding section of this essay).

The contention that it is impossible to *know* the conclusions of inductive arguments to be true or even probable is sufficiently important to be supported by quotation. (It is intended that it is *logically* impossible to know inductive conclusions to be even probable):

Hume was right in asserting that the conclusion of the inductive inference cannot be proved to be true; and we may add that it cannot even be proved to be probable. . . . The aim of knowing the future is unattainable, there is no demonstrative truth in-

―――――

[4] At any rate, in any sense of "probable" in which the conclusion can be confirmed or refuted by empirical test. I gave reasons in the earlier essay (*op. cit.,* pp. 68–74) for holding that recourse to probability provides no answer to Hume's problem.

forming us about future happenings [Reichenbach, pp. 475, 480].[5]

It is clearly a mistake to suppose that we can justify the procedure [which scientists follow] by showing that its conclusions are certainly true, for it is now a commonplace that its conclusions are only probable. And yet the attempt to justify induction by showing that its conclusions are probable also comes to grief, when we take 'probable' in the sense of the theory of chances [Kneale, p. 224].

> Hume's problem in its original form . . . is answered—inductive inference cannot be justified. . . . inductive inference, even when interpreted as a species of probable inference, cannot be justified [Wisdom, pp. 220, 221].

So far, then, these writers are quite as sceptical as Hume. According to each of them, we do not and cannot *know* that water is wet, that acorns grow into oaks or that monkeys never argue about induction. And if anybody were to say that pigs can fly, we should not *know* that he was wrong. The same must also be said, according to these writers, about probability statements. If they are right, you do not know that you are unlikely to win the Irish Sweepstake or that it will probably rain before the end of the year. I wonder whether anybody, not excluding Hume and his contemporary followers, has ever really been as sceptical as this?

The supposed circularity of all inductive arguments in support of inductive procedures is discussed separately in the next essay of this volume. The practicalists have no doubt on this point. They are, accordingly, firmly committed to the doctrine that experience has no bearing, one way or the other, on the soundness of inductive inference. As Kneale says, "This means that in order to justify induction we must show it to be rational without reference to the truth or to the probability of its conclusions" (p. 225).

This is a point of utmost importance to our argument. In ordinary life men constantly take for granted that repeated

[5] Notice how Reichenbach, like Hume, equates knowledge with "demonstrative truth."

success in making predictions is a good reason for trust in the reliability of the methods used in making such predictions. And because this is so natural a thought (and, as I think, one free from the circularity imputed to it) there is a constant temptation to revert to it in considering philosophical arguments for and against inductive methods. For inductive methods do work—and we know it. I cannot, therefore, insist too much upon the fact that the writers we are to discuss are in no position to use this natural line of argument in support of induction. They have renounced from the outset any appeal to experience in support of their methods; and this should always be borne in mind when appraising their arguments.

We are to suppose, then that induction needs justification, that conclusions about matters of fact cannot be known to be true or even probable, and that no appeal either to demonstration or experience will serve to establish the bona fides of induction. Are we then doomed to a barren scepticism? No, answer the practicalists. For in ordinary life we constantly encounter situations in which we must *act*, in ignorance of the truth of the suppositions required for action. Their program is to show that similar, "practical," considerations make it "rational" to act in accordance with the customary rules of inductive inference, albeit in ignorance of the *truth* of these principles. This is the outline I must try to make more definite.

4. *The inductive policies to be considered.* We are supposed to be searching for good reasons for *acting* as we do when relying upon inductive inferences. In other words, the task of justifying induction can be thought of as that of justifying certain inductive *policies*. It will be good to have some fairly precise policies before us and I think the following will sufficiently serve our purpose: [6]

[6] My formulation of the policies is mainly based upon Kneale's discussions, though there are divergences. He says, "The policy which we

(a) *Inductive policy for uniform generalizations:* If all observed instances of some character A have so far been found to
be instances of B, act as if all A's were B, i.e., expect any further
A that is encountered to be a B. Meanwhile, however, continue
to search for counter-instances, i.e., instances of A's that are not
B. If, as a result of search, some A's are found that are not B,
try to find another character C such that all instances of AC are
B. Continue to search for counterinstances of the new generalization.

(b) *Inductive policy for statistical generalizations:* If among
the n observed instances of A's, m have been found to be instances of B, expect that m/n A's are B. Meanwhile, however,
continue to search for further instances of A and constantly
modify the estimated ratio (m/n) as new data accumulate.

---

follow in the induction of laws consists of two articles: (a) to search for
new conjunctions of characters and (b) to assume the impossibility of
conjunctions which are not discovered by continued search" (p. 227).
His policy for "probability rules" is: "When we have observed a number of a things and found that the frequency of β things among them is
f, we assume that $P\ (a,\ \beta) = f$ [i.e., the probability that an a thing shall
be β is taken to be f]" (p. 230).

Reichenbach's "rule of induction" is as follows: "If an initial section
of n elements of a sequence x_i is given, resulting in the frequency f^n,
and if, furthermore, nothing is known about the probability of the
second level for the occurrence of a certain limit p, we posit that the
frequency f^i ($i > n$) will approach a limit p within $f^n \pm \delta$ when the
sequence is continued" (p. 446). By a "posit" Reichenbach means a
"wager." More precisely, "A posit is a statement with which we deal as
true, although the truth value is unknown" (p. 373). Thus Reichenbach's
rule asks us to assume provisionally (i.e., "posit") that the relative frequency of occurrence of a given character in a given infinite series con-
verges to a value close to the observed value of that relative frequency in
an initial segment. There is a good and less technical explanation of this
rule and its relation to the problem of induction in Reichenbach's *Experience and Prediction* (Chicago, 1938), pp. 339 ff.

Another elaborate form of a rule of induction may be found in C. I.
Lewis, *An Analysis of Knowledge and Valuation* (La Salle, Illinois,
1946), p. 272.

(c) *Inductive policy for probability judgments:* (Preliminary definition: When m out of n observed A's have been found to be B, we say that the *chance* that an A will be B, on the evidence available, is m/n.) Suppose a choice has to be made between expecting an A to be B_1 or expecting it to be B_2, where B_1 and B_2 are mutually exclusive characters; and suppose that the chance that A shall be B_1 or B_2 are k_1 and k_2 respectively: Expect A to be B_1 rather than B_2 if and only if $k_1 > k_2$.

These three policies can be briefly, but less accurately, stated as follows:

(i) Where characters are found to be conjoined in all of a number of examined instances, the first policy, (a), requires us to expect, until shown otherwise, that the conjunction will hold in all instances. (This is, of course, nothing more than "simple enumeration" or "pure induction." [7])

(ii) Where a character is found to occur in a certain *proportion* of the examined instances, the second policy, (b), requires us to expect, until shown otherwise, that the same proportion holds universally.

(iii) The numerical value of this proportion is defined as measuring the *chance* that the character in question will occur in the next instance to be examined. (This is a frequency definition of "chance" of the simplest imaginable sort.)

(iv) When we have to choose between hypotheses about the occurrence in a new instance of one or the other of two mutually exclusive characters, our choice is to be guided by the relative values of the respective chances, as previously defined.

Perhaps nobody would be found to argue seriously that these policies alone adequately represent the principles that guide reasonable men in inductive inquiries; but they may sufficiently serve the purposes of illustration.

5. *Shortcomings of these policies.* There are some fairly obvious deficiencies in these policies.

[7] "All inductions are reducible to induction by enumeration" (Reichenbach, p. 433).

(i) No consideration has been given to the degree of support that a generalization receives from *coherence* with accepted empirical theory. In practice, however, this test is most important: and a generalization fitting easily into an extensive and well-buttressed theoretical system will be accepted on the basis of far fewer confirming instances than one that stands relatively isolated from accepted empirical theory.

(ii) The policies have been framed in terms of sheer expectation or nonexpectation, no provision being made for *degrees* of expectation. But in fact we do normally generalize with greater or less degrees of assurance (see also the next essay, section 3 (ii)).

(iii) In choices between mutually exclusive alternatives, the considerations used by good judges are more complex than policy (c) would suggest. To consider only one point, the expected *utilities* of the outcomes are as important as their relative chances of realization.

(iv) Even if these objections are brushed aside on the ground that we are dealing with a first approximation to the policies that should regulate inductive inquiries, it may still be objected that plausibility requires the details of the policies to be modified. (In (b) for example, it would surely be more rational to locate the expected frequency in some *interval* $m/n \pm \delta$.)

Such criticisms would be much to the point if we were chiefly interested in presenting the logic of choice situations. But they need not detain us here, since the practicalists' defense of inductive policies is largely independent of the particular forms in which those policies are stated. For this reason also, the writers we are considering agree for the most part in the arguments they present in justification of inductive policies, however much they differ about technical details.

Plan of the following discussion. A scrutiny of the "practicalist" arguments that have been recently offered in support of inductive policies will show that they fall into one or another of three broad types. I shall consider these in turn. In

[166]

each case, I shall first state the defense informally in my own words, and then append citations from the writers concerned to show that I have not seriously misrepresented their position. Then I shall pass, in each section, to specific criticisms. When this work of attrition has been completed, I shall give a more general analysis of the type of defense in question. And I shall try to explain why such "solutions" of the "problem of induction" are bound to fail.

6. *The contention that induction is bound to be applicable.* I begin by stating and criticizing an argument that is not used by the four writers I mentioned above (see footnote 2) but is sufficiently close to their general position to be in place here.

It runs:

Either induction works, so that by using it we do in fact discover true generalizations (uniform or statistical) and in that case all is well. Or on the other hand, the universe might be too disorderly for any generalizations to hold. In the latter case, we should still be able to discover this "disorderliness"—and by induction. For the evidence of our repeated failures to generalize and predict correctly would eventually reveal the irregularity of the universe. So induction is bound to be applicable, no matter what the universe is like.

The following citation is relevant:

At least we should [in case generalization proved to be impossible] presumably come to possess the very important generalization that the maximum of novelty may confidently be expected. We should organize all our conduct on the principle that "lightning seldom strikes twice in the same place" and "history never repeats," with subsequent advantage to ourselves [C. I. Lewis, *Mind and the World Order* (New York, 1929), p. 388].

Criticism: (i) It is hard to see how, on the basis of inductive policies like those formulated above, anybody could ever be entitled to say that induction had proved unsuccessful. As we shall see in the next section, a different argument contends that the inductive policies are indefinitely adaptable to ad-

[167]

verse circumstances—so that they can be followed *no matter what happens.* And as we have seen, practicalists are committed to holding that experience has no power to discredit the inductive policies. Thus a practicalist is never in a position to say that he is justified in abandoning his policies. He must say, like Mrs. Micawber, that he will never desert the principles to which he is wedded—though like her, he may find his devotion increasingly arduous.

(ii) But suppose there is some answer to this. Perhaps reflection upon the continual refutation of all generalizations provisionally adopted in accordance with the inductive policies might, after all, entitle a man to say he was justified in abandoning further attempts. This renunciation could not itself be an act of following one of the inductive policies stated above. Our policies (a), (b), and (c) make no provision for failure—nor could any modifications of those policies do so. It is absurd to regard the abandoning of inductive policies (as here construed) as itself an act of inductive policy—just as absurd as it would be to say that a decision to abandon the use of a budget is an act of budget-making.

7. *The contention that the inductive policies are self-correcting.* This is, roughly speaking, the view that the inductive policies "always work." It might be expressed as follows: "If we have observed that n A's are all B, the inductive policy for uniform generalizations requires us to act as if all A's without exception were B. If all A's are in fact B, we shall have discovered a true generalization. If not, and we find some A's that are not B, we can always find *some* character C that all the examined A's that are B have in common. So the policy requires us to act, thereafter, as if all AC were B. We see the inductive policy need never be abandoned though it may produce generalizations (provisionally adopted) of constantly increasing complexity. The policy for uniform generalization continually corrects itself.

"It is even plainer that the policy for statistical generalization need never be abandoned. No matter how many A's we examine, there will always be a definite proportion of B's among them. So we can always use policy (b) to calculate the chance of another A being B, and constantly use policy (c) in deciding between alternatives on the basis of such calculations of chances. That the values of these chances constantly change as the evidence changes is a merit, not a defect: the policies are self-correcting."

The following statements to this general effect are drawn from our authorities:

The inductive procedure, therefore, has the character of a method of *trial and error* so devised that, for sequences having a limit of the frequency, it will automatically lead to success in a finite number of steps. It may be called a *self-corrective method,* or an asymptotic method [Reichenbach, p. 446, italics in original].

We have an additional reason for persevering, namely, the consideration that our procedure is self-correcting [Kneale, p. 235].

Since the inductive method is self-corrective, it is the most flexible device conceivable for the adaptation and readaptation of our expectations [Feigl, p. 138].

Such references to the alleged "self-corrective" power of induction probably stem from Peirce, who repeatedly made the same point. A characteristic statement of his refers to

. . . the constant tendency of the inductive process to correct itself. This is of its essence. This is the marvel of it. The probability of its conclusion only consists in the fact that if the true value of the ratio sought has not been reached, an extension of the inductive process will lead to a closer approximation [*Collected Papers* (Cambridge, 1932), 2.729].

Criticism: The first and most obvious retort is that the notion of "correction" is one of replacing an incorrect estimate by a correct one—or, at any rate, one that is nearer to the truth. Suppose a weather forecaster constantly changed his predictions whenever they proved to be wrong, pluming himself meanwhile upon the self-correcting character of his procedure. If his predictions continued to be invariably wrong,

[169]

we should have every right to laugh at his pretensions. If alteration *after the event* were all that was needed to make a forecast respectable, prediction would be as easy as reporting.

The defense before us involves just this confusion between correction and alteration. No assurance is held out that the inductive policies will bring us success in prediction (or even the probability of such success): indeed we were told at the outset there can be no question of any such assurance. The only comfort proferred is that if the generalizations prescribed by the policy prove to be mistaken, other generalizations can always be tried. It is the old maxim of the optimist, "You can always try again, can't you?"

The term "self-corrective" is a misnomer. The proper account is that the inductive policy provides for *modification* or *alteration* in the generalizations prescribed. A man who follows the policy can expect the estimates he adopts as a basis for action to need constant *revision*. But before such revisions could properly be called "corrections," i.e., changes for the better, it would be necessary to show these changes to be *progressive*, there would have to be some assurance that they were moving in some direction—and not the wrong one. And this assurance is quite lacking.

In order for the revisions in the estimates to count as improvements, it would be necessary, first, that there should be some "objective" value of the proportion of *B*'s among the *A*'s in general and, secondly, that the distances of the estimated ratios from this true value should show a tendency to diminish. Neither requirement is satisfied by the inductive policies. There can, in the nature of the case, be no assurance of any "true" proportion of *B*'s to *A*'s (indeed if the numbers of things involved are infinite, it is hard to see how this ratio could be uniquely defined) and even if the ratio of the number of *B*'s among the observed *A*'s were to converge to a limit, this would afford no assurance that the estimates drawn from finite samples would not continue to oscillate wildly so long as observations continued. The most we should be entitled to say would be that if the number of observations were to be

[170]

enlarged *indefinitely,* and if the ratio of B's to observed A's converged to a limit, the inductive policies would *in the long run* [8] yield the correct ratio. But the "long run," like the foot of the rainbow, is never reached. The vaunted "self-corrective" tendency of the inductive policies is an illusion. The best that can be said, on the evidence presented, is that the estimates offered by these policies *vacillate.*

"But at any rate, the successive modifications of the policy for uniform generalizations cover a larger number of instances. If 'All A's are B' fails to agree with the new instance, the more complex generalization does." Well, the new generalization is certainly tailored to fit the new cases, but what about all the old ones that have to be discarded (the A's that are not also C's)? And even if the policy could be so framed that *all* the examined instances could be brought successively within the scope of the constantly modified generalizations, it would be at best a policy of *describing the examined instances.* Nobody who observed the continued failure of the inductive policy to make correct predictions (as might happen on practicalist principles) ought to feel the least inclination to continue to regard it as a policy of prediction at all.

For the sake of comparison, let us formulate what might be called a *counter-inductive policy.* Let us consider the situations envisaged in the formulation of the inductive policies (b) and (c) above, i.e., situations in which m out of n observed A's

---

[8] This was recognized by Peirce. "The justification for believing that an experiential theory which has been subjected to a number of experimental tests will be in the near future sustained about as well by further such tests as it has hitherto been, is that by steadily pursuing that method *we must in the long run* find out how the matter really stands" (*Collected Papers* [Cambridge, 1932], 5.170). But notice how he moves from talk about the "near future" to talk about the "long run." Elsewhere, Peirce recognizes that the "long run" must be taken to be "endless." "But the fact is that the probability of the die turning up a three or a six is not *sure* to produce any determination of the run of the numbers thrown in any *finite* series of throws. It is only when the series is endless that we can be *sure* that it will have a particular character" (*ibid.,* 2.667).

have been found to be B. Our policies called for assuming that the true proportion of A's among all B's was m/n, and for using that same fraction to define the "chance" that another A would be a B. However crude these estimates may be, they agree pretty well with what we should normally, in the absence of countervailing considerations, regard as good inductive practice. But now suppose some eccentric individual insists upon adhering not to our policies (b) and (c) but to the policies— (b′) and (c′) say—that we get by substituting in our formulations the ratio $(n - m)/n$ for our original ratio m/n. Let us call him a "counter-inductionist." He is a congenital pessimist, as it were. When most A's have been B, he expects the next A *not* to be a B; and the more A's have been B in the past, the more firmly he anticipates that the next A will *not* be a B. Whenever *we* choose between alternatives according to calculations based on principle (c), *his* definition of chances leads him to make a choice exactly opposite to ours.

I have no wish to suggest that a "counter-inductionist" would be behaving rationally (though anybody who could explain in convincing detail why this should be so would have mastered the most important problems in the philosophy of induction). But the reader may be pressed to notice that so far as the aspect of "self-correction" goes, the counter-inductionist is in as good case as the "inductionist" whose predictions are more orthodox. The counter-inductionist has just as much right to pride himself upon the "flexibility" and the "adaptability" of his procedure. For his estimate of the chance of an A being a B varies with the accumulating evidence, no less than the orthodox estimate does (though the two never agree). He, too, can boast that *nothing* that happens can require him to abandon his policies. But the strangest thing is that, for all we are supposed to know on practicalist principles, the counter-inductionist might actually be more successful in his predictions than the orthodox forecaster. For we have seen that practicalist defenses of inductive policies are intended to work independently of any successes that those policies may have.[9] To say that those policies are "self-correcting" is not to say that they tend to have more successes than their competitors in the long run. And so we must not allow ourselves to be swayed at all by the reasonable conviction that the counter-inductionist would in fact be a hopelessly inaccurate forecaster. Perhaps he might. But if so, he need not be in the least disturbed. His policies would not be one whit the less "self-correcting" for all that. (And of course the same would be true for any policies that differed from our (b) and (c) only in the substitution for the ratio m/n of any other function of m and n whose value is always less than 1 and which always changes whenever m or n changes.)

I conclude that the claim that the inductive policies are "self-correcting" is a misleading one. It is true that the estimates called for by the policies are constantly *modified* by experience, and it *is* essential that any inductive policies that deserve to be followed by a reasonable man should have this feature. But this feature is also shared by indefinitely many "policies," some of which would exemplify willful folly.

8. *The contention that the inductive policies are the only way of achieving the aims of cognitive inquiry.* This is the most plausible of the arguments offered in support of the inductive policies.

I will express the argument as follows: "Let it be granted that there is not and cannot be any guarantee that the inductive policies will actually achieve the aims of cognitive inquiry (i.e., of science). But if these policies fail, so will all others—indeed all other policies must be tested by applying the inductive policies. Thus the inductive policies are the only way in

---

[9] Suppose the inductionist and counter-inductionist are both betting (according to their respective policies) on red and black at roulette. Then the two will always make opposite bets. So a crooked operator who could control the wheel might arrange for the counter-inductionist to win every time and for the inductionist to lose every time. Cf. also the essay "How Difficult Might Induction Be?" below.

which to achieve knowledge of the future, supposing that such knowledge can be obtained at all. If we follow them we can be sure of having satisfied the *necessary* conditions of scientific inference. It would be better if we could satisfy some *sufficient* conditions, but this is not within our power."

The following are relevant statements by some of our authors:

The assumption that there is a limit of the frequency must be true if the inductive procedure is to be successful. But we need not know whether it is true when we merely ask whether the inductive procedure is justified. It is justified as an attempt at finding the limit. Since we do not know a sufficient condition to be used for finding a limit, we shall at least make use of a necessary condition. In positing according to the rule of induction, always correcting the posit when additional observations show different results, we prepare everything so that if there is a limit we shall find it. If there is none, we shall certainly not find one—but then all other methods will break down also [Reichenbach, p. 475].

Primary induction is a rational policy, not because it is certain to lead to success, but because it is the only way of trying to do what we want to do, namely make true predictions [Kneale, p. 235].

No method of attaining foresight could conceivably be successful if every sort of induction were bound to fail. Perhaps there are alternative techniques of foresight that might be even more efficient or reliable than the laborious method of scientific generalization. . . . But our confidence in such "alternative" techniques of foresight would therefore ultimately be justifiable only on the basis of normal induction [Feigl, p. 137].

Criticism: Our verdict upon this group of arguments will depend absolutely upon how we define the aims of what I have, with deliberate vagueness, called "cognitive inquiry."

Suppose a doctor who is treating a certain disease with sulfa drugs were to say that no other measures could achieve the aims of the treatment, i.e., that it was *necessary* to use sulfa drugs to achieve the aims desired.[10] If the doctor informed us

[10] Reichenbach uses the example of a physician (p. 481).

that his aim was to *cure* the patient (by any means efficacious) his assertion that sulfa drugs are necessary to achieve that aim would be interesting and significant. But suppose he were to say that his aim was the narrower one of *curing the patient solely by means of sulfa drugs*. In that case, the contention that sulfa drugs are necessary would become trivial. It is an uninteresting tautology that if you intend to use sulfa drugs in effecting a cure, you must use sulfa drugs: the assertion is both uncontroversial and pointless.

Parallel considerations apply to the case in hand. If practicalists define their aim as that of making predictions about the unobserved *by means of their designated inductive policies*, the contention that adherence to these policies is a necessary condition for success in achieving this aim is trivial, uncontroversial, and pointless. If what is said is to deserve attention, the aims to be served by the policies must be more broadly defined. And in fact, being sensible men, practicalists do so define their aims, at least half the time. The chief aim of the inductive procedures (if we neglect our interest in systematic and coherent knowledge) is *successful prediction*. But if this is accepted, it is no longer an empty tautology that the only way to achieve it is by using the inductive policies.[11] A further argument is then needed, else the claim that the inductive policies satisfy at least the necessary conditions for successful prediction is left without foundation.

Such an argument is indeed supplied by the practicalists, as the quotations displayed above will show. It amounts to

[11] Reichenbach says: "Scientific method pursues the aim of predicting the future; *in order to construct a precise formulation* for this aim we interpret it as meaning that scientific method is intended to find limits to the frequency" (p. 474, italics added). He is narrowing the aim, not just formulating it more precisely. This narrowing of the aim makes it possible for Reichenbach to view the search for limits of the frequency as a necessary condition for the success of inductive method. But anybody who says he wants to predict the future but is not interested in finding the limits of relative frequencies of occurrence of characters in infinite series is not contradicting himself. Reichenbach is not analyzing scientific method but redefining it for his own purposes.

saying that *any* attempt to predict the unobservable—whether by soothsayer, or medium, by divination or "second sight"—*must* be judged by inductive standards. We do not and should not trust the soothsayer unless he has a high "success rate," i.e., unless we find him to be correct in his forecasts more often than not.[12] But in so testing his claims we are in fact applying an inductive test—presumably in accordance with our inductive policies. Thus even if we believe in what may seem at first sight to be alternative ways of predicting, we find on closer examination that we are still faithful to our inductive policies. (From this standpoint, appeal to a reliable soothsayer might be regarded as the use of a human *instrument* of prediction, whose reliability has to be established by the usual inductive procedures.)

[12] "We would ask the soothsayer to predict as much as he could, and see whether his predictions finally converged sufficiently with the frequency observed in the continuation of the series. Then we would count his success rate. If the latter were sufficiently high, we would infer by the rule of induction that it would remain so, and thus conclude that the man was an able prophet . . . the soothsayer may refer us to the future, declaring that on continuation of his sequence the prediction of a limit may still come true. Although clairvoyants favor such an attitude, finally even the most ardent believer no longer places any faith in them. In the end the believer submits his judgment to the rule of induction" (Reichenbach, p. 476).

"Whenever we try to extrapolate beyond experience, we must rely on some supposed law or probability rule; for even the attempt to make predictions without the help of science involves a kind of pseudo-science. If anyone decides to guide his life by prophecies, he must use some criterion to select those statements about the future he will adopt as prophecies, and in so doing he shows his reliance on some supposed law or probability rule, even if it be only the assumption that whatever comes into his head first is most likely to be true" (Kneale, p. 234).

Part of the time these writers seem to be telling us what people *in fact* do. But it is surely an over-optimistic view of human behavior to suppose most people are in fact guided by considerations of "success rates." Many a false prophet continues to be trusted by his disciples. Part of the time, at least, the practicalists tell us what a reasonable man *ought* to do: they say that a reasonable man *ought* to check all other methods of prediction by the inductive test of relative success. And whether this is right is the very question at issue.

[176]

This argument has won surprisingly wide acceptance. Let us test it by means of the following fiction. An inductive logician visiting a distant land finds a tribe who have a lively interest in the future but refuse to appeal to past experience at all. Instead they refer to a special dignitary whose title might be approximately rendered in English as "The Lord High Forecaster." Less reserved than the ancient oracles, this sage is prepared to entertain any and every question about the future when approached with the proper ceremonies. To any specific inquiry he responds in one or other of the following three ways: by an affirmative, by a negative, or by silence. And the dicta of the L. H. F. are referred to by his compatriots by an expression we can best translate as "trustworthy prediction."

Suppose next that our visiting inductive logician, well schooled in practicalist arguments, investigates the "success rate" of the L. H. F.'s predictions. Now either that success rate proves to be high, or it proves to be low. If the first is found to be the case and the logician sets his seal of approval upon the local methods, his hosts are liable to retort (perhaps with some irritation) "Of course! Didn't we tell you that this is how trustworthy prediction is obtained?" And no doubt they snigger behind the visitor's back at his barbaric (not to say irreverent) attempt at investigation without the proper rites and ceremonies. They tolerate the logician's approval because his verdict agrees with their own more dignified routine; and are strongly inclined to regard his success as mere fluke or coincidence.

But what if the logician discovers the success rate of the L. H. F. to be low and reports accordingly? Is this any reason for the locals to abandon their practice—or even to feel insecure? I think not. Within their system, the alleged report of the foreigner has no official standing until submitted to the L. H. F. for confirmation. Perhaps they dare to ask the oracle whether the success rate of his procedure is indeed low. He may disdain to answer, in which case the question can no longer be discussed without impiety and the natives proceed with an excellent conscience as in the past. But imagine the case in which the L. H. F. condescends to answer—and in the affirmative! There is still no reason for alarm. When the oracle is asked whether he should continue to be trusted in the future, he may still reply in the affirmative, although he has already announced that his success rate is low. Now all this might seem very strange to us, who are not practicalists, because we do set store upon the *success* of the inductive policies. But the logician we have imagined is, in this respect, in as bad case as the oracle-worshiping natives. Their method may be criticized for being closed against all criticism—but then so is his.

There is nothing to stop the elders of the tribe from arguing, quite in the manner of the practicalists: "Only in *our* way can the aim of trustworthy prediction be achieved. Of course, nothing is certain in this precarious world and we have no guarantee that we shall in fact achieve our aims. The proper ceremonies may be neglected, the oracle may take umbrage, perhaps deceive us deliberately, and so on. But if trustworthy prediction is *possible*—which we sincerely hope—this is the only way to get it. And if some foreign devil approaches us with another way of forecasting, we know in advance that the only way to establish his bona fides is to check his pretensions by consulting the oracle."

No doubt, in such a case the inductive logician would reproach the tribesmen with using a closed system of principles, impervious to the lessons of experience. But the same can be said of his own position. Our oracle-consulting natives have a most telling retort against their critic. "You claim to be criticizing us on the basis of experience" they might say, "but in fact your own defense of induction is intended to be independent of experiential considerations. Is it not pharisaical to accuse *us* of ignoring experience?"

The same point can be made by considering an argument between the practicalist and a "counter-inductionist" (see page 171 above), i.e., somebody whose estimates of the chances of future events are exactly opposite to the conventional estimates. Anybody who regularly uses the occurrence of a majority of observed A's being B as a reason for *not* expecting the next A to be B is certainly irrational. But how can the practicalist show this? As we have seen, he is in no position to maintain that the counter-inductionist is bound to be or is even likely to be less successful in his forecasts. Nor can he say that the counter-inductionist is not fulfilling the necessary conditions for *prediction,* since predictions would constantly be made by both parties to the dispute. There is no point, either, in pointing to the greater success of inductionist principles in the past for—circularity apart—this would be an excellent reason on counter-inductionist principles for *not* continuing to pursue orthodox inductive policies! [13] All that is left for the inductionist to say is that his opponent fails to respect the necessary conditions for success of the *inductive* policies. To which the other may retort, "Quite so. What else would you expect?" And he, for his part, may say that the inductionist fails to observe the necessary conditions for the success of the *counter-inductive* policies.

These criticisms seem to me to be decisive. The claim that all methods *must* be tested by the inductive policies is without substance. There are alternative ways (and systematic ones) of attempting to make predictions, and each such method can be defended by considerations parallel to those advanced by practicalists. No adherent of such a self-contained system is in a position to show that he is respecting the necessary conditions of cognitive inquiry. Anybody can claim—for what the claim is worth—that his method alone can satisfy the aim of attaining knowledge attainable by his method alone.

9. *The contention that the inductive policies alone can be known to satisfy the necessary conditions for achieving the aims of cognitive inquiry.* There remains one last resource for

[13] As Arthur Burks has pointed out in his valuable paper, "The Presupposition Theory of Induction" *(Philosophy of Science,* 20 [1953]: 177–197), the counter-inductionist could regard past successes of the orthodox policies as being at worst the occurrence of a series of events that, on his principles, was very unlikely to occur.

the practicalist which I will express informally as follows: "We can admit that other modes of prediction—e.g., those of your oracle-worshiping tribesmen—*might* permit successful anticipation of the future, might even prove more successful than the orthodox methods. But we have no way of knowing that they will, indeed no reason to suppose they will. Now the same can be said of our policies. But at least we can *know* that these policies satisfy the necessary conditions for achieving the aims of cognitive inquiry. And not even this can be said of the alternative methods. Thus our policies have a clear superiority in this respect over all competitors."

The following are relevant citations:

The rule of induction, or one of its equivalents, is the only method that can be used in the test of the other methods of approximation, hence it is the only method *of which we know* that it represents a method of approximation [Reichenbach, p. 477, italics in original].

The method of induction is the *only one for which it can be proved* (deductively!) that it leads to successful prediction *if* there is an order of nature, i.e., *if* at least some sequences of frequencies do converge in a manner not too difficult to ascertain for human beings with limited experience, patience and ingenuity [Feigl, p. 137, italics in original].

Criticism: This impresses me as the weakest of all the considerations that have been advanced by practicalists. In order for it to have any force at all, the inductive policies must first be admitted to satisfy the necessary conditions for cognitive inquiry. In the last section, I have tried to show that this is not so, and that all that can be demonstrated is the triviality that inductive policies satisfy the necessary conditions for the use of the inductive policies. The new defense is a variation upon the same uninformative tautology. We are told that the inductive policies are the only policies *which can be proved* requisite for—well, for achieving the aims of prediction by means of the inductive policies. And what of it, we might ask? As much could be said of any other methods. And so this defense fails, like all the others.

[180]

10. *The general character of practicalist defenses of induction.* We have now surveyed the various arguments of a "practical" or a "pragmatic" character that have been presented in the hope of showing it is reasonable to follow inductive policies. We have heard it said that the inductive policies are bound to work in all possible worlds, that if they don't work only the use of those very policies can teach us so, that the policies are "self-correcting," that only they can achieve the aims of prediction (so that if they fail so must all other policies), that all alternative policies must be tested by procedures based upon the inductive policies, and so forth. If I am not mistaken, each of these attempted "justifications" has some fatal flaw. And now the time has come to see why the kind of "justification" we have been examining is misguided *in principle.* I hope to be able to show that *this* kind of "justification" can contribute nothing to the solution of the "problem of induction."

Whatever plausibility attaches to the "practicalist" arguments results from their resemblance to certain arguments that we customarily and properly use when required to act upon insufficient information. It will be as well to have one or two such cases before us.

(i) Suppose, first, that a man is suffering from cancer. His physician may argue, quite properly, "If we operate, there is no guarantee that his life will be saved. But if we don't there is every reason to suppose he will die anyhow. We have nothing to lose—so the operation is justified." This is a sound argument (the argument of the "forlorn hope") and the policy it supports is justified even if its adoption results in no benefit and the patient dies.[14]

(ii) Imagine, next, that a certain motorist, driving at night in a strange territory, arrives at a fork in the road with no signpost or any other indication of the correct route. He may argue, with perfect propriety, "My errand is too important for me to wait in the hope of some passer-by arriving with the information I need to proceed. There is absolutely nothing to show which of these two roads is the right one. But *this* one has

[14] Reichenbach uses a similar example (p. 481).

the better surface, at least, so I am justified in taking it." This, too, is a sound argument, even though the choice made by the motorist may take him away from his destination.

According to the practicalists, the position of all of us with regard to the adoption of the inductive policies is like that of the surgeon or the motorist in the cases I have concocted. Either we have no choice except to follow inductive policies if we are to achieve the aims of prediction and generalization —or perhaps we do have a choice between alternative methods, none of which can be known to have a better chance of success than the others, so that we are entitled to fall back upon considerations of practical convenience in preferring orthodox induction. In either case the "justification" is supposed to be that we have nothing to lose by following the inductive policies (nothing to lose but our hypotheses) even though we do not know and can never know that those policies will be successful.

But the "practical situations" instanced above deserve closer attention. In the first illustration, the soundness of the train of argument depends upon the following conditions being satisfied: (a) the surgeon must want to save the patient's life (must "have an interest" in *this* outcome), (b) he must have good reason to believe that the policy to be adopted (the operation) has *some* chance of success, and (c) he must have good reason to believe that the alternative (not performing the operation) has a smaller chance of achieving the desired aim. If any of these three conditions fails, the course of action described is not reasonable.

Let us suppose that the surgeon does wish to save his client's life. In order for the second and third conditions to be satisfied, the surgeon *must* rely upon *judgments of probability,* based upon his previous experience of similar situations. It is in the light of his clinical experience, and what he has learned from the experience of others, that he decides, rightly or wrongly, that the operation promises the patient a better hope of survival than inaction would. And in the absence of such experience, a decision to operate would rightly be condemned as irresponsible and improper. In short, the surgeon relies upon *inductive* considerations to justify the estimates of success upon which his final decision is based. It is this reference to inductive considerations that gives his line of argument its "practical" character.

Much the same can be said of our second illustration. Let it be taken for granted that the motorist has an overriding interest in reaching his destination. Even so, he must decide whether the *probable* consequences of choosing the wrong road outweigh the *probable* risks attending inaction; and he must judge whether the observable differences in the roads ahead (for they will surely be different in some observable respects) are *probably* irrelevant to his aim. To estimate these probabilities he has no other guide than his past experience; and unless he can use such experience, his choice is arbitrary. If he must decide in *total* ignorance of the relevant factors, no choice is more reasonable than any other. So he, too, like every man in like circumstances, uses inductive considerations to ground his "practical" decisions.

To appreciate the consequences of the absence of such relevant experience, consider the following artificial case, which approximates to choice in complete ignorance. Suppose I am told in some intelligence test that my examiner has some "things," all of which are "*A*'s"—and not otherwise identified by him; and let me be further informed that all these "*A*'s" are also, each of them, "*B*," though I am not told and am not allowed to discover anything further about the meaning of the labels "*A*" and "*B*." And now, suppose I am ordered to "decide" whether the next *A* to be chosen by the examiner will or will not be a *B*—with a heavy penalty for refusing to make a decision. Would it be more rational for me to choose the affirmative rather than the negative answer? I cannot see that it would. If I am expressly denied all further information as to the "*A*'s" or the "*B*'s," I am offered no basis at all for my decision, and I would deceive myself if I fancied the forced choice could be other than arbitrary. This is not a situation in which I could make a reasonable "practical" decision, because the nature of the case prevents me from making any use of what I have learned through experience. When there are absolutely no precedents, one choice is just as arbitrary as any other, and if compelled to choose, I might just as well toss a coin. Here is a case where it is the better part of reason not to reason.

If the reader is inclined to dispute this, let him consider, first, whether he would genuinely regard a negative answer to the question I have described as less reasonable than the affirmative. And if, after searching his conscience, he is still prepared to say that he *would* regard the one answer as more reasonable than the other, let him try to give reasons for his preference. I do not know what more I could say to persuade him—but I would like to hear his reasons.

I have been arguing that if a choice has to be made between alternative courses of action, in a case where it is impossible to consult experience of the outcome in similar situations, no choice is more reasonable than any other. According to the practicalists, this very case arises when a philosopher tries to convince himself that he has good reasons for adhering to the inductive policies.

The very conditions we found to be *essential* to the possibility of rational choice in truly "practical" situations are here *expressly excluded.* Any possibility of supporting inductive policies on inductive grounds has been blocked, on the basis of circularity. What remains is not a practical situation, to which considerations appropriate to practical decisions may be applied, but a travesty or parody of such situations. If our predicament with regard to inductive policies were indeed as these writers depict it, the choice of those policies would be as arbitrary as any existentialist could desire: the most that could be said for such a "choice" would be that every other would be equally arbitrary. But if the practicalists were right, even the term "arbitrary" would be a misnomer. For "arbitrary" is opposed to "reasoned." On the view here discussed, there could be no such thing as a reasoned choice of a policy for prediction, since appeal to past precedents and the estimation of future chances would always be impossible.

A good way of seeing the difference between genuinely "practical" arguments and the supposedly "practical" ones that we have been considering is the following. In an everyday situation in which a man is called upon to decide what action he shall take, the conclusion of the argument is, typically, not entailed by the premises, i.e., the argument is not deductive.[15] The evidence available indicates with some *degree of assurance* what the proper action should be; but if a man who fails to see the cogency of the argument proposes to take some opposite action there can be no question (even if the original argument is sound) of charging him with self-contradiction. The practicalist arguments in defense of inductive policies *are*, however, *deductive*—and are even intended as such by their proponents.[16] The various contentions we have been examining (e.g., that inductive policies are the only way to achieve systematic anticipation of the future) are all supposed to follow strictly—in the deductive sense of "follow"—from the definitions of the key terms employed.

Deductive arguments using necessary statements about

[15] Deductive connections between propositions may, of course, be relevant to the decision, but unless inductive considerations also enter, the argument would be felt to be trivial and not genuinely practical. Practical decision requires *good judgment* as well as logical acumen.

[16] "An empirical assumption is not used for the justification . . . the relation between the inductive procedure and the aim of knowledge . . . is analytic. The recognition that a tautological justification of a synthetic inference can be given makes the solution of the problem of induction possible" (Reichenbach, p. 479).

"This statement [the one "justifying" induction] is of course a tautology" (Feigl, p. 137). "We know furthermore (as a matter of logical necessity or tautology) that *if* success can be had at all, in any manner whatsoever, it can certainly be attained by the inductive method" (Feigl, p. 138). Wisdom says his justification is tautological, except for a "fact" (?): "The fact is this: the universe may be favourable or it may be unfavourable to the deductive-hypothetico method" (Wisdom, p. 229). I would have supposed this, also, to be a tautology.

[185]

problematic or recondite notions may have great value in philosophical analysis.[17] For in this way we can sometimes discover the interconnection of our ideas. It would therefore be foolish to nurse a prejudice against deductive arguments that are based upon the definitions of key terms like "probable," "good reason," "rational," "knowledge," and so on. But in order for such arguments to be illuminating, they need to be nontrivial. Like any interesting mathematical or logical proof, they must reveal connections which were unknown to us antecedently. If we were to take at face value the "proofs" (as we should now call them) that are offered by practicalists, the conclusions would be startling enough. A demonstration that systematic prediction of the future is impossible except with the help of designated inductive policies would certainly be sufficiently unexpected to command our rapt attention. But in proportion as these "proofs" are surprising we have found them to be fallacious. And if we reinterpret the statements of the practicalists in such a way as to make their proofs sound, we are left with unexceptionable but uninteresting banalities.[18] For, reduced to its simplest terms, the so-called "pragmatic" *proof* that the inductive policies are "reasonable" amounts to no more than this: "These inductive policies are the only ones that could achieve the aims distinguishing these inductive policies from all other policies," and this is not only a tautology but a useless one. Still more simply, what

---

[17] To take a simple but important example from the philosophy of probability: We can *prove* that from statements of probability nothing follows about the actual frequencies in samples, but only statements about the relative probabilities of such frequencies. This is a tautology, but one sufficiently complex to have been overlooked, with disastrous results, by some of the early theorists in this subject.

For a more elaborate example, see "Additional Notes," section 4.

[18] To be fair to the writers here criticized, I should add that they have much to say about *sophisticated* types of induction that is stimulating, and certainly not banal. This applies especially to Reichenbach's notions about the "concatenation" of inductions and to Kneale's ingenious attempts to show the mutual relations between the inductive policies for uniform generalization and statistical generalization.

such proofs amount to is the assurance "You can always go on trying, can't you?" It is the spider's advice to King Bruce all over—"If at first you don't succeed, try, try, again." [19] But even Bruce would hardly have taken the advice seriously if he had thought that there could be no question of his having any likelihood of success.

My quarrel with the practicalists, then, is that the "proofs" they offer, if they are to count as valid, must have the trivial form "If X then X." Such a "proof" could at best count as clarifying the main ideas involved, and not as in some sense justifying their application. That such clarification can sometimes be valuable I have not the least doubt; but to label it "justification" is to invite confusion by popularizing the use of a misnomer.

11. *There is no problem of justifying induction.* There is every reason to suppose that anybody who approaches the "problem of induction" as Reichenbach and the other practicalists do is bound to end in an impasse. The chief steps are the following: (a) Imagine the analysis of the principles of inductive inference carried so far that we can state "first principles" of inductive inference, i.e., principles that cannot be *deductively* inferred from simpler principles. (b) Insist now that these principles (or the corresponding policies) need "justification." (c) Exclude any *inductive* arguments in their support on the score of circularity. All that can be expected to result from this program is a *trivial* deductive inference of the form "If X then X." And this will have no real title to be called either a genuine justification or a genuine clarification of ideas. It is not a genuine clarification, because it throws no

---

[19] "We may compare our situation to that of a man who wants to fish in an unexplored part of the sea. There is no one to tell him whether or not there are fish in this place. Shall he cast his net? Well, if he wants to fish in that place I should advise him to cast the net, to take the chance at best. It is preferable to try even in uncertainty than not to try and be certain of getting nothing" (Reichenbach, *Experience and Prediction*, p. 363).

light on the hidden connections between problematic or recondite notions: and it is certainly not a "practical" or "pragmatic" justification, because it violates the conditions that have to be fulfilled in order for there to be a genuinely practical situation (see section 10 above).

A sufficient reason for the impasse is the extreme abstractness of the manner in which the "problem of induction" has been traditionally formulated. Sceptical critics of inductive procedure, from Hume to Russell, are always asking us how we know the sun will rise tomorrow.[20] But the philosophical critic is not interested in this *special* question, as he himself would readily agree. We are not really being asked specific scientific questions, e.g., whether the accepted laws of physics can be known to apply to stars beyond the reach of our most powerful telescope, or whether we really know enough about the future of the universe to make intelligent long-term plans. All such genuinely open questions are too special, too concrete, for the sceptical critic. The "sun" to which he refers is anything you please—a mere dummy decorated with sunbeams. He asks us quite simply, "What reason is there to suppose that if a number of observed A's are all B, all A's are therefore B?" And the answer, so far as I can see, is that *in general* there is no reason. It all depends upon the A's, the B's, and what we already know about them. If the A's are specimens of a new strain of corn, selected according to a well-tested sampling procedure, there may be excellent reasons for expecting the generalization to hold. But if the A's are objects of which all we know is that they resemble one another in respect of being instances of B, a reasonable man will refuse to draw any conclusion. To insist that there must be a conclusion would be like saying that because a good chess player knows what move to make in a game of chess, he ought to be able to know what move to make when presented with a chessboard containing

[20] "We must either accept the inductive principle on the ground of its intrinsic evidence, or forgo all justifications of our expectations about the future. If the principle is unsound, we have no reason to expect the sun will rise to-morrow" (Russell, *The Problems of Philosophy* [London, 1912], pp. 106–107).

only a single piece. But this is not a problem of chess and there is nothing the chess player could do to solve it. The problem of what to infer when we know *only* that some *A*'s are *B* is not a genuine inductive problem; and there is no way to solve it except by recognizing that it would be improper to try.

But we are never in this situation of almost total ignorance if we are in a position to raise "the problem of induction." We really do know a good deal about the sun, and anybody who can intelligently ask a question about its rising tomorrow also knows a good deal about empirical regularities. For the very young child or the very ignorant savage, there really may be a question whether there is any material body to be called "*the* sun"—since perhaps all that he sees is a celestial radiance that appears and disappears at irregular intervals. But at least he knows all kinds of things about other material bodies. If my questioner already knows *some* empirical generalizations (e.g., that there is a material body called "the sun") I can teach him about other matters of fact in perfectly familiar ways. But a man who averred that *no* matters of fact had already been established would be somebody with whom rational discourse would be impossible. The ordinary words that I would want to use (words like "man," "sun," and "tomorrow") would seem to him to involve presuppositions that begged *his* question. For to use a word like "sun" is to presuppose [21] the regularities that give point and purpose to the use of that word. And the paradigms that we use in teaching a young child the meanings of "good evidence," "reasonable estimate," and the other terms needed for prediction and the appraisal of evidence about matters of fact, would likewise be unacceptable to our sceptic. I could no more argue with such a man than I could with a foreigner ignorant of my language.

Some philosophers will say this merely shows in another way that the "problem of induction" is insoluble. But we ought to bear in mind two possibilities. The first is that the problem is too difficult for solution; the second, that the "problem of induction" is not a genuine problem at all, because its terms have been so framed as to render solution impossible.

[21] See the second essay in this book.

If a man insists that I go from Ithaca to Timbuktu in the shortest possible time, he is setting me a difficult task. But if he goes on to insist that I must get there in no time at all, he is not rendering the task infinitely difficult. On the contrary, he is so framing the conditions that it becomes logically impossible for anybody to conform. The infinitely difficult task is no task at all.[22]

Something similar may be said about the problem of induction. To justify the principles upon which all inductive inference is supposed to rest seems immeasurably more difficult than showing that the sun will rise tomorrow or establishing any *particular* matter of fact. But upon reflection we can see that *no* conceivable way of attempting the supposed task will be allowed to count as compliance. The use of inductive methods to establish the principles is condemned as vicious circularity. Deductive proofs are inadmissible since the principles are recognized to be not self-evident. Finally, practical considerations, such as we use in ordinary life in solving particular inductive problems, are out of place. For either the defense will rest upon considerations of what can reasonably be expected on the basis of past experience and it will then be open to the old charge of circularity, or else it will simply rely upon the consequences of the meaning of "induction" and other key terms and will then be at best a clarification of meaning but no justification. But what remains? All conceivable avenues of investigations are blocked at the outset. It is as if we were told to go to Timbuktu, but neither by sea, nor on land, nor in the air. Nothing remains but to throw up our hands and deplore the unreasonableness of the original demand.

Professor Broad, in a famous phrase, once referred to inductive reasoning as "the glory of Science" but "the scandal of Philosophy." [23] Perhaps it is on the verge of becoming scandalous that this ancient tangle of confusions should still be regarded as a "problem" that needs a solution.

---

[22] Cf. the discussion of the "task" of counting an infinite collection, in essay VI above.

[23] *Ethics and the History of Philosophy* (London, 1952), p. 143.

XI

The Inductive Support of Inductive Rules

1. *The view to be examined.* It is very commonly said that any attempt to "justify" induction by means of an inductive argument must beg the question. The following are characteristic expressions of this view:

> It is impossible that any arguments from experience can prove this resemblance of the past to the future: since all these arguments are founded on the supposition of that resemblance [Hume, *Enquiry,* Section IV].

> All arguments which, on the basis of experience, argue as to the future or the unexperienced parts of the past or present, assume the inductive principle; hence we can never use experience to prove the inductive principle without begging the question [Russell, *The Problems of Philosophy* (London, 1912), p. 106].

> Though it is true that the inductive inference has been successful in past experience, we cannot infer that it will be successful in future experience. The very inference would be an inductive inference, and the argument would be circular. Its validity presupposes the principle that it claims to prove [Reichenbach, *Theory of Probability* (Berkeley, 1949), p. 470].

It would be hard to find any writer who disagreed with these statements.

I want to distinguish two views that these writers may be advocating: (a) The first is that *no* inductive argument ought to be regarded as correct until a philosophical justification of induction has been provided; and, hence, induction must not be used in the attempt to provide such a justification. This is not the view that I wish to discuss in this essay.[1] (b) It may be

---

[1] I have discussed the general problem of the justification of induction in Chapter 3 of *Language and Philosophy* (Ithaca, 1949).

held that if all inductive arguments are conducted according to one and the same inductive rule, *inductive* inference in support of *that* rule is bound to be circular. (If *several* logically independent inductive rules are admitted, there need be no circularity in using one of them to support another.) This second view may seem as obvious as (a), but it is certainly a different contention. (a) arises from sweeping doubts about any and every induction; but a philosopher might take *some* inductive arguments to be correct and still agree with (b). Indeed, (b) looks almost self-evident.

Nevertheless, I shall try to show that the view I have called "(b)" is mistaken. The conclusion I wish to establish is that if all inductive arguments were to be conducted according to one and the same inductive rule, an inductive argument in support of that rule might still be "correct," i.e., might satisfy all the tests that render an inductive argument acceptable.

2. *Examples of inductive arguments.* The following are simple examples of good inductive arguments:

(i) That egg has been boiling for twenty minutes, so it is bound to be hard by now.

(ii) My car has never failed to start when the temperature was above 30—it is pretty certain to start today.

(iii) There are a thousand tickets in this lottery and only one prize: almost certainly, this ticket will not win the prize.

(iv) All kinds of acids under all sorts of conditions have invariably turned blue litmus red: hence, acids turn blue litmus red.

(v) In a random selection of housewives interviewed, four out of five were found to play bridge; probably the proportion of bridge players among all housewives is close to four-fifths.

These examples may serve to remind us of the wide variety of arguments that are commonly called "inductive." [2]

---

[2] The lack of numerical precision in the examples is deliberate. A good deal of harm has been done in the philosophy of induction by the choice of sophisticated examples from highly developed sciences. We need to bear in mind throughout the discussion the extent to which inductive argument can be imprecise and inexplicit.

3. *Some features of inductive arguments.* I hold each of the following remarks to be true, though I shall not defend them here. (For the sake of brevity, I shall assume throughout that the premises, if there are more than one, are amalgamated into a single premise.)

(i) In no inductive argument is the conclusion entailed by ✗ the premise.

In other words, the conjunction of the premise and the negation of the conclusion is not a self-contradiction. This follows from the meaning of "inductive argument": that an inductive argument is not a special kind of deductive argument is a necessary truth.[3]

(ii) An inductive argument may indicate the *degree of support* that the premise gives to the conclusion. ✗

Sometimes, the conclusion may simply be presented as following from the premise (see example iv of the last section) with no indication of the strength of the premise; but very commonly the "degree of support" is explicitly shown by the use of expressions such as "pretty certainly," "probably," "extremely likely," and so on. When this happens, the conclusion is still asserted *with* a certain degree of support, and in the cases here considered is not *about* that degree of support. (There may, however, be second-order arguments about degrees of support.) In this respect, inductive arguments differ sharply from deductive ones. The latter either establish their conclusion or they do not—*tertium non datur.* An inductive argument, however, may offer stronger or weaker reasons in support of its conclusion.[4]

(iii) Some inductive arguments are "correct," i.e., the conclusion in question is established (perhaps with an indicated ✗ degree of support) by the premise.

I use the word "correct" in preference to "valid," reserving the latter for deductive arguments. It is to be presumed that the

[3] This point is argued in detail in the earlier discussion referred to in footnote 1 above. See especially pp. 66–68.

[4] What is here being called "degree of support" may be the same as what other writers have meant by "degree of confirmation."

reader can recognize some instances of inductive correctness; if not, this essay will be of no value to him.

✗ (iv) A correct inductive argument may have a true premise and a false conclusion.

Suppose we argue: "This pack of cards has been shuffled, so probably nobody will get thirteen hearts in the deal." If the pack of cards has been shuffled but somebody does get thirteen hearts in the deal, this does not show that the argument is incorrect. But of course, if this happened very often, the case would be altered.

(v) Every correct inductive argument belongs to a class of arguments (call it the "associated class") all of which are correct, and every incorrect argument to a class all of which are incorrect.[5]

Roughly speaking, correctness and incorrectness are properties of the members of *classes* of inductive arguments. In a limiting case, the *associated class* might be a unit class. I shall not discuss the defining properties of such classes.

(vi) All the members of a class of associated arguments conform to the same *rule of argument*.

The rule has the form: "To argue from such-and-such a premise that (probably, certainly, very likely, etc.) such-and-such a conclusion holds." It will be convenient to say that the argument is *governed by* the corresponding rule.

✗ (vii) In order for an inductive argument to be correct, the rule to which it conforms must be *reliable*. (degrees)

A rule is reliable if it yields true conclusions in *most* cases in which it governs arguments having true premises. If a rule governs an argument with a true premise and a true conclusion, it may be said to be *successful* in that instance; if it governs an argument with a true premise and a false conclusion, it may be said to be

---

[5] This assertion involves some degree of idealization. Try formulating the membership of example (i) of section 2, for instance. (Yet that argument, as it stands, is a perfectly good example of inductive argument and does not need the addition of further "assumptions.")

unsuccessful. Thus a rule is reliable when its successes outnumber its failures. Clearly, we can also speak of *degrees* of reliability.

(viii) From any inductive rule there may be derived a corresponding principle.

If the rule is, "To argue from X (with certainty, high or low probability) that Y," the corresponding principle is, "Whenever X, then Y."[6] A principle, unlike a rule, has a truth value, but the principle corresponding to a correct argument need not be true. For we demand only that the rule be reliable (see iv and vii above).

(ix) If a principle corresponding to a rule is true, it is a contingent truth, not a necessary one.

For otherwise the argument would be deductive, not inductive.

(x) A sound inductive inference need not involve the formulation of the rule governing the argument used.

I distinguish between an inference and an argument. In the former, the speaker *asserts* the premise and treats it as a reason for asserting the conclusion. He is then using an argument. If his inference is to be sound, the argument must be used *legitimately,* in a sense to be explained later (see Section 9). But the conditions of legitimate use do not include explicit formulation of the rule governing the argument. If the rule is formulated, the argument and the inference may be said to be *formal.* Not all sound inductive inferences are formal.

(xi) There is no single rule governing all correct inductive arguments.

The writers we are to discuss deny this, so I shall conduct the discussion on the supposition that it is false. Yet I am inclined to believe that many of the difficulties in this subject can be traced back to the incorrect supposition that there is a supreme inductive principle.

[6] Suppose the argument has the form "X, so probably Y." An alternative way of proceeding would be to consider the statement "Whenever X then probably Y" as the "associated principle." I do not believe this would make any difference to the conclusions I have tried to draw in this essay.

4. *The inductive rules to be considered.* As I have already said, the writers quoted assume that there is a single supreme inductive rule or principle which governs all correct inductive arguments and has to be shown to be true (or at least probable) if any inductions are to be sound. Now it is not easy to find plausible candidates for the role of such a supreme rule or principle, and writers on the foundation of induction have proposed many alternatives. But I hope to conduct the discussion in such a way that it may apply with little or no modification, no matter what formulation is chosen for the alleged first principle or rule. For the sake of definiteness in what follows, I propose to consider separately the following rules alone:

R_1: To argue from *All examined instances of A's have been* B to All A's *are* B.

R_2: To argue from *Most instances of A's examined in a wide variety of conditions have been* B to (probably) *The next* A *to be encountered will be* B.

The first of these may be taken to express a rule governing arguments by "simple enumeration." It will be remembered that many philosophers of induction hold that the justification of induction depends in the end upon the justification of this unsophisticated type of inductive argument.[7] The second rule has been included so that we may have one example before us of a type of rule governing arguments in which the conclusion receives a greater or lesser degree of indicated support from the premise (cf. the use of the word "probably").

Both R_1 and R_2 are somewhat crudely expressed. Some readers may be troubled by the temporal references in their formulation; and others might reasonably demand something less vague than the phrase "a wide variety of conditions" that occurs in the phrasing of R_2. Such niceties will not affect our argument, however.

[7] Mill and Nicod are two of the best-known examples of this.

5. *Two self-supporting arguments.* Let us now formulate two inductive arguments designed to support R_1 and R_2, respectively.

(a_1): All examined instances of the use of R_1 in arguments with true premises have been instances in which R_1 has been successful.

Hence:

All instances of the use of R_1 in arguments with true premises are instances in which R_1 is successful.

We may remind ourselves that we have agreed to call a rule successful if it is used in an argument having a true premise and a true conclusion. So the conclusion of (a_1) says that no argument governed by R_1 and having a true premise ever has a false conclusion. This amounts to saying that R_1 is perfectly reliable, and hence we can parallel (a_1) with the following less exact argument:

(a_{11}): R_1 has always been reliable in the past.

Hence:

R_1 is reliable.

The argument in support of R_2 that we propose to consider runs as follows:

(a_2): In most instances of the use of R_2 in arguments with true premises examined in a wide variety of conditions, R_2 has been successful.

Hence (probably):

In the next instance to be encountered of the use of R_2 in an argument with a true premise, R_2 will be successful.

There is no simplified form of this argument that will exactly parallel (a_{11}) above. But the following will serve our purpose:

(a_{22}): R_2 has usually been successful in the past.

Hence (probably):

R_2 will be successful in the next instance.

[197]

The arguments have been so formulated that (a_1) is governed by R_1, and (a_2) by R_2. Thus the first maintains in its conclusion the (perfect) reliability of the rule to which that very same argument conforms; and the second maintains in its conclusion the continued success of the rule to which the argument itself conforms. I shall call these arguments *self-supporting*.

Our task accordingly narrows itself down to determining whether and in what sense either (a_1) or (a_2) is guilty of circularity.

6. *The alleged circularity is not that of "petitio principii."* When the charge of circularity is made against an argument, one of two things is commonly alleged to be wrong. It may be that one of the premises is identical with the conclusion, or is, perhaps, that same conclusion in different words. In a more subtle version of circularity, at least one of the premises is such that it is impossible to get to know its truth without simultaneously or antecedently getting to know the truth of the conclusion. "The premise unduly assumed is generally not the conclusion itself differently expressed but something which can only be proved by means of the conclusion" (H. W. B. Joseph, *Introduction to Logic* [Oxford, 1916], p. 592).

Can the charge of circularity against our arguments (a_1) and (a_2) be construed in accordance with this normal meaning of "circularity"? Let us see, first, whether the conclusion of the first argument appears—perhaps in disguise—as a premise. The conclusion of (a_1) is that the rule R_1 is always successful (when applied to arguments having true premises). There is here only one premise, to the effect that R_1 has always been successful in all cases of its application to arguments having true premises *so far examined*. Clearly, this premise is entailed by the conclusion, but not vice versa. Hence (a_1) is free from the first kind of circularity, that arises when a premise duplicates the conclusion.

But could the premise of (a_1) be known to be true, without the conclusion of (a_1) being simultaneously or antecedently

[198]

known to be true? Well, I suppose that the premise (R_1 has always been successful when applied to arguments having true premises) might easily be found to be true by the use of observation and memory, i.e., without the use of *any* inductions conforming to R_1. But in order to have the most unfavorable case before us, let us suppose that the evidence in favor of the premise of (a_1) was itself obtained by means of inductions conducted according to the same rule R_1. Even so, there would be no circularity. For in none of these arguments could the statement, *R_1 is always successful*—or, what is the same thing, *R_1 is reliable*—have been a *premise*. All of these arguments were *governed by* R_1, but this did not require them to assert that the rule to which they conformed was reliable. (I do not checkmate a king in a game of chess unless my move is legal, but in making the move I do not *announce* that the move is legal, nor is any such announcement required in order to make that move legal.)

Now precisely similar considerations apply to the argument we called (a_2). Inspection shows that the conclusion is not entailed by the premise; so (a_2) is free from the more obvious type of circularity. And even if we suppose that the truth of the premise was established by means of inductions using R_2 itself, it is by no means required that a statement about R_2's reliability should have been a premise in any of those arguments. Thus (a_2), like (a_1), is free from each kind of circularity.

But we hardly need these details to establish our point. The following considerations are simpler and equally decisive. Any argument that is circular, in the traditional sense here in point, is a *valid deductive argument*, however worthless it may be for the purpose of getting new information from the conclusion. For if one of the premises duplicates the conclusion, it is logically impossible for all the premises to be true while the conclusion is false. And again, if it is impossible to know the premises to be true, without simultaneously or antecedently coming to know that the conclusion is true, this can only be because the conjunction of the premises entails the conclusion. So, if either of our "self-supporting" arguments really did "beg the question," it would have to be a valid deductive argument, and hence not an inductive argument at all. But whatever faults these arguments may be supposed to have, it is plain that neither is deductively valid—in neither case does the conjunction of the sole premise and the denial of the conclusion result in a self-contradiction. Hence, neither of them is deductively valid, and so neither of them can beg the question.

Of course, this is by no means the end of the matter. Our self-supporting arguments admittedly continue to look suspicious. Take (a₁) for instance. Its conclusion is that the very same rule used in arriving at that conclusion is reliable: more argument will be needed before we can be sure that there need be nothing logically reprehensible in this kind of proceeding.

First, let us convince ourselves that our self-supporting arguments can at least be correct, whether they have any cognitive value or not. (The reader will please remember that I am using "correct" as an analogue for inductive arguments of the term "valid," reserved for deductive arguments. Just as a deductive argument can be valid but cognitively worthless, so an inductive argument might conceivably be correct, but useless.)

7. *Self-supporting arguments can be correct.* Suppose, for the sake of the argument, that R_1 is in fact perfectly reliable, i.e., that every argument conforming to R_1, and having a true premise, will also have a true conclusion. Then, there is no reason why the premise of (a₁) should not be true; and if this is so, our assumption is that the conclusion of (a₁) will also be true. Thus, in this case, as in all others of the application of R_1, the argument that it governs will never lead from a true premise to a false conclusion, and such an argument will be perfectly correct.

We can perhaps make the situation more vivid by imagining that a machine has been constructed for delivering conclusions according to the rule R_1 from data supplied to it. Then, if the machine is informed that "All examined instances of the working of this machine upon true data have been instances of successful operation of the machine," it will deliver the conclusion "All instances of the operation of this machine upon true data are successful." And, upon our assumption, that R_1 is reliable, this conclusion will be true. There is nothing in the nature of the data fed to the machine upon *this* occasion to prevent it from drawing the right conclusion, here as always. No paradox results from the supposition that the machine makes true predictions about *its own* reliability.

Or again, suppose another machine drawing conclusions, this time according to the rule R_2. When informed "In most of the examined workings of this machine (in a wide variety of conditions) a true conclusion was derived whenever a true premise was furnished," the machine will report the conclusion: "(Probably) the next instance of the application of this machine to a true premise will result in a true conclusion." And there is no reason why this answer should not be true (at any rate, in a majority of such cases, which is all that we need).[8]

We are not machines, however. And we shall not regard the use of arguments (a_1) and (a_2) as justified unless certain other conditions are satisfied. For an argument may be "correct" in the sense explained above and yet its use by somebody may be held illegitimate. For example, suppose Smith believes some rule R to be usually unsuccessful, but nevertheless deliberately draws a conclusion from a premise in accordance with R. Now Smith might be mistaken in his belief and R might really be reliable, but this is no defense of his procedure. Though the argument he used was a "correct" one, his use of it was unjustified, and his inference was illegitimate. (Cf. the case of a man who inadvertently tells the truth while lying.)

We may say, following W. E. Johnson,[9] that before an infer-

---

[8] I owe the example of the machine to R. B. Braithwaite—see his valuable discussion of "The Justification of Induction," Chapter 8 of his *Scientific Explanation* (Cambridge, 1953). Braithwaite is one of the very few writers who do not think that inductive justifications of induction are viciously circular. But I think he is unnecessarily restrained in his conclusions on the matter and my own treatment follows somewhat different lines.

[9] *Logic,* pt. 2 (Cambridge, 1922): p. 8.

ence may be regarded as legitimate or "reasonable," certain "epistemic conditions" must be satisfied by the reasoner. Now it is conceivable that circularity of a kind more subtle than any we have yet considered might arise in the satisfaction of the epistemic conditions for the legitimate use of our self-supporting arguments.

8. *When is the use of a deductive rule of inference legitimate?* For the sake of comparison, let us begin by considering the epistemic conditions that must be satisfied before anybody's use of a *deductive* rule can count as legitimate. One might be tempted to say that no deductive inference is legitimate unless all the arguments governed by that rule are known to be valid.[10] But this is to demand too much: all we are entitled to ask is that the man who applies the rule shall have no good reasons to suppose that the rule ever governs an invalid argument. Many a deductive inference is made by a reasoner who has never consciously formulated the rule to which he was conforming, let alone considered whether there were any reasons for suspecting the rule to be untrustworthy. But consider the most self-conscious and deliberate deductive reasoning that you please: Suppose the reasoner has formulated the rule he is using, finds its validity self-evident, and after weighing any objections against it that he knows, still continues to find it self-evident.[11] Suppose, moreover, that he has gone to the trouble of considering whether it is deducible from, or is at any rate consistent with, other rules whose validity he finds self-evident. If the rule survives this process of critical scrutiny, the reasoner has done all that could be reasonably demanded according to the most rigorous standard of self-consciously

---

[10] A rule may be called valid if all the deductive arguments conforming to that rule are valid.

[11] As I have said before, this Cartesian attitude toward an argument is not needed in order to make that argument correct. To say otherwise would be to make all arguments, deductive and inductive alike, impossible. If I may take no step until I have proved I am entitled to, it becomes logically impossible for me to walk at all. First comes the correct reasoning—then, if need be, its justification.

rational employment of a deductive rule. But even this extraordinary and unusual procedure of preliminary cross-examination of the rule to be employed does not guarantee that all the arguments that conform to the rule shall be valid; for what seems self-evident after the most searching criticism may nevertheless still be false. Yet this process of prior test is the very utmost that can be demanded of a reasoner (and far less than this would normally be regarded as enough). If a man has done as we have described, then, so far as concerns the employment of the deductive rule in question, he has satisfied all the epistemic conditions.

9. *When is the use of an inductive rule legitimate?* Inductive rules are not self-evidently reliable, nor can their reliability be deduced from self-evident truths. Yet there is something in inductive reasoning that is analogous to self-evidence in deductive reasoning. Some inductive rules impress us as intrinsically trustworthy—so much so, that it calls for a very considerable effort of abstraction from the situations in which we use them to be able to entertain seriously the possibility that they may not be reliable after all. Unless the inductive rules we use "inspire confidence," as we might say, we are hardly reasonable in using them. But a severe critic of inductive reasoning may regard such untutored trust in a rule as very likely to lead to error. (For a deductive rule that looks self-evident may, after all, be not a tautology; and an industrious rule that we cannot help trusting may not be reliable—may produce false conclusions from true premises most of the time.) Very well, then—let us try to satisfy the most stringent demands that such a critic might feel called upon to make. Let us suppose we take the rule that initially "inspires confidence" and, not content with that, make the most painstaking examination of a wide variety of cases in which that rule has been used in the past, considering also all the objections that might plausibly be brought against the use of that rule. Suppose, now, that our rule has survived this searching cross-examination and still seems to us, as it did at the outset, worthy of our con-

[203]

fidence in its reliability. Then, surely, all the guarantees that could reasonably be asked of us will have been supplied. And our use of that rule will be legitimate, even if that rule should, after all, and in spite of our best efforts, prove unreliable. To demand more than this, e.g., that the rule should be *known* to be reliable before it is used, would be to render all genuine induction impossible. For if the rule were known to be reliable prior to its employment, we could adjoin the assertion that the rule was reliable to our other premises and *deduce* that desired conclusion. Thus, we seem to have stated sufficiently stringent conditions for the reasonable use of an inductive rule. The question that I now want to settle is whether the satisfaction of conditions as stringent as these will lead, in the case of our self-supporting arguments, to any kind of circularity or triviality.

10. *Can a self-supporting argument be correct without triviality?* We have already seen that (a_1) and (a_2) may be correct without begging the question. Suppose now that somebody using (a_1) tries to satisfy the stringent conditions outlined above. Suppose, in fact, that before he argues, he must first regard R_1 as reliable, must then have taken deliberate steps to check this spontaneous confidence in R_1 by examining previous instances of the use of R_1, possible objections to its use, and its logical connections with other rules that he trusts. If R_1 survives such a process of criticism, the man who uses it will, of course, have excellent reasons for holding it to be reliable. Now will this render the inference (a_1) superfluous?

Well, no doubt, inductive inferences will have been used in the course of finding good reasons for one's confidence in the reliability of R_1 (and many of these inferences may even have been conducted in accordance with that very same rule R_1). If that very same inductive evidence for R_1's reliability is now produced again as the premise of (a_1), (a_1) will indeed yield no new knowledge, and will then, indeed, lead to useless repetition of what was known at the outset. *But there is nothing in the specification of (a_1) that requires us to confine* *ourselves to the evidence that we previously had for* R_1*'s reliability.* Having evidence, K, say, that gives us excellent reason to hold R_1 reliable, and thus to make any employment of R in an inductive argument legitimate by the most stringent tests that might be demanded, there is nothing to prevent us going in search of further relevant evidence. If we find even one new argument in which R_1 has been successfully employed, and refer in formulating the premise of (a_1) to that new evidence as well as to the evidence we already had, that self-supporting argument may really be of value. For consider what would have been the result of our going in search of a new argument conforming to R_1 and finding that R_1 was in fact unsuccessful in that new instance. Then we should have discovered that although we did previously have good reason (indeed the best) to trust R_1, further experience had shown after all that R_1 was not perfectly reliable as we had supposed. And just because further experience might discredit R_1, the argument to the effect that further experience yielded a result favorable to R_1 has cognitive value.

The case we have made for the use of (a_1) is an artificial one. For experience does *not* show that R_1 is invariably successful and the rules that we use in legitimate inductive inferences have only a greater or lesser *degree* of reliability. And for this reason, (a_2) comes closer than (a_1) to representing the type of argument that we do sometimes have occasion to use in practice.

Suppose, as before, that some exacting critic of inductive reasoning refuses to allow us to use (a_2) until we have previously convinced ourselves by careful investigation that R_2 is trustworthy. We shall be satisfied if such investigation gives us good reason to suppose that R_2 has a sufficiently high degree of reliability. Suppose such evidence assembled. Then, if we simply repeat the evidence in the form of a premise for (a_2), that argument will certainly accomplish nothing except to remind us of what we already knew. But, as before, there is nothing to stop us going in search of further evidence in support of R_2. In favorable cases, such new evidence will not merely support the general conclusion as to R_2's reliability: it may *raise* the degree of the reliability of that rule. And it is precisely in this way that arguments like (a_2) have cognitive value.

For how do we in fact proceed in inductive inquiries? No doubt we are taught to argue inductively before we are ever in a position to reflect upon the reliability of the rules that we find ourselves already using. (And if not, how could there be any matter for reflection?) But as we become self-conscious and critical about the methods that we are using, we come to realize that it is of the essence of inductive method that the rules according to which it operates must be treated as being probably subject to qualifications and restrictions that are not clearly apprehended when those rules are used unreflectively. And it is precisely in rendering clearer such restrictions that inductive arguments in support of *particular* inductive methods find their greatest use in practice. It is by the application of inductive methods to those same methods that induction, in favorable cases, may become "self-correcting." And in all this, there is no more vicious circularity involved than there is in the truism that tools can be used to sharpen themselves. Inductive arguments in support of inductive rules can meet the tests that determine the acceptability of an inductive argument. Anybody who thinks he has good grounds for condemning all inductive arguments will also condemn inductive arguments in support of inductive rules. But he will have no good reasons for singling out what we have called self-supporting arguments for special condemnation.

11. *Summary.* We set ourselves the task of determining the correctness of the widely held opinion that any inductive support of induction must be circular. In order to accomplish this, we found it necessary to state some of the main features of inductive argument and to distinguish inductive argument from inductive inference. I took an inductive argument to consist of two propositions, an amalgamated premise and a conclusion, connected by a bond that indicates the degree

of assurance with which the conclusion may be asserted on the basis of the premise. Such an argument belongs to a class of similar arguments, all of which are correct or incorrect together. The class of associated arguments generates a rule of argument. Any use of one of these arguments in the course of an inference was said to conform to, or to be governed by, that rule, but we saw that the rule need not be stated in the course of the inference. A rule is said to be successful in a particular inference if it leads from a true premise to a true conclusion, and unsuccessful if it leads from a true premise to a false conclusion. A rule is said to be reliable if its successes outnumber its failures—or, more briefly, if it is *generally* successful. It was important for my position to stress that a sound inference need not be governed by a rule that is invariably successful. Indeed, we need to distinguish between *degrees* of reliability of inference.

Two versions of a "supreme rule of induction" were selected for examination and two corresponding "self-supporting" inferences formulated. I first considered the possibility that such an inference might "beg the question" in the traditional sense of that expression. This was rejected, mainly on the ground that it would require the self-supporting inference to be deductive—and, indeed, deductively valid—not inductive, as assumed.

Next, I tried to show that there was no reason to suppose that a self-supporting inference could not be "correct." Such an inference might very well draw its conclusion from its premise according to a rule that was in fact reliable and therefore probably successful in the particular instance.

There remained the possibility that such an inference could not be "legitimate" because circularity would enter in the satisfaction of the "epistemic conditions." I tried to state the most rigorous conditions (modeled on those holding for the case of deductive inference) that anybody using a self-supporting argument might be asked to satisfy. Even these conditions, stringent as they were, were found to be satisfiable without circularity. A reasoner could have, in fact, excellent reasons for regarding the rule of inference to be used in the self-supporting argument as reliable, *before* he drew the inference. Admittedly, he might confine himself in that argument to using the very same evidence that had already supplied him with good reasons for holding the rule to be reliable; and then the "inference" would indeed be trivial and could not lead to advance in knowledge. But the specification of the self-supporting arguments does not require this to be the case. It is also possible for new evidence to be sought, and then we have an inference that is both correct and legitimate, and one that really does support the conclusion about the rule's reliability. The interesting case is that in which the rule does not have perfect reliability, but rather a degree of reliability sufficient to accredit the inferences in which it is used. In this case (the one that usually occurs in practice) the "self-supporting" argument in support of the rule may, in favorable cases, be used in an inference that raises the degree of the estimated reliability of the rule. It is in this way that inductive procedures may, in favorable cases, be "self-correcting."

This discussion was not intended to be taken as an attempt to find an inductive "justification" of induction. For we could not accept the assumption that there is a single supreme principle of induction. And in any case, any philosopher who seriously questions the admissibility of induction will have equally grave doubts about *any* induction. Thus an inductive inference to the reliability of some inductive rule will still leave such a sceptical philosopher a prey to his sceptical doubts.

XII

How Difficult Might Induction Be?

THERE was once a demon who had read Hume and wanted to make the future unlike the past. If he were allowed to create anything that was *logically possible,* how difficult might induction prove to be?

This was an indolent demon, despising busybodies like "Descartes' mythical deceiver, who always guides our hands and eyes to non-representative samples" (Donald Williams, *The Ground of Induction* [Cambridge, Mass., 1947], p. 149). He yearned to produce a maximum of disorder by a single act of creation. Nothing would satisfy him but a prescription for chaos—an exact formula for generating a series of events so irregular as to baffle all attempts at prediction.

We might as well suppose the demon engaged in producing a single series of successive events, each consisting in the manifestation of one or other of just two characters. Such a series might consist of an indefinitely prolonged series of tosses of a coin, the outcome being either "heads" or "tails" each time— or an infinite sequence of male and female births—or any similar series in which each term is an instance of one or the other of exactly two characters.

Each event of such a series can be conveniently represented by a "1" or a "0," according to the character manifested in that event. So the demon's task can be regarded as that of defining an infinite series of digits, each of which must be either 1 or 0. Having once defined the numerical series, the demon can simply ordain that a corresponding series of events shall progressively come into existence—or he might even arrange for the digits themselves to appear in succession at some convenient site. If one such series proved too irregular to permit of inductive generalization, the demon might hope to make the universe increasingly disorderly by multiplying such series at pleasure.

To proceed with our fable. One fine night, astronomers are astounded to see a colossal 1 sharply etched upon the surface of the moon. The following night there is a 0, and on each successive night either a 1 or a 0, in no discernible pattern. The demon has started work. He has decided, once and for all, upon a series of 1's and 0's that is to be progressively revealed in the manner explained. Let us call this particular infinite series of 1's and 0's *the demon series*—or *"DS"* for short.

The demon has tried to define *DS* in such a way as to make predictions about terms yet to be revealed as difficult as possible. We suppose, therefore, that anybody making a prediction about *DS* will have partial or complete information about an *initial segment* of the series, consisting of all the terms that have so far been revealed in accordance with the demon's fiat. On the basis of such information, the predicter tries to forecast later terms of the series, while the demon hopes to defeat as many such forecasts as possible.

Not all forecasts could be defeated, for no plan of construction for *DS* could prevent correct guesses about particular terms of the series. If an astronomer and his wife always disagree about a term, one of them is bound to be right. Nor can the demon prevent guesses about any finite number of terms from turning out right: if 2^n men make different guesses about n terms of *DS*, one of them is bound to be right. So the demon concerns himself only with *general* predictions, i.e., those whose symbolic expression would require the use of quantifiers.

Simple examples of such general predictions are the statements "Three successive 1's are always followed by a 0" and "Every term whose rank is a prime is a 0." (By the "rank" of a term is meant the number indicating its place in *DS*. The rank of the first term is 1, of the second 2, and so on.)

Now some of these generalizations will refer only to a finite number of terms of *DS*—as is the case, for instance, with the statement "The first hundred terms of *DS* will contain at least five o's." Such a statement can be conclusively verified or falsified by examining a finite segment of *DS* (the length of which is specified by that statement) and is logically equivalent to a truth-function of particular predictions. For the reasons already explained, the demon cannot hope to defeat such *explicitly restricted* predictions. But these, too, will have to be regarded as guesses, since any evidence that would justify a restricted prediction of this sort would also justify an unrestricted generalization.

Suppose the first hundred terms of *DS* contain only five 1's and a cautious predicter therefore says, "The next hundred terms will contain no more than five 1's." Then he should be prepared to say, "Any sequence of a hundred terms containing no more than five 1's will be followed by a sequence of a hundred terms containing no more than five 1's."

If we exclude the cases already discussed, there remain for consideration generalizations that cannot be known in advance to be testable by a finite segment of *DS* of known length. Now some such generalizations could never be conclusively falsified by *any* finite segment, no matter what character the segment had. Simple examples are: "*DS* will contain an infinite number of 1's," and "No finite sequence of digits will occur only once in *DS*," and "The relative frequency of occurrence of the digit 1 in *DS* will tend to the limit 1/2." No observations could show any of these three assertions to be untrue. Since they are unfalsifiable, the demon (a good finitist) takes no steps to falsify them.

Many such statements will be false nevertheless, though not by premeditation. Thus we shall see that the definition of *DS* chosen by the demon does in fact ensure the falsity of the third of the three statements cited.

The demon does not regard inattention to unfalsifiable generalizations as a weakness in his plan. He agrees with Karl Popper (in his *Logik der Forschung* [Vienna, 1935]) that scientific generalizations must be falsifiable. And he will be content to make *scientific* prediction as difficult as possible.

We are left with an important class of generalizations about *DS* that are *never conclusively verifiable but constantly falsifiable* (in a sense now to be explained). Let G be such a generalization. Then, no matter what initial segment of *DS* is revealed at any stage in the progressive revelation of that series, there is always at least one finite prolongation of the segment such that, *if* it were to occur, it would falsify or further falsify G. There can never come a time when no possible finite prolongation of *DS* could falsify G. Let us call this kind of generalization an *acceptable theory* (about *DS*).

The following are all acceptable theories in the sense explained:
(a): "There are never more than two consecutive 1's in *DS*."
(b): "The digit 0 is always followed by a 0."
(c): "If a hundred consecutive 1's occur, the next digit but one is always a 0."
(d): "The sequence 101 is always followed by the sequence 101 or the sequence 010."
(e): "Take the decimal expansion of π, i.e., 3.14159 . . . Consider the third term of *DS*, then the first after that, then the fourth after that, then the first after that, then the fifth after that, and so on. These are alternately 1 and 0."

To illustrate the definition of "acceptable theory," suppose *DS* were to begin with the initial segment 11010. Then in that segment (a) would not yet have been falsified. But it would be falsified (for the first time) if the series were to continue with 111. Again, (b) would have been falsified once in the initial segment 11010. If the series were to continue with a 1, (b) would be falsified once again. Similarly for the other three examples. All five are "never conclusively verifiable" and "constantly falsifiable," as the reader can check for himself.

Every general statement that makes indefinitely many predictions about terms of *DS* will be an "acceptable theory" in the sense defined, for example, any statement giving the values of terms of *DS* as a mathematical function of the ranks of those terms. Thus acceptable theories can be of any desired degree of complexity, and the demon's decision to restrict himself to the falsification of *all* acceptable theories leaves him with a sufficiently grandiose project. Since all scientific generalizations about *DS* are "acceptable theories," the success of the demon's plan would be enough to wreck the scientific enterprise. And this should be enough to satisfy any demon.

The demon's project has now narrowed itself to an attempt to falsify as many acceptable theories as often as possible. The idea behind the attempted execution of the plan is a simple one. The demon argues that all the acceptable theories that could be formulated by the would-be predicters, *can be arranged in a single linear order.* Now every acceptable theory, as we have seen, is such that it *could* be falsified at every stage in the evolution of *DS*. The demon so constructs *DS* (in a way to be explained) that every acceptable theory shall in fact be falsified in turn. (We shall see eventually that each theory is indeed falsified an infinite number of times, and inductive generalization about the series becomes well-nigh impossible.) Once all acceptable theories have been arranged in a single predetermined order, it is not hard to arrange for each of them to be falsified in turn (as we shall be able to show).

Why can all acceptable theories be arranged in a single infinite linear order? Well, the predicters may be supposed to be using some determinate language, which contains a certain stock of simple symbols. Everything they might want to say about *DS* could be expressed, for instance, by means of sentences using the letters or other symbols to be found in the latest edition of the *Encyclopaedia Britannica*. This allows them to dispose of a finite vocabulary of uncompounded signs (though new signs could, of course, be introduced by means of explicit definitions, if convenient). Every acceptable theory must, therefore, be expressible as a finite string of signs selected from this finite store. Now it is well known that all such strings can be arranged in a single linear order, in a predetermined fashion. So the demon can assign an identifying number to every conceivable acceptable theory that could even be formulated for consideration by his victims. (And he could still do this even if, contrary to our assumption, they had an infinite stock of elementary signs upon which to draw.)

[213]

The elementary or uncompounded signs will consist of letters of the English, Greek, and perhaps other alphabets, logical and mathematical signs, parentheses, etc. Imagine these simple signs to be arranged once and for all in a linear order.

Each acceptable theory consists of a finite string of signs selected from the stock of simple signs (with repetitions permitted). Suppose T_1 is the string of simple signs $a_1 a_2 a_3 \ldots a_m$ (where each a is one of the simple signs in the language under consideration) and suppose T_2 is the string of simple signs $b_1 b_2 b_3 \ldots b_n$. Then if $m < n$, we put T_1 ahead of T_2 in the order in which the acceptable theories are to be ranged. Again, if $m = n$, let a_i be the first a which differs from the corresponding b; then if a_i is ahead of b_i in the order in which all the simple signs were arranged, we put T_1 ahead of T_2. This amounts to arranging the "theories" in an extended "alphabetical" order.

Notice that we count two different strings of signs as different theories—which may, however, be logically equivalent. According to this arrangement, statements making exactly the same predictions will occur in many different places in the order. For suppose T is any theory; then the statement having the form "T and the first digit of the series is either 1 or 0" (where "T" is supposed to be replaced by the formulation of T, the theory under consideration) will occur later in the order than T, but will obviously make exactly the same predictions. The two strings of signs will express logically equivalent theories. We see that there are infinitely many acceptable theories logically equivalent to a given acceptable theory.

The next step in the execution of the demon's plan calls for a determinate procedure for falsifying a given acceptable theory at any given stage in the formation of DS. Consider any initial segment, S, of the series, and any given acceptable theory, T. Since T is "acceptable," or "constantly falsifiable," there is at least one finite prolongation of S that would falsify T if it should immediately follow S. And if so, it is obvious that there must be infinitely many such "falsifiers" of S, as we may call them. It is not difficult for the demon to pick exactly one of these falsifiers (see below) which may accordingly be called "*the* falsifier" (for given S and T).

The demon defines "the falsifier" for given S and T as follows: Imagine all possible prolongations of the initial segment, S, arranged in this order:

0, 1, 00, 01, 10, 11, 000, 001, 010, 011, 100, 101, 110, 111, 0000, . . .

(This, like the order of the acceptable theories already chosen, is an "alphabetical" order, with o taking precedence over 1.) For the given initial segment, S, and the given theory, T, there must be exactly one of those possible prolongations that is the first in the order to be a falsifier of S. Let this be called *the falsifier* for that initial segment and that theory.

As an example, consider the theory "All terms of prime rank in DS are 1," and suppose the initial segment to be 11010. The theory has already been falsified twice in that segment, at the terms of rank 3 and 5 respectively. The next place where falsification can occur is the 7th term. Reference back to the order in which all possible prolongations were arranged will show that *the* falsifier (for the initial segment and the theory in question) is 00. Similarly, for the same initial segment, and the theory "The number of 1's always exceeds the number of o's," the falsifier is 0.

Notice that the falsifier may be taken to be defined also at the beginning of DS (for a null segment, S, as it were). Thus, at the beginning of DS, the falsifiers for the theories mentioned in the last paragraph are, respectively, ooo and o.

Our definition ensures that a given initial segment S and a given theory T between them uniquely determine the falsifier for that stage in the production of DS. For given T, the character of the falsifier will, in general, vary from point to point in DS (i.e., will vary with S).

Having now arranged all acceptable theories in a linear order and defined "the falsifier" for each given initial segment and given acceptable theory, the demon can proceed to define DS. The idea is simply this: First falsify T_1 (the first acceptable theory in the order) by the falsifier for the beginning of the series; then add the falsifier for the segment thus constructed and the acceptable theory T_2; then the falsifier for the new segment so defined and the *third* theory in the order; and continue in the same way. In this fashion, *every* acceptable theory will be falsified at least once.

[215]

To illustrate this procedure, suppose the first four theories in the demon's order to be the following (already used as examples above):

T_1: "There are never more than two consecutive 1's."
T_2: "The digit 0 is always followed by a 0."
T_3: "Terms of prime rank are always 1."
T_4: "The number of 1's always exceeds the number of 0's."

The falsifier for T_1 at the outset is 111, and the series would accordingly open with that segment. The falsifier for T_2 at the stage thus reached is 01, so the series now runs 11101. The first term of prime rank after these initial terms is the seventh. Hence the falsifier for T_3 at this stage is 00, and the series runs 1110100. The falsifier for T_4 is now 0. So, after the first four theories have been falsified, the series runs 1101000.

We spoke above as if the demon had first to specify an initial segment and then, in the light of that decision, proceed to specify another segment, and so on. But in fact there is no reason for him to remain engaged in active calculation. The outline definition given above could be converted into a perfectly rigorous and exact definition. The demon, if he wanted to take the trouble, could write out the definition, issue the decree, "Let *that* series unfold itself," and settle back to enjoy the fun without further meddling.

How much has the demon accomplished by constructing DS? Well, the plan he adopted made it certain that every acceptable theory about DS that his victims could consider would be falsified at least once. But in fact a much stronger result follows (as we shall now show): He can be sure in advance that every such theory will be falsified infinitely often.

We have already seen that for each acceptable theory there are infinitely many acceptable theories logically equivalent to it, i.e., making exactly the same predictions.

An alternative way of seeing this is the following. Suppose A is the theory "There are always more 0's than 1's in each initial segment," and suppose that A were falsified only a finite number of times, say not after the 100th term of DS. Let B now be the theory, "After the first 100 terms, there are always more 0's than

[216]

1's in each initial segment." Then, according to the demon's prescription, B must be falsified at least once. And this will produce a further falsification of A, contrary to our supposition. A similar argument can be applied to every acceptable theory.

We now see that anybody who makes an assertion about DS that *could* be falsified an infinite number of times (i.e., asserts an acceptable theory) is certain to make an infinity of incorrect predictions. If some theory were to make only a finite number of incorrect predictions, a predicter might hope, by starting sufficiently late in DS, to have an unbroken run of successes. But we now know that such a hope would be illusory. No matter how late in the series a predicter starts, and no matter how complex or how weak a theory he formulates, he is bound to be proved wrong infinitely often. And the demon knows this in advance.

This is bad enough, but there is worse to come. A predicter might be reconciled to the prospect of making an infinity of mistakes, provided he were right "on the whole" or "in the long run." Let us make this notion more precise. Suppose that on a given night, a given theory T has already made m correct predictions and n incorrect predictions; and let n/m be called the *failure-ratio* of T at that time. Then to say that T is right on the whole is to say that its failure-ratio tends to zero, as the terms of DS are successively revealed. And unless this condition is satisfied, T would surely be rejected by any reasonable man as too grossly discordant with the progressively revealed character of DS.

Now it is a remarkable (and demonstrable) property of the demon's series that even this modest requirement fails—and for each acceptable theory. No matter which theory is taken, *there is no upper bound to its failure-ratio.*

This result is not quite as obvious as those already obtained. In order to demonstrate it, we shall need to consider, first, exactly where the predictions of a given theory are tested.

With respect to a given term of DS, a given theory, T, may (a) make a correct prediction (i.e., correctly forecast its value), or (b) make an incorrect prediction, or (c) fail to make a prediction at all. In case (a) let us say T has a *success*, in case (b) a *failure* at the term in question. Terms at which case (c) arises are simply to be ignored in computing the failure-ratio of T.

Suppose a given acceptable theory has had m successes and n failures in a given initial segment of DS. And now suppose this segment is prolonged by adjoining the falsifier for that theory and that segment. Then it is easy to see that the number of failures of the theory is increased by one, while the number of its successes remains unchanged. In other words, the failure ratio is increased from n/m to $(n + 1)/m$.

The reason for this can be seen by considering a single illustrative example. Let T be the theory "There are never more than two consecutive 1's," and suppose the initial segment of DS to have been the following:

$$1 \ 1 \ \underline{1} \ 0 \ 1 \ 1 \ \underline{0} \ 1 \ 1 \ \underline{1} \ \underline{1} \ \underline{0} \qquad \text{(S)}$$

Failures or successes of T occur only at points in DS immediately following the occurrence of two consecutive 1's. In the given segment, these points are the third, seventh, tenth, eleventh, and twelfth terms (shown by underlining). The failure-ratio of T for S is easily seen to be $3/2$.

The falsifier for T and S is clearly 111, whose adjunction to S converts it into the following segment:

$$1 \ 1 \ \underline{1} \ 0 \ 1 \ 1 \ \underline{0} \ 1 \ 1 \ \underline{1} \ \underline{1} \ \underline{0} \ 1 \ 1 \ \underline{1} \qquad \text{(S')}$$

The first new testing place thus introduced is the last term. If a new testing place had been introduced sooner, there would be a shorter falsifier for S and T than 111, and 111 would not be *the* falsifier. Thus the adjunction of the falsifier does raise the failure-ratio from $3/2$ to $4/2$, as claimed.

The argument has not depended upon any special features of the theory and the segment chosen for the illustration. So we can always increase the failure-ratio of a theory from n/m to $(n + 1)/m$ by adjoining the appropriate falsifier.

Consider now any theory, T. Let T' be a statement of the form "After the nth term of the series (and for all values of n) there immediately follow no more than n^2 uninterrupted failures of the theory T (i.e., failures without intervening successes)." (In this statement, "T" is supposed to have been replaced by the formulation of T.)

Then T' is an acceptable theory in our sense of that expression.

[218]

For after any initial segment consisting of n terms, T' could be falsified by repeating more than n^2 times the operation of adjoining the falsifier of T. Hence T' is included in the demon's list of acceptable theories and must be falsified infinitely often. Suppose such a falsification occurs immediately after the kth term of DS (i.e., suppose a falsifier of T' for that segment does in fact follow). Since only k terms of DS have so far occurred, T at this point can have had at most k successes. Now a falsification of T' means that there immediately follow more than k^2 uninterrupted failures of T. Each such failure raises the number of failures of T by one without changing the number of its successes. Hence, when T' has been falsified, T must have at least k^2 failures, and its failure-ratio must have reached at least k^2/k or k. This must happen for infinitely many values of k, since T', like every acceptable theory, is falsified infinitely often. Hence, there is no upper bound to the failure-ratio for T, as was asserted above.

In view of this property of DS, the demon can say to a predicter: "Choose any acceptable theory you please. Now what ratio of failures to successes will induce you to abandon that theory? A million to one? I guarantee in advance that if you wait long enough you will be faced with that failure-ratio or a larger one. Or would a ratio of a billion to one be needed to discourage you? Just wait long enough and that too will happen." This boast can be made for every acceptable theory, and no matter which number is substituted for the "billion."

Of course, the construction of DS does not prevent the repeated arrival of occasions at which the number of successes of a given theory overwhelmingly outnumber the number of its failures (i.e., stages at which its failure-ratio is as close as may be desired to zero). Indeed, it is easy to see that this must happen, since for every theory there is a complementary theory whose "failures" are the first theory's "successes" and vice versa. But such triumphs are bound to be temporary: the failure-ratio cannot converge, and the demon has good reason to gloat.

On the other hand, the construction of DS does not tell us where the oscillations in the values of the failure-ratios occur.

[219]

The failure-ratio for a given theory might seem to be converging to zero for whole eons.

With the prospects of long-term inductive generalization now so dismal, a predicter might at least try to make the humble probability assertion, "The chance of a 1 occurring at any point of DS is $\frac{1}{2}$." If this assertion is intended to be understood on the "frequency interpretation," it implies that the relative frequency of occurrence of 1's in DS tends to the limit $\frac{1}{2}$, and is then demonstrably false.

The ratio of the number of 1's to the number of 0's in any initial segment of DS is the failure-ratio of the acceptable theory "Every term of the series is a 0." Since there is no upper bound to this failure-ratio, as we have seen, the relative frequency of occurrence of 1's does not tend to a limit and there is no such thing as the probability (in the frequency sense) that a term of DS shall be a 1.

Suppose we divide up an initial segment into consecutive sequences, each two terms in length, and count the number of them that have the character 00. Let the relative frequency of occurrence of this type of two-termed sequence be m/n. Then m/n cannot tend to a limit as n increases. For we can easily formulate an acceptable theory that is falsified when and only when the sequence occurs in the appropriate places. Since the failure-ratio of this theory has no upper bound, the result follows. In general, the relative frequency of occurrence of a definite sequence of k terms cannot tend to a limit in DS.

So far, everything has gone smoothly for the demon. He seems to have succeeded in his ambition of creating a series of events, with regard to which even the most modest inductive generalization is doomed to failure at the outset. The demon might be content to let ill enough alone but for one consideration that now threatens to nullify all his labors. Cannot the demon's own definition for DS be expressed in the "language of the *Encyclopaedia Britannica*"? And is there not a corresponding acceptable theory that states the value of each term of DS? And in falsifying *this* theory will not the demon be contradicting himself?

Suppose T is the theory (modeled on the demon's definition) that predicts the value of each term of DS. Since T is clearly "acceptable," it must occur somewhere in the demon's list of acceptable theories—so suppose it is T_{99}. Consider what happens when the demon, having already falsified theories 1 to 98, now finds himself called upon to falsify T_{99}. Upon consulting the prearranged order of theories, he discovers that T_{99} is the formula for the construction of DS. Hence, if he adhered to that formula he would be compelled at that point to falsify T_{99}, i.e., to falsify that very same formula. So the demon's procedure is apparently self-contradictory, and his victims can breathe freely again.

The contradiction here uncovered is similar to such well-known "semantical paradoxes" as Richard's paradox or the paradox of the least integer not namable in less than nineteen syllables.

For an account of such paradoxes see, for instance, Whitehead and Russell, *Principia Mathematica,* 1 (Cambridge, 1910): ch. viii, pt. 8.

If such a contradiction can be formulated, the language we have been supposing the predicters to be using is inconsistent. Accordingly, the demon may introduce distinctions of type into that language. He distinguishes (in familiar fashion) between (a) acceptable theories in which no reference is made to such theories, (b) acceptable theories in which reference is made to theories of the first kind, (c) acceptable theories in which reference is made to theories of the second kind, and so on. This additional complication means that he must take account, not of a single infinite array of acceptable theories, as in the first version of his plan, but of a doubly infinite array of such theories. But this is not a serious obstacle. It is well known that this doubly infinite array can be rearranged in a single infinite series, so the demon can proceed as before.

Let theories in which no reference is made to theories be said to be of type 0. Let theories in which reference is made to theories of type 0 be said to be of type 1, and in general, let theories in which reference is made to theories of type n be said to be of type

$n + 1$. Let a theory of type n be represented by a symbol of the form T^n in which the superscript indicates the type. Then the demon can represent all acceptable theories in a doubly infinite array as follows:

$$
\begin{array}{cccccccc}
T_1^0 & T_1^1 & T_1^2 & T_1^3 & T_1^4 & T_1^5 & \dots \\
T_2^0 & T_2^1 & T_2^2 & T_2^3 & T_2^4 & T_2^5 & \dots \\
T_3^0 & T_3^1 & T_3^2 & T_3^3 & T_3^4 & T_3^5 & \dots \\
T_4^0 & T_4^1 & T_4^2 & T_4^3 & T_4^4 & T_4^5 & \dots \\
T_5^0 & T_5^1 & T_5^2 & T_5^3 & T_5^4 & T_5^5 & \dots \\
\cdot & \cdot & \cdot & \cdot & \cdot & \cdot & \dots \\
\cdot & \cdot & \cdot & \cdot & \cdot & \cdot & \dots
\end{array}
$$

In this arrangement, all theories in the same vertical column belong to the same type. These can be arranged in a single infinite order by taking them in the following sequence:

$$ T_1^0 \ \ T_1^1 \ \ T_2^1 \ \ T_2^0 \ \ T_3^0 \ \ T_3^1 \ \ T_3^2 \ \ T_2^2 \ \ T_1^2 \ \ T_1^3 \ \ T_2^3 \ \ T_3^3 \ \ T_4^3 \ \dots $$

Now the demon can revert to his original plan, and every theory still gets its turn to be falsified.

With this modification of the original plan, the demon's own prescription for *DS* is no longer capable of formulation in the language of the predicters, and so he need no longer fear self-contradiction.

It might be said that the demon's own prescription is of the transfinite type ω. Alternatively, that the demon allows himself the privilege of exemption from the system of type distinctions he has introduced into the language of the predicters.

C. I. Lewis once imagined us as gambling against a "perverse demon whose sole purpose is to mislead us and render knowledge impossible" (*Mind and the World Order* [New York, 1929], p. 387). Suppose a mortal were to gamble against *our* demon, receiving a dollar every time he made a correct prediction about a term of *DS* and losing a dollar every time his prediction was incorrect. If the human player had a limited capital, no matter how large, he would be certain to lose it all if the game were sufficiently prolonged. Indeed if the demon had an indefinitely large capital, he could afford to offer any odds, no matter how seemingly disadvantageous to him. If he paid a thousand dollars for every correct prediction, while collecting only a penny for an incorrect prediction, he would still be certain to bankrupt his human adversary. This follows from what was said earlier about the absence of upper bounds to the failure-ratios of theories concerning *DS*.

In this type of game, rational calculation would be a waste of time, for every policy would lead to the same disastrous outcome if persisted in. If compelled to gamble with the demon, one might just as well neglect experience entirely and wager on the 1 every time. Lewis was too optimistic when he said it would be certain "that we should not lose *less* of our money if we intelligently observed past dealings and continually revised our betting on the basis of accumulated experience" (*op. cit.*, p. 389). We should not lose *less*, but we should certainly lose *all*.

These considerations show that the anti-induction demon might achieve an astounding measure of success with his machinations. But perhaps there is a loophole in his plan, after all. The point of weakness is, of course the assumption that the predicters are restricted to the use of a fixed and predetermined language (the language of the *Encyclopaedia Britannica*). Of course, the mere introduction of new symbols would not foil the demon, provided each of them could be defined in terms of the old symbols. For then any "acceptable theory" in the extended language would be logically equivalent to some acceptable theory in the original language, and nothing would have been gained.

But we have supposed the demon to be able to formulate a full prescription of *DS* in advance. In order to do this he must be exempt from the type restrictions by which the predicters are bound, since he is able to refer to every theory expressible in their language.

Now what demons can do without contradiction, mortals

can aspire to emulate. If the demon can, without contradiction, use an "essentially richer" language, there is nothing to prevent the playthings of his malice from doing likewise. Nothing, except the superhuman difficulty of the task.

Even if we knew that the demon had read this very essay and was following the same general plan (i.e., arranging in a single linear order all the acceptable theories we can at present formulate) we should be almost as helpless as before. For we would still have to determine the particular order which he had chosen.

The number of ways in which the $\aleph_0$ acceptable theories could be arranged is of the order of the continuum (c, not $\aleph_0$), so our prospect of hitting upon the particular order adopted is negligible. It is worth noticing that the hypothesis that the demon has adopted *some such* plan as has been outlined in this essay is not falsifiable. For *any* initial segment, no matter how long, could be supposed to be the falsifier of the first acceptable theory in the demon's order. In particular, his general plan of operation (successive falsification of all acceptable theories) is compatible with any degree of regularity in the initial segment. Does it follow that, for all we know, any regular sequence already investigated, no matter how uniform, may be the beginning of a *DS?*

The demon would, in fact, have very little to worry about. Long before we would be prepared to consider seriously such fantastic hypotheses as that of the existence of an anti-induction demon, we would have been justified in abandoning the inductive enterprise as too difficult to be worth further effort.

The foregoing considerations were intended to illustrate the point that there can be no a priori guarantee of the success or, indeed, of the reasonableness of inductive prediction. There is no a priori limit to the irregularity and the complexity of the phenomena with which a predicter might be called upon to cope. It is conceivable that the world might have been so complicated that the only reasonable thing would have been to abandon all hope of making reasonable predictions. But if we did abandon the inductive enterprise in any class of cases on such grounds, we could never be sure that we

[224]

had not stopped too soon. There would always remain the possibility that a law more complex than any we had yet considered would have been discovered if we had persevered a little longer.

Summary: In this paper I have introduced the fiction of an "anti-induction demon" in order to dramatize the logical possibilities of disorder in a series of events with which a scientific predicter might theoretically be called upon to deal. By an "acceptable theory" concerning such a series I meant any generalization concerning the series, based upon a given initial segment, and capable of further falsification at every point in the series. I tried to show that by arranging all the acceptable theories that can be formulated in a given language in a single linear order, it is possible to falsify each of these theories in turn. The series defined (the "demon series") had the following remarkable properties: (a) each acceptable theory about it is falsified an infinite number of times, (b) there is no upper bound to the "failure-ratio" (the ratio of the number of incorrect to the number of correct predictions) of any of these theories, (c) it is impossible to make probability judgments concerning the series. I have also tried to show that the definition of such a series need not involve its definer in self-contradiction. These results seem to refute the opinion, expressed by Lewis, and no doubt by others, that induction is always the best policy. If we were compelled to gamble upon the character of the terms of such a series, calculation would be as futile as the crudest guesswork. And there is no a priori reason, it seems, why such series should not occur.

4

Problems Connected
with Logic

XIII

Frege on Functions

The argument does not belong with the function, but goes together with the function to make up a complete whole; for the
function by itself must be called incomplete, in need of supplementation, or 'unsaturated.' And in this respect functions differ fundamentally from numbers.[1]

1. FREGE thought he was here formulating the basis of a distinction between a function and an "object" (*Gegenstand*)
that he regarded as "of the highest importance" (p. 54); yet
no passage in his writings is harder to understand. By a "function" Frege understood not only a function in the mathematical sense but also any property or relation. So his contention that all functions are incomplete would lead one to
suppose that he was making each of the following claims:
that the sine function is incomplete, the property of solubility
in water is incomplete, the relation of parenthood is incomplete. In fact, however, Frege intended not a single one of
these assertions to follow from his claim that functions are
incomplete.[2] At first sight, this seems to be inconsistent with
the customary conventions for the meaning of a sentence of
the form "All *A* are *B*"; and even the most sympathetic student of Frege's work may be hard put to it to explain Frege's
contention.

There is scarcely another instance where Frege's meaning

---

[1] *Translations from the Philosophical Writings of Gottlob Frege,* by
Peter Geach and Max Black (Oxford, 1952), p. 24. In subsequent references to this work, only the page number will be cited.

[2] In order to infer "The sine function is incomplete" from "All functions are incomplete," we should need the further premise "The sine
function is a function." We shall see (section 9 below) that Frege holds
this additional premise to be false.

[229]

is in doubt. Here, however, he explains that "complete" and "unsaturated" are mere "figures of speech" (p. 55) and asks the reader to meet him "half-way" in interpreting these "metaphorical expressions" (p. 115). "All that I wish or am able to do here is to give hints," he says (p. 55). We shall see later that on Frege's view it is logically impossible to express his thought literally and explicitly. If this is so, we seem to be committed to the quixotic task of trying to understand the ineffable. We must not be too hasty in assuming that this is what Frege required of his readers.

How shall we take advantage of the "hints" that Frege has supplied? The most obvious thing to do is to unravel the analogies suggested by his use of the word "incomplete." [3] The sense we make of Frege's claim that functions are incomplete will depend upon our success in transferring to this unusual context the meanings that "incomplete" would have in its *literal* uses. By considering the relevant features of such ordinary uses of "incomplete," as I shall do in the next section, it should become possible to see how much of the literal meaning can be preserved in the metaphorical use. Our purpose is to discover the extent to which Frege's metaphorical use of "incomplete" requires us to attach an extraordinary meaning to that word.

2. In nonphilosophical conversation or writing, the word "incomplete" can often be replaced, without substantial change of meaning, by the word "unfinished." Now if it makes sense to say of something that it is unfinished, it must make sense to say of that thing, however falsely, that it is finished. Again, we apply the word "finished" only to something that *takes time*—time to do, time to make, or time to happen. It is sensible to speak of finishing a speech, a painting, or a war; but it is logically absurd to talk of finishing a mountain, the number

---

[3] The same might be done for Frege's word "unsaturated" (*ungesättigt*), which he uses as an alternative to "incomplete" (*unvollständig, ergänzungsbedürftig*). I do not think this would substantially affect my argument.

seven, or the boiling point of water. In none of these last cases can there be any sensible question of the time needed. It would be the height of absurdity to ask, "How long did this mountain take?" or "Has the number seven lasted longer than the number five?" or "When was the boiling point of water finished?"

There is, therefore, a simple test for the applicability of the word "incomplete" in any sense in which it is roughly synonymous with "unfinished." If we are in doubt whether the word applies to some particular thing, we have only to ask whether any sense can be made of the question "How long does that thing take to do (or to make, or to happen)?" Only if this question makes sense will it be sensible (whether true or false) to call that thing unfinished; only then can we speak without absurdity of that thing being incomplete *because* it is unfinished.

Something that takes time to do, to make, or to happen—let us say "a process," for short—may be of such a character that it results in the existence of a relatively permanent thing. When the storm has ended, nothing remains; but when the chef has finished his work, he has a cake to show for his pains. In such a case, let us say the process has resulted in a "product," and if that product is the work of man or animal let us call it an "artifact." Since the production of a product takes time, there will be what we might call "preliminary stages" in the coming into existence of the thing in question. Very well: the word "unfinished" is often applied, not to the process, but rather to a preliminary stage of a corresponding product.

Not to any kind of product, however. If the reader will make a list of things that come most readily to mind as instances of the "unfinished" or "incomplete," he is likely to hit upon such things as *The Mystery of Edwin Drood,* or Cologne Cathedral, or Schubert's *Unfinished Symphony*—all of which are artifacts. In each of these cases, the process finishes when a certain goal has been reached: it "comes to completion," as we say, and does not merely cease or end. We have only to take instead some examples of processes that do not involve an active agent working toward some goal, to see the absurdity of using "incomplete" in such cases. There is no sense in speaking of an "incomplete gale" or an "incomplete earthquake." We do sometimes speak of "incomplete oxidation" or "incomplete fertilization"; but then it is we, the speakers, who set the goal and judge the natural process by its distance from that goal.

At this point, Frege might interrupt to protest that all this talk of "time needed," of "process," "artifact," and "goal," has nothing to do with what he wanted to say. Precisely. We can attach no sense to such sentences as "the sine function has lasted a thousand years," or "the property of solubility in water has taken a long time" or "the relation of parenthood is swift"—all of which would have been as repugnant to Frege as they are to us. But just because there can be no question of time in connection with functions in Frege's sense, there can be no question of a metaphorical transfer of the common senses of "incomplete" in which it can be equated with "unfinished." We can no more speak of functions being incomplete in these senses that we can of four o'clock being venomous.

There does remain another set of senses of "incomplete" in ordinary talk in which it is roughly equivalent to "having a part missing." This chess set is incomplete, because the king is not in the box; this specimen of *Gentiana crinita* is incomplete, because the stamens have become detached; this copy of the *First Folio* is incomplete, because the frontispiece has been lost. Even in these cases the thing most naturally called incomplete is still an artifact, judged to be incomplete or defective because it fails to meet a standard set either by its maker or by the speaker.

But let us try to exclude any such teleological considerations and suppose that Frege meant by "incomplete" simply "having a part missing," no matter if the thing in question could not sensibly be regarded as requiring human agency or resulting from a process. Even then, we must notice, the question "Is this incomplete?" needs further elaboration before it can have a determinate sense. To know whether a given thing is incomplete, in the sense of having a part missing, we must know with what kind of thing it is being compared: an incomplete chisel can be a complete handle, an incomplete sentence a complete clause, and so on. The question "Is this incomplete?" no more admits of an answer in the absence of further specification than does the question "Is this an ingredient?" We have to reply with further questions: "Ingredient of *what?*" and "Incomplete *what?*" Of course, the context itself often makes this unnecessary. If I am asked whether "this essay" is complete, I understand that the question is whether it is a complete essay—not a complete book or something else.

Too much philosophical lexicography becomes boring, so I will merely add two further features of the ordinary uses of "incomplete." (a) A cup without a handle is still a cup, but an incomplete sentence may be only a clause, not a sentence at all. But in both cases, the incomplete thing is the *same kind of thing* as the complete thing with which it is contrasted. Remove the handle and you still have a cup; remove the end of a sentence and you still have a set of words. On the other hand, it would be absurd to say that the redness of a red flag was incomplete with respect to that flag. For redness is not a flag, nor is it the same kind of thing as a flag. (b) When we say Schubert's symphony is incomplete, we mean something is actually missing: if the missing part were supplied, the symphony would cease to be unfinished. And so in general: A complete door is not composed of an incomplete door plus a handle—when the handle is added, the door *ceases* to be incomplete.

Let us now apply these considerations to Frege's claim that functions are incomplete.

3. Frege's reason for saying that a function is incomplete is a parallel contention about "function signs," i.e., the symbols or words by means of which we talk about functions. "The expression of a function," he says, *"needs completion, is 'un-*

saturated.' The letter *'x'* only serves to keep places open for a numerical sign to be put in and complete the expression; and thus it enables us to recognize the special kind of need for completion that constitutes the peculiar nature of the function . . ." (152).[4] This is why he concludes that the function itself must be incomplete. "The peculiarity of function signs, which we here call 'unsaturatedness,' *naturally has something answering to it in the functions themselves.* They too may be called 'unsaturated,' and in this way we mark them out as fundamentally different from numbers" (p. 115, italics inserted).

The line of thought that led Frege to regard the function sign as incomplete or "unsaturated" is substantially the following: In speaking of the sine function, say, a mathematician uses the symbol "sin *x.*" Here, however, the *"x"* merely serves the purpose of holding a place open for the insertion of a numeral. Thus the symbol is essentially "sin( )" where the empty place is shown without the use of a letter. Hence the function is incomplete (cf. p. 25).

I shall examine this argument later (section 6). For the time being, let us simply apply what we learned about the literal uses of the word "incomplete" to the assertion that the function sign is incomplete. We may begin by asking our old question, "Incomplete *what?*" The answer cannot be "Incomplete function sign," for Frege held that *every* function sign was "unsaturated"; if completed, it ceases to be a function sign. Whenever a function sign is completed by the insertion of a name in the empty place we always get what Frege called an *"Eigenname"* or, literally, a "proper name." We might accordingly suppose Frege to be asserting that a function sign is an incomplete proper name. But this, as it stands, is misleading, for reasons that must now be explained.

[4] A similar statement is this: "The sign for a function is 'unsaturated' (*ungesättigt*); it needs to be completed with a numeral, which we then call the argument-sign" (p. 113). Frege returned many times to these themes, using almost the same words each time.

4. To understand what Frege meant by *"Eigenname,"* we must turn to a crucial passage in his essay, "On Sense and Reference":

It is clear from the context that by 'sign' and 'name' I have here understood any designation representing a proper name, which thus has as its reference a definite object (this word taken in the widest range), but not a concept or a relation. . . . The designation of a single object can also consist of several words or other signs. *For brevity, let every such designation be called a proper name (Eigenname)* [p. 57, italics inserted].

By an "Eigenname," he means, accordingly, either a name or a definite description, provided however that it does not stand for either a concept or a relation (or, more generally, a function). The need for brevity hardly excuses the use of "proper name" in this most unusual sense; it would surely have been better, if an abbreviation was needed, to use the word "designation" (*Bezeichnung*). In what follows, I shall myself use the word "designation," to mean the same as "name or definite description," but with the important difference that, unlike Frege, I shall not stipulate that a function cannot have a designation.

Frege's view that a function sign is an incomplete designation is complicated by his view that declarative sentences are designations—either of "the True" or of "the False" (see pp. 62–63). The following argument seems to me to be a sufficient refutation of Frege's view that sentences are designations of truth values.

We may assume that if A and B are designations of the same thing the substitution of one for the other in any declarative sentence will never result in nonsense. This assumption would not have been questioned by Frege. Let A be the sentence "Three is a prime" and B the expression "the True." Now "If three is a prime then three has no factors" is a sensible declarative sentence; substitute B for A and we get the nonsense "If the True then three has no factors." The last form

[235]

of words has no more use than "If seven then three has no factors" or "If the third smallest prime number then three has no factors" or indeed any form of words containing an expression of the form "If X then . . ." where "X" is replaced by a designation. Hence, according to our assumption, A and B are not designations of the same thing—which is what we set out to prove. By the "truth value of a sentence," Frege said, he understood "the circumstance that it is true or false" (p. 63) and added: "There are no further truth values. For brevity I call the one the True, the other the False" (*ibid.*). He failed to notice that he had given a use for the expression "the **True**" only in conjunction with a given sentence (the "*it*" in his statement) and not in other uses.

5. In the light of our own conclusion that sentences are not designations, we must now distinguish two interpretations of Frege's claim about function signs, depending upon whether we take him to be saying that function signs are incomplete designations or incomplete sentences. Fortunately, we can accept both contentions. It matters little whether we take the function sign to be "sin x" or "sin( )" or just "sin" (and Frege vacillates on this point): we can, if we choose, look upon each of them as a stage in the construction of "sin 1," or similar numerical designations. It can hardly ever happen that in order to get "sin 2" a mathematician first writes down "sin x," then erases the "x," and only then writes down the "2." No matter—it could be done. A man might fill a mug of beer by first getting a mugful of sand, then emptying the sand, and finally inserting the beer; and looked at in this way, the mugful of sand would be a preliminary stage in the production of a mug of beer. Of course, if we start with "sin( )" or simply "sin," it is easier to look upon the function sign as an unfinished numerical designation. Similarly, we can look upon the predicate "is a parent of" as a preliminary stage in the construction of a sentence like "Tom is the parent of Dick." We are certainly entitled to say, and without a trace of metaphor, that a function sign is a designation with a part

missing—or, from another standpoint, that a function sign is a sentence with a part missing.

This interpretation is useless for Frege, however. For parallel assertions hold for designations. A name can be a part of a function sign, as in "$x + 2$"; and many sentences contain a name or other designation as a part. We have as much justification, so far, for saying that a designation is an incomplete function sign as for saying that a function sign is an incomplete designation; we have as much right to say that a designation is a sentence with a part missing as for saying the same about a function sign. Thus Frege's intention, to mark "a distinction of the highest importance" (p. 54) seems to have been unfulfilled and we must be on the wrong track.

6. Consider, next, how the ellipsis could be removed from Frege's assertion that the function itself, rather than the sign by which it is represented, is incomplete. To the question "Incomplete *what?*" the only answer now must be the paradoxical "Incomplete *object* (*Gegenstand*)."

The following statement is typical of several to be found in Frege's philosophical writings:

> The function is completed by the argument; I call what it becomes on completion the *value* of the function for that argument. We thus get a name of the value of a function for an argument when we fill the argument-places in the name of the function with the name of the argument. Thus, for example, '$(2 + 3.1^2)1$' is a name of the number 5, composed of the function-name '$(2 + 3.\xi^2)\xi$' and '1' [p. 153].

The "completed" thing with which the function is here contrasted is the number 5; so if the function is to be an incomplete anything, we must be prepared to say it is an incomplete number. Every function whose values are numbers will have to be called an incomplete number.

However, nobody has yet given any good sense, metaphorical or literal, to the expression "incomplete number" in its application to functions. There can be no question here of the creation of numbers, a process requiring time, or a resulting artifact. And to think of a function as a number with a part missing is to strain ordinary language beyond endurance. Of course, the words "part" and "whole" are commonly used in all sorts of ways, and so an ingenious man might perhaps give the expression "incomplete number" a plausible meaning. But the locution would be so unusual that it would have to be explained. We can not be expected to meet a writer half way if we do not know in which direction to move.

Frege seems to agree:

> . . . I have here used the word 'part' in a special sense. I have in fact transferred the relation between the parts and the whole of the sentence to the reference by calling the reference of a word part of the reference of the sentence, if the word itself is a part of the sentence. This way of speaking can certainly be attacked. . . . A special term would need to be invented [p. 65].

But to introduce a technical term will merely provide an unfamiliar word to stand for a mysterious idea; what we need is some explanation of what "part" can mean when used in Frege's extraordinary fashion. It is no help to be told that the term is used figuratively when the ground of the figure of speech is completely hidden.

We can be sure at least of this, that the expression "incomplete number" is a misnomer if it suggests that an incomplete number is a *kind* of number: a function is not a number at all. A door with a missing handle is still a door, but an incomplete object, in Frege's sense of "object" is not an object at all. This is most obvious in the case of truth values: it is perfectly absurd to think of "the True" or "the False" as being incomplete, or having a part missing, in any senses of "incomplete" and "part" suggested by the ordinary uses of those words.

I conclude that the ideas that the word "incomplete" is likely to suggest to us on the basis of its literal uses will mislead us as to Frege's intention. Let us, then, make a fresh start by examining in detail the argument by means of which Frege

[238]

thought he had established that the function sign must be "incomplete." For whatever the argument proves will be presumably what Frege wanted to say.

7. I have already summarized the argument by means of which Frege tries to show that a function sign is incomplete. Here is the argument in his own words:

It is precisely by the notation that uses 'x' to indicate [a number] indefinitely [e.g. '$2.x^3 + x$'] that we are led to the right conception [of a function]. People call x the argument and recognize the same function in

$$‘2.1^3 + 1’$$
$$‘2.4^3 + 4’$$
$$‘2.5^3 + 5’$$

only with different arguments, namely 1, 4, and 5. From this we may discern that it is the common element of these expressions that constitutes the essential peculiarity of a function; i.e. what is present in

$$‘2.x^3 + x’$$

over and above the letter 'x'. We could write this somewhat as follows:

$$‘2.(\ )^3 + (\ )’ \quad [\text{p. } 24].$$

If I say 'the function $2.x^3 + x$', x must not be considered as belonging to the function; this letter only serves to indicate the kind of supplementation that is needed; it enables one to recognize the places where the sign for the argument must go in [p. 25].

The expression for a function must always show one or more places that are intended to be filled up with the sign of the argument [p. 25].

From the third of these quotations, in conjunction with Frege's remarks elsewhere, we can arrive at the following interpretation of the claim that the function sign is "incomplete": A function sign, unlike a designation (*Eigenname*) must have gaps—places intended to be filled by designations; it is logically impossible to refer to a function except by means of a sign having such gaps or hiatuses.

This claim seems to contradict the possibility of using the traditional symbolism of free variables ("*x*," "*y*," and so on) which does not literally contain spaces to be subsequently filled. As the second quotation shows, Frege holds that the free variables are simply used to mark the gaps. He is thinking of the function sign as a kind of container—something, as he often says, that can be "filled up." From this standpoint, the function sign is like a frame without a picture, a glove without a hand, or an empty mold; and the free variable is like a lay figure, a mere dummy used to draw attention to the way in which the gap might be filled. Perhaps the etymology of *"vollständig"* or its Romance equivalents, *"complet"* and "complete," encourages a tendency to think of anything incomplete as an empty container or mold, intended to be completed by being "filled up."

Now is it really necessary for the function sign to include some indication of empty spaces that are intended to be filled up? We must notice, first, that the use of such a sign can be demanded only when the function sign is used separately, and is not attached to a designation to form a complex designation of an object. As Frege said, his notation of gaps is needed "only for the exceptional case where we want to symbolize a function in isolation" (p. 114, *fn.*). The case is so exceptional in the formal development of a deductive system of calculus as never to arise; there is constant need for it, however, in Frege's remarks *about* symbolism and the world. Only in examples like "The function $\xi^2 = 4$ can have only two values" (p. 154), and "The function $x^2 + y^2$ has numbers as values" (p. 39), where we want to talk about the function itself, can there be any question of the function sign necessarily containing hiatuses. It would be too farfetched to regard an expression like "log 2" as containing a gap or space in addition to the signs "log" and "2." This would be like saying that a bottle of wine consists of the empty bottle, the wine, and the space filled by the wine.

Suppose now that it should be logically impossible to refer to functions in isolation. In that case, it would be impossible to use Frege's notation of "spaces," and instead of saying that a function sign must contain a hiatus, we should have to say a function sign can never have a hiatus. If this were so, our present question—whether there must be gaps in a function sign used in isolation to refer to a function—would simply not arise. If there cannot be empty rivers, the question of whether an empty river must contain a space fails to arise; if there can be no reference to a function, the question whether a sign referring to a function must have gaps fails to arise. We shall see there is serious reason to suppose that on Frege's view this is indeed the situation (see sections 9 and 10 below).

For the time being, however, let us suppose there is no objection to the use of such sentences as "Log x is continuous," in which there seems to be reference to the function itself and not to one of its values. To find out whether it is essential for an empty space to be indicated, we need only consider what information is actually conveyed by the use of the free variable or an equivalent device in such contexts. When we have a clear idea of the work done by the free variable or the hiatus, it will not be too hard to decide what *"must"* be the case for this work to be done.

In the statement "Log x is continuous," the free variable *"x"* is used to convey the following information: (a) We are reminded that the preceding word "Log" stands for a function. (b) The fact that *"x"* occurs, rather than *"(x,y)*," say, tells us that a function of only a single variable is in question. (c) The design of the symbol "Log x" may remind us that values of the function will be log 1, log 4, log 5, etc. In more complex statements, a free variable may also be used to "identify variables "—as in *"F(x,x)"*—but we shall not need to refer to this.

Can these three items of information be conveyed by Frege's gap notation? In "log( )" the work of indicating that "log" is a function sign is performed by the brackets: I doubt that Frege would have been happy to say that the function sign *"must"* be accompanied by brackets whose presence shows something about the "essential peculiarity" of functions;

[241]

functions are not *that* peculiar. If the hiatus is to show that we have to do with a function of one variable, it will have to do so in virtue of the absence of a comma, such as we have in "F (,)." What a remarkable empty space, as Frege might have said. The fact is that the gap symbolism effectively draws attention to *one* feature of such a symbol as "Log"—the possibility of combining it with numerals to get numerical designations. But we are certainly not compelled to use a gap to remind us that a function has values; nor are we compelled to use letters from the end of the alphabet to communicate the information conveyed by the traditional symbolism of free variables. That a symbol is a function sign can be shown in all sorts of ways—by the use of special type, numerical subscripts, and so on; and the same is true of information about the number of variables involved. As for being reminded that the function has values, this may be, and usually will be, quite irrelevant to the assertion we are making with the aid of the function sign. To use the sign "log" correctly, we must of course know its "logical grammar," that is to say, the rules governing its correct use. But the demand that this grammar shall always be explicitly symbolized in the case of every sign used obviously leads to an infinite regress. If it is legitimate to omit explicit symbolization of, say, restrictions upon admissible values of the function (an important feature of the grammar of the corresponding sign), why should it not be equally admissible to omit explicit indication of the relation of the function to its values?

Alternatively, if it is held that the logarithmic function must be symbolized by "log x" or "log ( )" because it is part of the essential nature of a function to have values, we might reply that it is just as much a part of the essential nature of objects that they can combine with functions. This line of thought might lead us to insist, with no less justification than Frege did in the case of function signs, that all designations shall be accompanied by brackets and gaps. To understand the use of numerals in higher mathematics is to know, *inter alia,* how they may be substituted for variables and otherwise used in combinations. Neither designations nor function signs have any use in isolation, and to know how to use them is to know how to combine them with their associates. When it comes to demanding that logical "grammar" be explicitly indicated, all signs are on an equal footing. To be vividly reminded of part of the grammar of a sign may be useful— or it may be a paper-wasting nuisance; we shall certainly go astray if we try to draw philosophical inferences from such purely practical considerations.

There is, indeed, something absurd in trying to base inferences about the logical structure of reality upon any physical characteristics of the signs we use. Yet Frege comes near to doing so. At times he seems to think of the sign "log( )" almost as literally containing a hole, and one which is preserved in every symbol by which it could be faithfully translated. But the physical gap between the brackets is of no ontological interest: exactly the same information might be conveyed by allowing the brackets to approach, overlap, or disappear. All that is "essential" to the function sign is that we recognize it correctly, without confusing it with other signs: a particular pattern of ink traces may help us in this, but no design can guarantee understanding, nor does "the nature of things" (p. 41) impose any restrictions whatsoever upon the character of the signs that we can successfully use. Once we see that there is no necessity for the function sign to be regarded as an empty container, it is to be hoped that the metaphor of the function itself as a kind of container will lose whatever appeal it might have had.

8. Yet another metaphorical basis for the contention that functions are incomplete is expressed in the following passage:

Not all the parts of a thought can be complete; at least one must be 'unsaturated,' [5] or predicative; otherwise they would not

[5] Notice that here a "part" of an existing whole is called "unsaturated." We have seen above that if a B is actually a part of some inclusive whole, an A, it is improper to speak of the B as an incomplete A. This is another instance of how Frege plays fast and loose with the underlying metaphors.

hold together. For example, the sense of the phrase 'the number 2' does not hold together with that of the expression 'the concept *prime number*' without a link. We supply such a link in the sentence 'the number 2 falls under the concept *prime number*'; it is contained in the words 'falls under,' which need to be completed in two ways—by a subject and an accusative; and only because their sense is thus 'unsaturated' are they capable of serving as a link (*Bindemittel*) [p. 54].

This can be paraphrased as follows: "No series of designations constitutes a sentence. So they must be united in order to form a whole. This can only be done by having an 'incomplete' sign with 'spaces' or 'holes' which the designations can 'fill up.' " Then the train of thought is carried over to what the signs signify: the sense of the sentence could not "hold together" unless something "unsaturated," a function, were to complete the sense of the designations.

Here the picture is that of a "bond" or "link" holding the parts together. The following is a crude physical analogue of the way in which Frege was here thinking of the relation of subject to predicate in a sentence: Two men side by side do not make up a whole—they "hold aloof from another" (p. 55); but this can be remedied by a pair of handcuffs. Just because the handcuffs have a pair of empty spaces that can be filled up, they can unite the two men into a single unified whole. (The very crudity of this picture will help us to see better the logical blunder involved.)

The picture has only to be taken seriously in order to appear inept. Even as a paradigm of physical connection, the image of the separate objects that need a "link" immediately proves inadequate. The fact that more handcuffs are not needed to join the handcuffs themselves to the men is enough to show that some physical bodies "hold together" without benefit of intermediaries. The string around a parcel does not have to be attached by string; nor does glue need an invisible superglue in order to be effective. (If we had superglue, what purpose would be served by the ordinary stuff?) As soon as we realize this, however, the archetypal image loses its attraction. If a hand and a glove can "hold together" without assistance from a third object, why should we not be content to say that a designation and a function sign may combine to form a sentence, without either being "unsaturated" or incomplete?

Of course a sentence is not a mere series of designations; but neither is it a chain with links. Consider the following analogy. A chessboard with pieces standing on its squares is what chess players call a "position." Now a philosopher might be inclined to say that a chess position is not merely a board *plus* the pieces; the position, he might say, "has a kind of unity." But in fact nothing is needed to "bind" the board and the pieces together. The fact that they stand upon the board is enough to make them a "position," and if they have been so placed in the course of a game, they constitute a "real" or "actual" position. If the chessboard had grooves into which the pieces had to fit, one might be tempted to call the chessboard "incomplete"; but what would be gained by this?

Similarly for language. What gives the series of sounds used in a genuine assertion its "unity" is simply the fact that they are used by a speaker in accordance with the rules for correct speech of the language in question. To put it another way, the series of sounds "I am going for a walk now" is what we call a sentence according to the correct use of English (and parallel remarks apply to German or any other language). As Frege saw, no link or copula between the words is needed. Names, predicates, and other expressions are abstractions from sentences: the question "How do they hold together?" has no more sense than the question "How do the bricks and mortar of a wall hold together?" When bricks and mortar are put together under certain conditions, it is simply a fact that they adhere. When an English speaker says the four words "I am going home" (in that order, with appropriate intonation, in the right circumstances, and so on) it is simply a fact that he makes himself understood and does not leave his audience waiting for more information. If we imagine the continuous band of sound dissected into segments that are then

separated from one another, we may be able to puzzle ourselves with the question "How do they hold together?" But
to answer "Because one of them has an empty space waiting
to be filled" is to practice self deception. We are saying, in
effect, "Because one of them has the power of combining with
the others." There is no good use for the idea of the function
as a kind of ghostly grappling hook.

9. There remains one final interpretation of Frege's thought,
suggested by the following remarks:

> It is clear that a concept cannot be represented independently
> as an object can but that it can occur only in combination (*in
> Verbindung*). One can say that a concept can be distinguished
> (*unterschieden*) in a combination but not separated (*abgeschieden*)
> out of it. All apparent contradictions which one can come upon
> here result from treating a concept as an object, contrary to its
> incomplete nature ["Uber die Grundlagen der Geometrie," *Jahres-
> bericht der Deutschen Mathematiker-Vereinigung*, 12 (1903): 372,
> *fn*.].

This interesting statement suggests one perfectly clear and
quite unmetaphorical meaning for the contention that functions are incomplete. It might be taken simply to mean that
it is logically impossible to make a function the subject of
an assertion. This view was once held by Russell and was very
clearly stated by him:

> The essence of a substance, from the symbolic point of view, is
> that it can only be named—in old fashioned language, it never
> occurs in a proposition except as the subject or as one of the
> terms of a relation . . . Attributes and relations, though they
> may not be susceptible of analysis, differ from substances by the
> fact that they suggest a structure, and that there can be no signifi-
> cant symbol which symbolizes them in isolation. All propositions
> in which an attribute or a relation *seems* to be the subject are only
> significant if they can be brought into a form in which the at-
> tribute attributes or the relation relates. If this were not the case,
> there would be significant propositions in which an attribute or
> a relation would occupy a position appropriate to a substance,

which would be contrary to the doctrine of types and would produce contradictions ["Logical Atomism," in *Contemporary British Philosophy; Personal Statements,* First Series (London, 1924), pp. 375–376].

I do not think that all Frege meant by saying that functions are incomplete was that functions cannot be designated; but he was at least implying this. Yet he still wants to use expressions of the form "the function F," and therefore tries to show that such expressions are not really designations of functions at all. This, as we shall soon see, is the crux of his theory.

Frege's argument is, briefly, (a) that functions (including "concepts" as a special case) can never be referred to by a name or definite description (i.e., cannot be designated), (b) that nevertheless we often need to make assertions about functions, (c) that consequently the grammatical subjects of such assertions do not really stand for functions, as they seem to do, but refer to objects representing those functions.

The three words 'the concept "horse"' do designate an object, but on that very account they do not designate a concept, as I am using that word [p. 45].

In logical discussions one quite often needs to assert something about a concept and to express this in the form usual for such assertions—*viz.,* to make what is asserted of the concept into the content of the grammatical predicate. Consequently, one would expect that the reference of the grammatical subject would be the concept; but the concept as such cannot play this part, in view of its predicative nature; it must first be converted into an object, or, speaking more precisely, represented by an object. We designate this object by prefixing the words 'the concept'; e.g.:
'The concept *man* is not empty.'
Here the first three words are to be regarded as a proper name, which can no more be used predicatively than 'Berlin' or 'Vesuvius' [pp. 46–47].

It must indeed be recognised that here we are confronted by an awkwardness of language, which I admit cannot be avoided, if we say that the concept *horse* is not a concept, whereas e.g. the city of Berlin is a city and the volcano Vesuvius is a volcano [p. 46].

By a kind of necessity of language, my expressions taken literally sometimes miss my thought; I mention an object, when what I intend is a concept [p. 54].

Over the question what it is that is called a function in Analysis, we come up against the same obstacle; and on thorough investigation it will be found that the obstacle is essential, and founded on the nature of our language; that we cannot avoid a certain inappropriateness of linguistic expression; and that there is nothing for it but to realize this and always take it into account [p. 55].

It would be most unsatisfying if a theory about symbolism and its connection with reality had to culminate in lamentations about the inescapable inadequacy of language. Frege does not notice the disastrous consequences for his own formulation of the view that it is logically impossible to refer to a function. If the expression "refer to a function" is nonsense, as it needs to be on his view, then the sentence containing that expression "It is logically impossible to refer to a function" is also nonsense: if Frege's view implies that the very formulation of that view is nonsensical, no further refutation is needed. Of course, it would remain open for him to say, simply, "The expression 'refer to a function' is without sense," but this is not what he intended.

The view that expressions that seem to refer to functions are not nonsensical, because they really refer to objects, escapes the objection just made, but is open to equally serious criticism. Consider, for example, the statement "Log *x* is incomplete." If the grammatical subject of the sentence is taken to designate some object (*Gegenstand*) the statement becomes not false, but nonsensical. Frege said it was "impossible, senseless" (p. 50) to assert of an object what could be asserted of a concept—or, more generally, of a function. "What . . . is asserted about a concept can never be asserted about an object" (p. 50), and "The assertion that is made about a concept does not suit an object" (p. 50). Now the statement "Log x is incomplete" is intended to suit a function, and hence the predicate, "is incomplete," does not "suit" an object. On the other hand, if "Log x" really stands for some object, as Frege suggests, then the predicate cannot mean what it seems to mean; it must express some other sense appropriate to an *object*. (Perhaps it is for that reason that Frege says "functions are incomplete," but not "log x is incomplete.")

The position would then be that in trying to say of functions that they are incomplete we should succeed only in saying something else about objects [6] that in some unexplained way managed to go proxy for the functions. Frege's own assertion about the incompleteness of functions would have to consist in the attribution of unknown characters to unidentified objects. Could mystification go further?

Even if the assertion "Functions are incomplete" had a sense on this farfetched construction, Frege would have succeeded only in recognizing some character of *objects*—and would have failed to make the desired distinction between *functions* and objects. Suppose that in saying, "Functions are incomplete," we are really predicating some character K of certain objects. Some objects, but not all, will then have the character K. So, in saying that functions are incomplete, we are really distinguishing between two kinds of objects, those that have and those that do not have K; we fail utterly to explain or characterize the difference between objects and nonobjects (functions). The reason is plain enough: we cannot say anything about functions without talking about them, and if we insist that we are talking about something else we

[6] The only object uniquely associated with a given function in Frege's system is the corresponding value-range (*Werthverlauf*). Now the value-range is never defined, and is introduced solely for the purpose of making possible what Frege's doctrine about functions forbids, viz., reference to and quantification upon functions. No wonder that Frege regarded the existence of value-ranges as "indemonstrable" (p. 26)—or recognized this as a weak point in his system (p. 234).

shall at best succeed in saying something that we hadn't intended.[7]

10. The proper course for Frege to have taken was to forbid the
use of expressions of the form "the function *F*" except in statements which, as Russell put it in the quotation used above,
"can be brought into a form in which the attribute attributes
or the relation relates." For instance, in the statement *"The
property of being* a man *is exemplified,"* we can treat the
whole italicized part as synonymous with "Something is," so
that the sentence is taken to mean the same as "Something
is a man." [8] On this construction, the expression "a man"
occurs predicatively, and we need not suppose that the grammatical subject of the original sentence (i.e., the expression
"the property of being a man") stands for anything at all.

[7] I think Frege's general position on sense and reference could have
been made consistent with the view that "the concept *C*" does refer to
a concept, and "the function *F*" does refer to a function. Why not say
(a) in a statement like "Bucephalus is a horse" the words "is a horse"
express the property of being a horse, so that that property is the sense
(*Sinn*) of the predicate; but (b) in the statement "The concept *is a horse*
is often realized" the expression "The concept *is a horse*" *refers* to the
property (has that property as its reference or *Bedeutung*)? The expression "is a horse" would, in the latter case, occur in what Frege calls "indirect reference" (p. 59)—which would incidentally explain why, as
Frege pointed out (p. 46), one naturally italicizes or puts quotation marks
around the expression. This way of looking at the matter would have
the merit of removing some of the mystery from Frege's notion of *Sinn*.
Frege allows that a *Sinn* may be referred to, in indirect reference; hence
the *Sinn* cannot be a function. But what other kind of object recognized
by him would serve instead?

[8] The example is taken from P. T. Geach, "Subject and Predicate,"
Mind, 59 (1950): 472–473. Geach differs from Frege in not regarding
"the property of being a man" as designating anything at all. He does not
observe that this makes it impossible to construe most of his own interesting remarks about properties, functions, and so on. Expressions like
"the property of being a man" can usefully be treated as mere circum-
locutions for predicative uses of the predicates contained within them
only so long as one is content not to generalize about properties, relations, and functions.

[250]

Now this way of handling sentences containing the expression "the function F" will work only when "F" has no free variable attached: in order that "F" shall be used predicatively there must be either a designation or a quantifier attached to the function sign. But we have already seen that the only cases which Frege had in mind when he claimed that functions are incomplete were those in which the function sign occurs "by itself," as he said, i.e., without attached designation or quantifier. If one insists that function signs shall be used only predicatively, all such locutions become nonsensical.

This policy would put a gag upon any attempt to generalize about properties, relations, or functions. We would have to count as nonsensical such characteristic statements of Frege himself as "What a name expresses is its sense" (p. 154), "An object is anything that is not a function" (p. 32), "Relations are functions" (p. 142), and so on. Even the main contention of the theory itself, "A function is incomplete," would have to be regarded as nonsensical. For this contention has the form "(x) (If x is a function, x is incomplete)." Now nothing can be properly substituted for the "x" in "x is a function": the name of a function cannot be substituted, since functions, according to Frege, cannot be designated; and if we substitute the name of an object we get a statement that is "impossible, senseless." Hence the functional expression "x is a function," is ill formed and any attempt to generalize by binding the free variable is absurd. The same, of course, applies to the second clause, "x is incomplete." Now a doctrine that reduces philosophy to silence might conceivably be correct; but nobody can reasonably be expected to accept a theory which, on its own showing, is trying to say what cannot be said.[9]

11. Let us end by considering what reasons Frege had to offer for the paradoxical view, from which so many unwelcome

[9] One may be reminded of Wittgenstein's position in the *Tractatus*. He was showing, however, that his own metaphysical statements were senseless. Frege had no such intention.

consequences flow, that an expression of the form "the function F," cannot designate a function. In order to designate, the expression would have to be what Frege called an *Eigenname* ("proper name"). Now if the reader will refer back to Frege's definition of *"Eigenname"* (section 4 above) he will find that functions are expressly excluded from being referred to by an *Eigenname*. To put the matter in another way, Frege so *defines* "designation," "object," and "function" that it is impossible for a function to be designated. But this tells us only how he has chosen to use these words. It by no means follows that it is wrong to begin a sentence with an expression of the form "the function F"; nor does it in the least follow, as Frege mistakenly supposed, that the definite description must then stand for what he called an object.

Nothing that I have said in this essay is intended to deny the validity of the distinction that Frege points out between names (and expressions that can be substituted for names), on the one hand, and predicates or functional expressions, on the other. That these two classes of expressions have different "logical grammars," i.e., are controlled by different rules of meaningful usage, is obvious upon the most cursory inspection. But this can be understood without recourse to mystifying and misleading metaphors about the "incompleteness" or "lack of saturation" of what the functional expressions are confusedly supposed to stand for. In fact, the muddle arises, I suggest, because Frege, in spite of this clear distinction in the uses of the two types of expressions, still wants to think of the functional expressions as *names* for functions (cf. his use of the term *"Functionname"* and his tendency to say that function names and function expressions "stand for" something). Of course, if one intends to use the term "name" in such a way that "objects" can, but functions cannot, have names, and yet thinks of the functional expression as after all still, somehow, naming a function, confusion will be bound to result; one will try to speak of functions as if they were and at the same time were not "objects." The use of the figurative expressions *"unvollstandig"* and *"ungesättigt"* is an attempt, but an unsuccessful one, to have the matter both ways—to call functions objects, albeit peculiar, "unsaturated," ones. As to the question whether "the function *log x*" *really* refers to a function, I do not see how this is to be answered in the absence of any criterion for "really" referring to anything. I would suppose that we have uses for expressions like "the function *log x*" and that if they were banned much of what we now succeed in saying in mathematics, logic, and philosophy would become impossible of utterance. If a reader desires a more profound justification than this, I cannot help him, and he must look elsewhere for satisfaction.

12. *Summary and conclusions.* I have tried in this essay to understand Frege's contention that functions are incomplete and the considerations that led him to make it. In its literal uses, "incomplete" is usually a synonym for "unfinished" or "having a part missing"; only the second set of uses can provide a plausible basis for Frege's metaphors, since the first involves reference to a temporal process or a resulting product. In ordinary usage, "this *B* is incomplete" is always an ellipsis for "this *B* is an incomplete *A*" where either *A* is identical with *B*, or *A* and *B* are species of a common genus. Frege's assertion that a function *sign* is incomplete might, accordingly be taken to mean that a function sign is an incomplete *Eigenname* ("proper name"). Since I found reason to reject Frege's view that a sentence is an *Eigenname*, I had to consider separately the assertion that a function sign is an incomplete designation and the assertion that it is an incomplete sentence. Both assertions can be taken to be *literally* true, but only in trivial senses which do not serve to distinguish function signs from designations. On the other hand, the suggestion that the function itself might be considered as an incomplete object (*Gegenstand*) had to be rejected as absurd. The metaphors of the function sign as container or link were examined and found wanting. Nor could I find any good reason to agree that the function sign "must" show empty places. Frege's theory finally breaks down in its implication that "the function *F*"

[253]

cannot refer to a function. This seems to imply the impossibility of generalizing about functions and thus the impossibility of formulating the theory itself.

The major difficulties of the theory seem to have arisen from incompatible inclinations to count function signs both as being and not being designations and this, in turn, may have something to do with Frege's relative neglect of all symbols that are not "names" or parts of names. If Frege had not been so impressed by the importance of "names," he might have avoided the whole imbroglio.

XIV

Carnap on Semantics and Logic

Sie sprechen eine Sprache
Die ist so reich and schön
Doch keiner der Philologen
Kann diese Sprache verstehen

1. *Introduction.* The technical language of "semantics" [1] and the wider subject of "semiotic" of which it is a part must be agreed to be both rich and mathematically elegant—if the shade of Heine will pardon this misapplication of his rhyming sentiment. Yet many beside philologists are puzzled today by the new language and the discipline whose instrument it is. We may discount as much as we please the mere technical difficulties of mastering a symbolism which makes the language of *Principia Mathematica* seem transparently lucid by comparison. There remains, even for those philosophers for whom gothic letters are no impediment, a more serious cause for disquiet. If the interest aroused by the birth and growth of semantics has been tinged with perplexity, the reason is largely the difficulty of understanding the full import of the primitive

[1] The best elementary exposition of semantics is included in Professor R. Carnap's monograph, *Foundations of Logic and Mathematics* (Encyclopedia of Unified Science, vol. 1, no. 3, Chicago, 1939). Professor Alfred Tarski's article on "The Semantic Conception of Truth and the Foundations of Semantics" (*Philosophy and Phenomenological Research,* 4 [1944]: 341–375) is very useful, likewise Professor Charles Morris' *Foundations of the Theory of Signs* (Encyclopedia of Unified Science, vol. 1, no. 2, 1938) which provides a general setting for the whole subject. A more exact exposition is Carnap's *Introduction to Semantics* (Harvard University Press, 1942). I shall refer to these works by the abbreviations, *"F.L.M.," "S.C.T.," "F.T.S.,"* and *"I.S.,"* respectively. In referring to Carnap's earlier *Logical Syntax of Language* (English ed., 1937), I shall use *"L.S.L."*

assumptions which determine the character of the subject and its potential usefulness.

It is, of course, easy to forget that semantics has many precisely distinguished subdivisions—and, so forgetting, to submit irrelevant criticism.

It would be idle, for instance, to complain that in *pure* semantics the crucial terms may receive no definition, being introduced perhaps by means of rules or postulates that determine only how the words are to be used in the subsequent deductive elaboration of a system defined by those very same rules; or to lament the fact that in *pure* semantics the objects under discussion are whatsoever elements may happen to satisfy the axioms—"signs" only by proleptic courtesy. For such abstractness and indefiniteness of reference are necessary in any discipline which aspires to be "pure"; the hopes of positive achievement in semantics, *qua* formal algebra of meaning, rest upon just such self-imposed limitations; and to charge it, in the mathematical aspects of its work, with lack of empirical reference would be quite to misconstrue its purposes.

But semantics is hardly interesting enough as pure mathematics to be pursued for its own sake; and, but for the wider claims of philosophical relevance which have been made on its behalf, the subject would have aroused little interest outside the ranks of specialists in symbolic logic. When a well-wisher claims that "the recent discovery of semantics is of fundamental philosophical importance"[2] it must be presumed that the reference is to *descriptive* semantics rather than to a branch of pure mathematics. The department of semantics for which such claims of philosophical relevance are made must then be prepared, like any other empirical discipline, to demonstrate the adequacy of its basic concepts and the fruitfulness of its empirical and analytical procedures in the solution of the problems that define its purposes.

A comparison of descriptive semantics with some other empirical subject—the theory of optics, perhaps, or the psychol-

[2] A. Hofstadter, "On Semantic Problems," *Journal of Philosophy*, 35 (1938): 232.

ogy of sign-using behavior—leaves an impression of relative poverty of factual data and conceptual analysis. The basis for the three-fold analysis of the sign-using situation into *sign-vehicle, designatum,* and *interpretant* ("that which acts as a sign, that which the sign refers to, and that effect on some interpreter in virtue of which the thing in question is a sign to that interpreter" [3]) seems to be nothing more searching or epistemologically sophisticated than common observation. And this simple conceptual framework becomes still further attenuated in *semantics,* where all reference to the interpretant, the locus of all that is distinctively human in the use of signs, is excluded by definition. When a still more advanced level of abstraction yields the subject of *syntax,* in which reference is made neither to designata (extralinguistic entities) nor to interpretants (acts of interpretation), Berkeley's quip about the "ghosts of departed quantities" receives a new application.

Initial hesitations such as these—and more specific qualms concerning the usefulness of the blanket application of primitive terms such as "designatum" to a heterogeneous diversity of items—are best resolved by reference to the degree of success of the new subject in the solution of its problems. But what are these problems—apart from the interesting, but for the present purposes irrelevant, technicalities of pure semantics?

An answer is suggested by Professor Hofstadter's claim that "with the appearance of semantics as a new scientific discipline, those problems which could not be handled with the apparatus provided for in earlier statements of logical empiricism are now in the way of receiving definite treatment." [4] For among the most important of such problems I take to be those that have in the past troubled all plausible versions of empiricism; those that arise whenever the attempt is made to account, in a manner consistent with exclusive reliance upon experience as a source of knowledge, for the privileged cognitive status of the so-called "necessary" truths of mathematics,

[3] Charles Morris, *F.T.S.,* p. 3.   [4] A. Hofstadter, *ibid.*

logic, or for that matter, philosophy itself. "Logical Empiricists" of the Vienna School, inspired by the stimulating oracular pronouncements of the earlier Wittgenstein, have constantly sought some linguistic interpretation of "necessary truth"; the promise offered by semantics of completing what has been called the "vindication of analyticality" [5] accounts for the honored place of the subject in the affections of those who wish to be consistent empiricists.

Instead of making further preliminary comment while loitering at the entrance to semantics, the more useful procedure suggests itself of tracing in detail the contributions of the new subject to the linguistic interpretation of necessary truth and more particularly, for the purpose of this essay, to the linguistic interpretation of *logic*.

But here we meet an initial difficulty. In spite of the philosophical importance of the thesis that logic can be subsumed without remainder under semantics, it is impossible to find either a sufficiently clear statement of the meaning of the thesis or a reasoned defense of its truth.

My first task in this essay should be, then, to try to *formulate* with reasonable precision a claim of the linguistic character of logic, in a manner conforming to the intentions of logical empiricists. I shall be content, however, to do this for a single illustrative proposition belonging to logic; the aim will be to test the plausibility of "the linguistic thesis" (as I shall say by way of abbreviation) in its application to a particularly simple and perspicuous example. Since the simplification of semantical method which this procedure will require need not involve misrepresentation of the methods applicable to more complex instances, we may hope that the conclusions may also apply to the more general thesis.

The sections which follow are arranged in the following way: First (section 2) I reproduce some statements made by Professor Carnap (to whose views the discussion will be confined) in order to establish significant variations in the linguistic thesis according as logic is identified *either* with syntax

[5] G. Bergmann, *Mind*, 53 (1944): 243.

or with semantics. Next (section 3), I describe the simple proposition that is to serve as a test case for the validity of the linguistic thesis, and meet some preliminary objections. In section 4, *a syntactical* version of the linguistic thesis is described in a presentation free from all unnecessary technicalities. Section 5 outlines criticisms of the syntactical version. Finally, in section 6, I try to show that the *semantical* version of the linguistic thesis is, in certain essential respects, identical in import with the syntactical version, and needs, therefore, to answer the same objections.

In view of the restriction of the discussion to a particular application of semantics, it may be as well to say explicitly that I have no wish to belittle the value of a mathematical approach to the morphology of linguistic systems. Some of the methods already developed (for instance by Gödel and Tarski) have considerable interest in the study of the structure of deductive systems. But we are here concerned with the philosophical value of semantics—which has yet to be established.

2. *Carnap's formulations of the linguistic thesis.* It will be convenient to assemble a number of alternative statements of the type of position to be further examined in this essay; I have chosen passages from books written by Professor Carnap [6] at different stages in the development of his opinions concerning the functions of "scientific philosophy" and its methods of "logical analysis."

. . . we must acknowledge [says Carnap] that all questions of logic (taking this word in a very wide sense, but excluding all empirical and therewith all psychological reference) belong to syntax. *As soon as logic is formulated in an exact manner, it turns out to be nothing other than the syntax either of a particular language or of languages in general* [*L.S.L.*, p. 233; italics in original].

. . . 'non-formal logic' is a *contradictio in adjecto.* Logic is syntax [*L.S.L.*, p. 259].

[6] Carnap has written the most fully and explicitly upon these topics. But his views are, of course, shared by many logical empiricists and others.

These quotations are typical of many statements in *The Logical Syntax of Language* in which logic is summarily identified with syntax. A related insistence, common to positivists from Hume onward, is that logic is nonfactual; or, as Carnap more explicitly says, logical and mathematical theorems:

. . . do not possess any factual content. If we call them true, then another kind of truth is meant, one not dependent upon facts [7] [*F.L.M.*, p. 2].

In Carnap's more recent work, reference to semantics almost, but not quite, replaces the earlier reference to syntax:

. . . logic, in the sense of a theory of logical deduction and thereby of logical truth, is a special part of semantics [*I.S.*, p. 56].

. . . logic is a special branch of semantics . . . logical deducibility and logical truth are semantical concepts. They belong to a special kind of semantical concepts which we shall call *L*-concepts [*I.S.*, p. 56].

But we are also told, in a similar context, that the equation of logic with semantics

. . . does not contradict the possibility of dealing with logical deduction in syntax also [*I.S.*, p. 60].

As syntax is a special branch of semiotic (distinguished by the absence of explicit reference to designata) there need be no inconsistency between the later and the earlier formulations. The earlier statements were made at a time when Carnap did not yet hold reference to extralinguistic designata, which is characteristic of semantics, to be an acceptable part of the new disciplines which were to replace "the inextricable tangle of problems which is known as philosophy" [8] (*L.S.L.*,

---

[7] The further arguments of the monograph make it clear that Carnap intends to establish the "theorems of logic and mathematics" as what is technically described as "*L*-true statements of semantics" (Cf. *F.L.M.*, p. 15).

[8] Cf. the characteristic early statement ". . . all theses and questions of logical analysis and therefore all theses and questions of philosophy

p. 279). His gradual relaxation of the methodological restrictions necessitated by earlier positivist criteria of meaningfulness of utterance has clearly not shaken his acceptance of *some* form of what I am calling a "linguistic interpretation" of logic; the "theory of logical deduction" is still, as in the earlier days, regarded as "not dependent upon facts" *because* it deals, at least in part, with the consequences of *linguistic* rules. The intelligibility and plausibility of such a doctrine clearly depend upon the extent to which its advocates can make precise the senses of logic, language, and dependence upon language to which they are committed; and for this purpose of mere clarification of the linguistic thesis, the shift of emphasis from semantics to syntax is no less significant than the constancy of the general mode of approach. It will be a major concern of this essay to discover what addition is made to the plausibility of the linguistic thesis by the admission of semantics into the company of reputable philosophical disciplines.

First, however, let us pause to ask what Carnap means by "logic."

It seems that he wishes the term to be used so broadly as to cover not only the theory of valid deduction and the construction of "modal" logics but even questions, more commonly assigned to metamathematics, concerning the structural relations between axiom systems (*L.S.L.*, p. 233). But in any case, in presenting an analysis of propositions belonging to what he calls a "theory of logical deduction" *he must surely wish the sentences expressing these same propositions to be understood in some customary meaning.*

If the linguistic thesis were intended as a definition of what was arbitrarily designated as "logic"—independently of what that term is already, and with more or less consistency, established to mean, its philosophical import would be negligible. And the defense of what would in that case be asserted would

---

(in our sense of this word) belong to logical syntax. The method of logical syntax, that is, the analysis of the formal structure of language as a system of rules, is the only method of philosophy" (*Philosophy and Logical Syntax*, 99).

be supremely easy; there is nothing easier than to assign our own meaning to a sentence (whether by using terms of semantics or those drawn from any other subject) if we are free to ignore how the words of the sentence are already used; and if this were Carnap's contention he might with equal justice and as little relevance to philosophical problems contend that logic was a part of mathematics, legal theory, or systematic genetics.

None of this would, I presume, be denied by Carnap or those who agree with him in presenting a linguistic interpretation of logic; they would agree, no doubt, that philosophical inquiries into the nature of logic must concern themselves with the *present usage* of the sentences expressing the propositions to be analyzed. And we must also concede the justice of the possible retort that "present usage" is often confused, indefinite, and in need of revision. But such welcome unanimity of opinion on this elementary, but quite fundamental, initial issue, cannot be allowed to obscure the neglect, *in practice,* of this very need to relate logical analysis to current linguistic usage. I shall try to show, indeed, that this is one of the main defects of Carnap's attempted identification of "logic" with syntax or semantics; that, in short, what he thereby *calls* "logic" has, in certain essential respects, very little connection with what, on the basis of current practice and the philosophical claims of significance for his procedure, we might reasonably have supposed him to be analyzing.

3. *The definition of a test case for the linguistic thesis.* I propose to test Carnap's versions of the linguistic thesis by tracing in some detail what implications his view would have for the interpretation of some simple necessary statement. It is difficult, however, to describe the kind of statement which I have in mind without using language which would seem unfairly to beg the question of the validity of the linguistic thesis. The kind of statement I wish to present is one which might naturally be described as the assertion of a relation between a couple of propositions such that the first is a valid

consequence of the second. Sometimes this is expressed by saying, "*q could not be true unless p* were true," or again, "It is impossible that *p* should be true and *q* false," or, "*q* follows from *p*," or, "*p* entails *q*." On replacing "*p*" by "Smith is a man" and "*q*" by "Smith is a husband," we obtain, as an example of the kind of statement by which I propose to test the linguistic thesis, the statement "That Smith is a husband entails that Smith is a man" or, in more colloquial form, "Smith could not be a husband unless he were necessarily also a man."

Now the objection that is likely to be made to the formulations which I have just used is that the colloquial forms are elliptic and the technical ones question-begging and vague. We may be asked whether the statement about Smith and his status as a man and husband is intended to express a relation between sentences, propositions, "propositional attitudes," classes of mental events, or complex aspects of "sign-using behavior." And if we should incautiously reply that we mean a relation between propositions (perhaps intending to emphasize primarily that we do not seem to be talking merely about sentences as a grammarian might), the semanticist may accuse us of so *defining* our instance as to make it impossible for him to present a linguistic interpretation; and enemies of flabby names will raise a determined objection to the very mention of entities so repugnant as propositions should be to all good pragmatists.[9]

In order to anticipate such objections, it is necessary to make clear that the statement to be presented for analysis is not itself such as to imply *any* theory concerning its correct analysis. It makes for linguistic convenience to be able to say, "The *proposition* that Smith is a husband entails that Smith is a man," but this form of words need not—and in the context of this essay will not—carry the implication that propositions are or are not subsistent entities; or again, that they are or are

---

[9] See John Dewey and A. F. Bentley, "A Search for Firm Names," *Journal of Philosophy*, 42 (1945): 5–6; and the spirited examination of "proposition" in the latter author's "On a Certain Vagueness in Logic. I," *ibid.*, 10–14.

not classes of mental events. There need be no imputation of any sort concerning the ontological status of propositions or the proper analysis of statements in which the word "proposition" occurs.

All I contend is that there is some truth, however analyzable, quite properly expressed by one or other of the sentences which I have cited. One may hear a person mentioned in conversation as being somebody's husband and say at once, "Well, in that case he's a man"; now just such truths as the one perceived by the author of this ejaculation are the stuff of which logic as a theory is fashioned. Any philosophical theory concerning the nature of logic, aspiring as it will to give an adequate account of the more complex generalizations and principles of logic, must a fortiori be prepared to give an intelligible and persuasive analysis of humble statements of logical entailment of one proposition by another. If it can be shown that the linguistic interpretation breaks down in such a case, there will be no need to proceed further with the critical examination of the linguistic thesis.

In order to have a definite instance of the form "p entails q," it will be desirable to choose an example in which the sentences expressing the two component propositions exhibit an obvious and simple morphological interrelation. For Carnap will want to argue that the chosen statement is to be analyzed, more or less directly, into a statement referring explicitly to a morphological or "formal" relation between the sentences by which the propositions are expressed; it is therefore desirable to choose an example which is not obviously refractory to his proposed interpretation. I shall accordingly take as a standard test case the true statement:

(1): Smith cannot be in New York without necessarily being either in Paris or New York.

From this point onward it will be assumed that the reader has identified the truth which the statement (1) is intended to assert, recognizes it as a truth of logic, and understands that

[264]

the statement is intended to require no prior commitment to any view, linguistic or otherwise, concerning its correct analysis. I shall refer to (1) occasionally as a "statement involving logical implication."

Since we shall have occasion to refer constantly to (1), it will be convenient to introduce a few symbols. Let *"P-or-N"* and *"N,"* accordingly, be names of the *sentences* "Smith is in Paris or New York" and "Smith is in New York," respectively (where the symbols used may help to remind us of the morphological part-whole relation between the sentences in question). Then it is characteristic of Carnap's view that he proposes to replace (1) by a sentence of the form

(2): *P-or-N* is a consequence of *N,*

which he will assert to have the very same meaning as (1). The term "consequence" will prove to have somewhat different meanings according as it is taken to belong to semantics or syntax, so that we are offered not one, but at least two sentences equivalent in meaning to (1); and the sentence (2) will in each case prove to be misleadingly elliptical. But however we repair these ambiguities and omissions in (2), the overt reference to *sentences,* through the presence of *"P-or-N"* and *"N,"* will remain; it is this which stamps Carnap's translation of (1) as linguistic. (I shall not discuss the interpretation of (1) in "absolute semantics" in which no reference is made to sentences. This nonlinguistic interpretation has difficulties of its own.)

4. *The syntactical interpretation of statements about logical implication.* Our task is now to learn what translation is offered in *syntax* for the statement

(1): Smith cannot be in New York without necessarily being either in Paris or New York.

(Later we shall try to discover what difference is made by adopting a semantical rather than a syntactical translation.) The tentative translation previously offered was

[265]

(2): *P-or-N* is a consequence of *N*,

with the understanding that supplementation and further specification would be needed. The first addition to be made is the insertion of explicit reference to some "language" or calculus; for the term "consequence," as Carnap uses it in his syntactical studies, is defined only in relation to some language or calculus to which it applies; we can no more speak of "consequences" in general than we can in legal theory describe some act as a felony without explicit or implicit reference to the legal code in which the act in question is properly so designated.

Carnap explicitly generalizes this point to apply to every syntactical concept:

> With regard to every sentence of syntax, and consequently every philosophical sentence that it is desired to interpret as syntactical, the language or kind of language to which it is referred must be stated. If the language of reference is not given, the sentence is incomplete and ambiguous [*L.S.L.*, p. 299].

This intentional relativity in the meaning of "consequence," as of other syntactical notions, requires us to change our formula into some such assertion as:

(2*a*): *P-or-N* is a consequence of *N*, in the calculus *K*.

But we have still to specify the reference of "*K*," i.e., still to say in *which* calculus we propose to establish the relation between *P-or-N* and *N* asserted to hold by (2*a*). (And afterward, of course, we shall still need to explain what is meant by "consequence" in that calculus.)

In deciding what "*K*" shall mean, there are two radically different courses that may be adopted. We might choose *K* to be some calculus whose elements and combinatory rules were arbitrarily defined by us, without any attention to the concrete exemplification of that calculus anywhere in the world; or again we might choose that "*K*" should mean an idealized and formalized version of some empirically given language.

If the first choice were made, we should have an interpreta-

[266]

tion of (1) by means of a statement belonging to *pure* syntax, for:

Pure Syntax is concerned with the possible arrangements (of any elements whatsoever), without reference either to the nature of the things which constitute the various elements, or to the question as to which of the possible arrangements of these elements are anywhere actually realized (that is to say, with the possible forms of sentences, without regard either to the designs of the words of which the sentences are composed, or to whether any of the sentences exist on paper somewhere in the world). In pure syntax only definitions are formulated and the consequences of such definitions developed [*L.S.L.*, p. 7].

I have mentioned this first possibility—of translating statements about the logical relations between given propositions into statements belonging to pure syntax—only in order to reject it immediately. Let us remember clearly the logical truth which was intended to be conveyed by the sentence (1); and let it then be understood that the "translation" offered in *pure* syntax could amount at best to an assertion that in some arbitrarily constructed system of symbols, two arbitrarily chosen elements had a certain specified relation. Whatever the correct analysis of the proposition expressed by the sentence (1), the meaning of the sentence is at least *definite;* now the proposed surrogate from pure syntax will have the form "Some X has a certain relation to some Y," where "X" and "Y" are variables; or, in a slightly more plausible variation, "In accordance with certain definitions of 'consequence,' any X satisfying a certain condition A will be in the relation of consequence to any Y satisfying another condition B." In the first case we are offered a sentential form, in the second a generalization—but in neither case an adequate analysis of our original sentence.

Probably nobody would want to defend the version of the linguistic interpretation of logic here rejected, once its implications were clearly apprehended. But so very large a part of the work of Carnap and other writers on semiotic is concerned with *pure* syntax, and so much of their work consists in elaboration of the "consequences of definitions" [10] that some philosophers have made the mistake of supposing these researches to provide a direct answer to the philosophical problem of the analysis or interpretation of necessary statements.

Supposing the first version of the syntactical interpretation to be rejected, we are led to adopt the second alternative, and so to make our syntactical statement refer to some *empirically given* language; and in this way we shall obtain a statement of *descriptive* syntax. For this subject, we are told ". . . is concerned with the syntactical properties and relations of empirically given expressions (for example, with the sentences of a particular book)" (*L.S.L.*, p. 7). The empirical reference needed in the context of our own problem is, of course, not to the usage of a single author, as exemplified in "the sentences of a particular book," but rather to the wider linguistic usages of those speakers and writers whose sign-using behavior sets the currently accepted standards of "correct" English.

In place of the calculus, K, whose rules contain variables making reference to any elements which may happen to satisfy the definitions and axioms of the calculus, we have now to imagine a language,[11] E, say, whose rules are constructed in close conformity to the *actual* usages of those speaking correct English. The proposed translation of our original sentence now becomes:

(2b): *P-or-N* is a consequence of *N*, in the language *E*.

Before we proceed to the last part of our task of exposition, the explanation of the meaning of "consequence in E," let us become a little clearer concerning the character of the "language" E.

In accordance with the general specifications for a "lan-

---

[10] Only in *F.L.M.* (pp. 5–11), where a "fictitious language . . . very poor and very simple in its structure" is analyzed, have I been able to find anything approaching a detailed discussion of the syntax or semantics of "historically given languages."

[11] Carnap uses the terms "language" and "calculus" as approximate synonyms. In this paper the former term will be restricted to refer to what Carnap calls "historically given languages."

guage," as understood in semiotic, E will consist of a vocabulary, rules for combination of the vocabulary into admissible expressions (the so-called "formation rules"), and rules for transformation of admissible expressions into other expressions.[12] For our purposes, the vocabulary must be taken to include such words as "Smith," "is," "in," "Paris," "or," and so on, regarded as identical with certain words to which reference is made in standard English dictionaries. Thus the symbol "N" is, in the present interpretation, no longer the name of some complex object, not otherwise identified except as satisfying certain conditions of an abstract calculus; it refers instead to the specific sentence, "Smith is in New York," belonging to the English language as correctly spoken today; it refers to that sentence and to no other object, linguistic or otherwise, in the universe. Similar considerations apply to the rules of combination of E; they, too, must refer not to some imagined, or hypothetical, or abstractly delineated rules obeyed by "any elements whatsoever," but quite concretely to just those grammatical usages which are currently acceptable as characteristic of "good English." If the rules of E tell us, as they must, that "Smith is in Paris" is, while "Smith Paris is in" is not, a correctly formed expression, the reason must be found not in the freedom of action of the constructor of the calculus so to define his rules, but rather in the circumstances that the rules of combination in question do closely reflect the manner in which words are combined in current English usage.

We are ready, at last, to learn the meaning of "consequence" as it is used in ($2b$); for it is by means of the transformation of rules that "we determine under what conditions a sentence is a *consequence* of another sentence or sentences (the premises)" (*L.S.L.*, p. 27). In the present connection, where we are discussing a language E, intended to be modeled upon actual linguistic usage, the term "transformation rule" is liable to mislead us at the very outset. For it is bound to suggest some

[12] In semantics, further semantical rules of meaning will also be needed. See section 6 below.

process of *replacement* of one sentence by another by the users of the language; just as a chess player literally *transforms* one position into another by each move he makes, so we might reasonably suppose that a rule of E to the effect that some sentence S_1 can be transformed into S_2 is justified by some habitual removal of S_1 in favor of S_2 on the part of those who speak good English. Now this seems to be no part of the intention of those who use the term "transformation rule" in speaking of descriptive syntax.[13] To say that S_2 is a transform of S_1 in E is to assert *only* that S_2 is in a certain relation to S_1 and *nothing more;* a "transformation rule" is an assertion to the effect only that a certain sentence (or class of sentences) *stands in* a certain relation to certain sentences (or classes of sentences).

What the relation in question is can here be described only in vague and general terms (since further details would call for fuller specification of the transformation rules of E). The relation is, in the first place, what Carnap calls a formal [14] relation, i.e., one which can be established on the ground merely of the kinds and orders of occurrence of symbols of which the relevant sentences are composed; negatively, therefore, a formal relation between sentences cannot be grounded upon any reference to the *meaning* of the sentences.

Let us pause to consider a few examples of formal relations between symbols; that one word (in the English language) contains more syllables than another; that two sentences have at least one word in common; that one is a part of another; all

[13] The nearest that Carnap comes to assigning nonformal meaning to "transformation-rule" is in a suggestion that a transform of a proposition may *sometimes* be " 'thought' simultaneously with it" (*L.S.L.*, p. 27). There is elsewhere (*F.L.M.*, p. 6) a suggestion implied that the empirical basis of a proposed transformation-rule may depend on whether certain sentences are simultaneously *"acknowledged* as correct assertions."

[14] "An investigation, a method, a concept concerning expressions of a language are called *formal* if in their application reference is made not to the designata of the expressions but only to their form, i.e., to the kinds of signs occurring in an expression and the order in which they occur" (*I.S.*, p. 10).

these are instances of formal relations, in the sense explained, since in all the cases the holding of the relation in question can be established by sole reference to properties of the "design" or "form" of the symbols concerned. Let us especially notice that our overworked sentences, *P-or-N* and *N,* can be regarded as connected by a certain formal relation, namely, that which holds between two sentences whenever the first is a compound sentence composed of any sentence followed in turn by the word "or" and then by the second sentence. The relation is clearly formal, since to establish its exemplification we need to compare only two sentence designs without any attention to considerations of meaning. For this particular relation I shall coin the term "typographical alternation," in the hope that its very oddness may remind us that in saying *P-or-N* is *typographically alternate* to *N* we are saying that the former has the structure ". . . or *N*" and are saying *nothing more.* Now we can suppose the transformation rules of *E* to say in part that any sentence which is typographically alternate to a sentence shall be regarded as being a "consequence" of it.

What has been said about the relation of typographical alternation must now be imagined extended to apply to many other cases of formal relations between sentences of *E*. We have to suppose for instance that the rules of transformation provide that *N* shall be a consequence of *N-and-P, if-not-P-then-N* a consequence of *P, not-both-P-and-N* a consequence of *if-P-then-not-N;* and so on for a great variety of cases. In each of these many cases, the relation in question will be "formal" and might if we wish be appropriately labeled by a name of the form "typographical . . ."; and the rules of transformation of *E* can be summarily described as asserting that all cases of typographical alternation, typographical conjunction, typographical contraposition, etc., etc., through an extensive list of defined formal relations, *and those alone,* are cases of the relation of consequence.[15]

[15] But other ways of defining "consequence" would be technically more convenient in any systematic syntactical investigation of languages as complex as E. I have deliberately omitted as unnecessary for the present

After this explanation, we should at last be able to know what is being asserted by the sentence (2b), offered as a translation of our original example. We may perhaps paraphrase the sense of (2b) as follows:

(2c): *P-or-N* and *N* are expressions composed of symbols belonging to the accepted vocabulary of "correct English"; they are, moreover, correctly formed sentences of that language; and finally, they stand in a certain general formal relation, for whose holding between them it is a sufficient condition that the first should be composed of the second with the addition of the word "or" and another sentence.

The reader should by this time have no trouble in seeing how this type of interpretation could be so generalized as to apply to such statements as "Each proposition of form *A-or-B* is a consequence of the corresponding proposition *A*" and to other generalizations belonging to logic.

4. *Objections to the syntactical interpretation of statements involving logical implication.* I shall present objections to the view just outlined in summary form, adding to each case some further explanatory comment:

(i) *Supposing it could be shown that (2b) was true when and only when (1) was true—or let us say that a "linguistic correlate" of (1) had been produced—and supposing further that by a similar procedure a linguistic correlate could be produced for every statement of logic; it would still not have been established that logic requires a linguistic interpretation.*

What I am here supposing is that, with sufficient ingenuity, in every case in which we present a proposition "belonging to logic" a corresponding proposition could be produced in which reference was made only to relations between syntactical designs of *sentences*. Even then, it might still be argued that the evidence for a linguistic interpretation of logic was

discussion all reference to such complications as the need for distinguishing between a "definite" concept of "derivability" and the "indefinite" concept of "consequence" (Cf. *L.S.L.*, pp. 172–173 and *passim*).

inconclusive. For the sentences, such as (1), which *ostensibly* make no reference to linguistic entities *also* belong to "correct English"—if we grant philosophers the compliment of being supposed to speak correctly. If the parallelism between the ostensibly material sentences and the ostensibly formal sentences is evidence that the former are "really" linguistic, it might be argued, by parity of reasoning, that the parallelism is also good evidence for the ostensibly linguistic propositions being "really" concerned with nonlinguistic objects. There may be quasi-syntactical sentences no less than quasi-material sentences.[16]

Nevertheless, I regard this type of objection as having, on the whole, little force; and a detailed demonstration of linguistic parallelism (such as only a full development of the theory of syntax could be expected to furnish) should be regarded as good *prima facie* evidence for the linguistic thesis.

(ii) *Some statements involving logical implication, however, appear to have no linguistic correlates.*

A simple instance of such a statement is "My pencil cannot be red unless it is colored," which appears to involve exactly the same logical relation between propositions as our original example; there is of course no difficulty in multiplying similar instances of entailment or logical implication between *atomic* (uncompounded) propositions. In this case there is at least no obvious "typographical" relation between the sentences "My pencil is red" and "My pencil is colored," and the linguistic interpretation seems to break down irreparably.

I can think of only two even moderately plausible replies to this objection: (*a*) that the cases cited do not belong to logic and (*b*) that, if they do, there really is a syntactical relation of an *indirect* sort between the corresponding sentences. The first type of answer is quite arbitrary and, by defining logic as the totality of propositions admitting of linguistic interpretation,

---

[16] Cf. C. J. Ducasse, "Concerning the Status of so-called 'Pseudo-object' Sentences," *Journal of Philosophy*, 37 (1940): 309–324, especially section 8 of the paper.

comes dangerously near to reducing the linguistic thesis to triviality. On the other hand, I do not see how the second type of reply is to be made good except by providing that the rules of transformation of the language in question shall specify that any sentence of design "X is red" shall be regarded as a consequence of a sentence of design "X is colored." But if *this* type of relation between sentences is to be legitimately regarded as "formal," then *every* two sentences whatsoever can be regarded as standing in relevant formal relations; and all empirical propositions, no less than those of logic, will admit of linguistic interpretation in this extended sense.

I am not denying that the relation between "My pencil is red" and "My pencil is colored" *could be* formalized; there would be no technical difficulty in including, among the transformation rules of the "language" to which the sentences are assigned, one rule which would permit the second sentence to be recognized as a "consequence" of the first on the basis of inspection of the corresponding sentence designs, without appeal to meanings. For the practice of descriptive syntax permits us to obtain definite descriptions (without reference to meanings) of unique sentences.[17] Since we are permitted to refer to unique sentence designs, without overstepping the boundaries of formal treatment, we can certainly introduce a formal rule to the effect that one designated sentence is a consequence of another.

Unfortunately, the same method can obviously be extended in such a way as to make any statement whatsoever a consequence of any other arbitrarily designated sentence. It would be easy enough by appropriate revision of the transformation rules of E to make the categorical imperative a "consequence" of the third law of thermodynamics, without thereby rendering the relation of consequence any less "formal."

This appears to be conceded by Carnap when he asserts that the rules of transformation of a language may also include what he calls "physical or P-rules" (*L.S.L.*, p. 180)—the "so-

---

[17] Cf. *L.S.L.*, p. 155, where paragraph B_3 illustrates "Description of an expressional design by means of syntactical terms."

called laws of nature," and even "empirical observation-sentences." He explicitly tells us moreover that the *P*-rules are formal: "It is a matter of convention whether we formulate only *L*-rules, or include *P*-rules as well; and the *P*-rules can be formulated in just as strictly formal a way as the *L*-rules" (*L.S.L.*, p. 186).

I submit that this represents an extension of the linguistic thesis to a degree that removes any plausibility it might initially have had. So long as some sentences, but not others, are agreed to stand in certain "typographical" or formal relations, there is a possibility of using the distinction as a basis for discriminating logical from empirical assertions. But as soon as we are told that empirical statements "can be formulated in just as strictly formal a way" as logical statements, there remains no basis within syntax for distinguishing one kind of statement from the other. If it is just a matter of convention whether empirical statements too are regarded as validated on formal grounds, the linguistic thesis suffers a truly portentous inflation. We might well inquire whose convention is to determine the linguistic status of statements (such as those of logic themselves), the proper interpretation of which is still a matter for debate? If the logical or syntactical analyst chooses that logic shall be linguistic, his remarks tell us more about himself than about the nature of logic; but if his reliance upon "convention" is a covert appeal to some more stable postulational procedure by a concrete speech community, we are left quite in the dark as to the location and authority of the justification thereby invoked.

What has been occurring in this extension of the linguistic thesis follows a pattern which is all too familiar in philosophical discussion. The critical term "formal" had initially a relatively narrow but correspondingly well-defined reference; to say that statements of logic had the same truth conditions (were equivalent to, could be translated into) statements of *formal* relation between *sentences* was, therefore, to make a relatively well-defined, though paradoxical, assertion. In the simplest cases of linguistic interpretation (such as that of the transla-

[275]

tion of the trivial example used in this paper), the term "formal" retains its initial meaning. But as more complex instances of logical statements are successively presented for linguistic reinterpretation, the initial meaning of "formal" proves no longer adequate, and begins to suffer a sea change which ends by robbing it of all definite meaning. We end, as we began, with the assertion that logic is syntax, but in so diluted and "tolerant" a sense of the latter term that only by the grace of the "convention" of persons unknown are we prevented from including physics or any other body of empirical truth in the same hospitable discipline.[18]

(iii) *Given sentences stand in many formal relations to one another, yet there may be no parallel relations between the corresponding propositions; the criterion of logical relation between propositions must therefore be that there is a special kind of formal relation between the corresponding sentences; yet there seems to be no way of properly delimiting the appropriate class of formal relations.*

The sentence "Roosevelt is President" has a certain formal relation to the sentence "Churchill is President," viz., that both sentences have the same number of letters; yet nobody would want to claim that the truth so expressed belongs to logic. How then are the formal relations between sentences used in defining "consequence in E" segregated from those

[18] But after all, it might be said, is there not some striking significance in a demonstration that the "theory of logical deduction" *can* be "formalized" (supposing that proves to be the case)? And has not Carnap some justification for regarding this demonstration as being of "fundamental importance" (*F.L.M.*, p. 17)? I do not deny its technical importance, especially to those who are interested in the construction of comprehensive and useful logical calculi; but I fail to see any "fundamental" philosophical importance in the enterprise. There is a temptation to argue that if logic *could be* formalized it must *really be* a formal discipline. But this is no better than it would be to argue that a man who claims to be frightened by unidentified objects is *really* frightened by tigers—using as a reason that *if* a tiger were to be introduced in just those cases in which the man is frightened we *could say* he was frightened only by the presence of tigers.

[276]

other formal relations which have no relevance to logic? It is of course no defense to say that "consequence in *E*" is *defined* in the way which it is defined, for the question here is what basis, other than arbitrary fiat, there can be for such a definition. The only alternative appears to be to claim that the transformation rules are established by empirical observation of just those instances in which English speakers do assert statements of logical implication.[19] Now this view has the defect of rendering such statements as (2*b*) empirical. For the proposed translation will now amount to this:

(2*d*): The sentences, *P-or-N* and *N*, stand in one of the syntactical relations which observation shows to be exemplified in instances in which those speaking correct English claim that one proposition entails or logically implies another.

I feel a strong reluctance to accept this sociological view of the criteria for the "truth" of propositions of logic. I cannot help feeling that if all users of the English language except one were taught to assert that *N* could be true while *P-or-N* was false, they would be wrong and he, though in a minority of one, still right. But perhaps this is just a lingering after-effect of addiction to metaphysics and insufficient schooling in language tolerance.

(iv) *The validity of a linguistic interpretation of logic finally rests upon the extent to which it reflects the testing procedures actually used by us in establishing the truth of logical statements; the linguistic thesis fails to meet this test.*

This last objection gathers up many of the criticisms already made. It has already been argued that the linguistic thesis obliterates the commonly accepted distinction between empirical and logical propositions, locates the justification of logic in some equivocal and ownerless "convention," and requires constant *ad hoc* extension of the meaning of "formal," "syntactical," or related terms used in the formulation of the linguistic

---

[19] So far as I can tell, this is Carnap's view in *F.L.M.* (pp. 26–29), where he argues that in one way of regarding logic we are "bound in the choice of the rules in all essential respects."

thesis. These points are objections only in the light of some settled notion of our own as to how the statements which we identify as belonging to logic are used in actual practice. We must not fall into the error of claiming that no statements are properly interpreted as "linguistic," or that no statements claimed by their authors to be nonempirical do "in fact" refer to the fruits of observation and experience, or even that many statements in good standing in philosophy and the sciences are not so vague as to require definition by more or less arbitrary convention as a preliminary to philosophical interpretation. If, therefore, we claim that these hedging generalities should give no comfort to the defender of a linguistic interpretation of logic, our defense must be that we have a relatively clear notion of the procedures actually used in establishing logical propositions and obtaining agreement as to their validity.

I do not feel called upon, however, to provide here a positive account of the manner in which logical propositions are used in communication and the acquisition of knowledge; it is sufficient, for the purpose of criticism, to draw attention to the ways in which the implications of the linguistic thesis deviate from current practices of testing logical propositions. And once again I can think of no better way to demonstrate such deviation than by invoking concrete illustrative cases.

Let us return, and now for nearly the last time, to our exemplary instance of the relation between *P-or-N* and *N*. Suppose we were trying to teach an elementary student the truth commonly expressed by "*N* entails *P-or-N*," our original statement (1). If we were fully persuaded of the truth of the linguistic thesis, honesty would require us to present the so-called "truth" as if it were a maxim of etiquette or decorum. We should say, perhaps, "Observe the relation of this typographical design to that and remember that in such cases we speak *by convention* of the first being a consequence of the second." In order to proceed from this definition to any assertion capable of being true or false, I suppose we should add something of this sort: "You are to bear in mind, further, that it is a convention of the language which I am teaching you to master, that whenever *A* is a consequence of *B*, anybody who asserts *B* will be taken to be likewise asserting *A*." And so, if our student at last asks, "Why should I speak *this* language?" we must reply, "You *need* not—there are no 'obligations' in logic—but common prudence should restrain you. Only a fool will subject himself to the penalties of social nonconformity."

I suppose logic *might* be so taught and learned, as a branch of prudent social behavior, as I imagine physics might be taught as the art of imitative flattery of expert physicists. But I cannot help feeling that in either case the pedagogical technique would be peculiarly misguided; that when the unregenerate teacher of logic says, "Reflect upon the meaning of this proposition and that and you will then *see* that it is impossible for the one to be true and the other false"—that in such a case the logician is not simply investing a social precept in the spurious attraction of a mythical validity but is rather appealing to a source of evidence which still eludes the ingenious analysis of the semiotician.

4. *The semantical interpretation of statements involving logical implications.* The criticisms so far made apply only to the syntactical versions of the linguistic thesis. But, as we have already seen, Carnap nowadays also offers a *semantical* version of the thesis; we ought therefore to examine whether the interpretation of logic within this more extensive branch of semiotic is able to meet the objections we have produced.

For the reasons already presented in rejecting a linguistic interpretation of logic in *pure* syntax, we may ignore any suggestions that logic is to be interpreted as *pure* semantics. We argued that no satisfactory interpretation of a specific assertion involving the logical implication of one proposition by another could be provided by assertions containing variables, as in the case of those belonging to pure syntax. Statements belonging to pure semantics will resemble statements belonging to pure syntax in containing variables; they will therefore be able to refer only to whatever objects of arbitrary character and properties can satisfy the defining axioms or abstract postu-

[279]

lates of the subject. And, for exactly the same reasons as were used in rejecting the eligibility of the interpretation in pure syntax, we shall need to reject also the interpretation in pure semantics. The only version of a semantical interpretation having sufficient initial plausibility to deserve extensive consideration is one involving an attempt to translate statements about logical implication into sentences making reference to a specific language system modeled upon the actual sign-using behavior of those speaking correct English.

Thus in translating our original sentence, (1), according to the new version of the linguistic thesis, we shall once again be making reference to a formalized and idealized system of the actual rules of good English usage. The first difference made by the transition from the syntactical to the semantical standpoint is that the rules which we took to define E are now supplemented by certain characteristic "semantical rules" of truth; to mark the distinction we shall call the new system E'. E' will contain, in addition to the rules previously described above, some further "semantical" rules to be described immediately. We must become further acquainted with the character of the semantical rules of E' if we are to understand how the relation of consequence (or rather a substitute for it) is defined in the *semantical* interpretation of statements involving logical implication.

One distinctive feature of a semantical rule, differentiating it from the rules of formation and transformation to which previous reference was made in our discussion of syntax, is the explicit mention of the *truth* of sentences. Thus the simplest kind of semantical rule, of the type approved by Carnap, is an assertion that a sentence having the form "A is true" is logically equivalent to a related sentence from which reference to "truth" is absent.[20] As an illustration, we may suppose E' to contain these semantical rules:

[20] For further discussion of this and related matters see Chapter 4, "The Semantic Definition of Truth" of my *Language and Philosophy* (Ithaca, 1949).

(α): ("Smith is in Paris" is true) if and only if (Smith is in Paris).

(β): ("Smith is in New York" is true) if and only if Smith is in New York).

(in whose formulation the parentheses are used merely as marks of punctuation). It will be noticed that each of these has the form we have claimed; the second, for instance, presents the sentence "*N* is true" as logically equivalent to the sentence *N* in which reference is made to an individual and a city but no longer to the truth or any other relational characteristic of a *sentence*.

In general, the structure of these two semantical rules, and the many others of equally simple type which we must suppose *E'* to include, is such as to make it possible to *eliminate* the word "truth" in simple contexts, without alteration of the truth value of that context. In virtue of the form of (α), any assertion in which "*N* is true" occurs can be replaced by an equivalent assertion in which the sentence *N* occurs instead; and in the same way the rule (β) allows us to substitute *P* for "*P* is true" without altering the truth value of assertions in which the latter occurs.

The semantical rules of *E'* must also include rules in which *more complex* sentences of the form "*A-or-B* is true," "*A-and-B* is true," "*If-A-then-B* is true," etc., occur. As illustrative of these we may suppose *E'* to contain:

(γ): ("(Smith is in Paris) or (Smith is in New York)" is true) if and only if (("Smith is in Paris" is true) or ("Smith is in New York" is true)).

(δ): ("(Smith is in Paris) and (Smith is in New York)" is true) if and only if (("Smith is in Paris" is true) and ("Smith is in New York" is true)).

Each of these presents a statement concerning the truth of a complex sentence (in the first case *P-or-N*) as logically equivalent to an assertion concerning the truth of simpler sentences (*P* and *N*, respectively, in both cases).

What has already been said should be sufficient to suggest

[281]

how the four rules, (α), (β), (γ) and (δ), can be supplemented so as to permit the occurrence of the word "true" to be eliminated from other and, if necessary, still more complex contexts without alteration of the truth-value of the total assertions from which it is eliminated. It should be clear, for example, that E' might be supposed to contain rules sufficient to ensure that the sentence

(N is true) and ((P is true) or (N is true))

becomes, in accordance with the rules, logically equivalent to

N and (P or N).

We have to suppose, then, that E' contains not only the rules cited (or more general ones of which these will appear as special cases), but also many others to ensure the elimination of the word "true" (without change in truth value) in many other possible contexts. But for the purpose of illustrating the suggested translation of our simple example, the rules cited will suffice.

The importance of having semantical rules in which reference is made to truth arises from the fact that Carnap chooses so to define the relation to be substituted for logical implication, that explicit mention is made of the truth of the statements concerned. He names the relation "*L-implication*" and explains that the phrase "T_2 *is an L-implicate of* T_1," means that "the semantical rules exclude the possibility of T_1 being true and T_2 false" or, in an equivalent formulation, "according to the semantical rules, if T_1 is true, T_2 must be true" (*F.L.M.*, p. 14). Instead of saying that some proposition is logically implied by another, we are invited, in the semantical version of the linguistic thesis, to say some sentence is an *L*-implicate in E' of another or, in other words, that *appeal solely to the semantical rules* will determine that one sentence follows from the other.

We can illustrate the meaning of *L*-implication by verifying that, according to the explanation just given, it is in fact true that

P-or-N is an *L*-implicate of N (in *E'*).

For, according to the explanation, this statement will be true if and only if

If (*N* is true) then ((*P-or-N*) is true)

follows solely from the semantical rules of *E'*. Now appeal to (γ) reduces the last assertion to

If (*N* is true) then ((*P* is true) or (*N* is true))

and then appeal to (α) and (β) reduces that in turn to

If *N* then (*P-or-N*).

Finally, an elementary principle of deductive logic assures us that the last statement is true. In summary, we have used the normal procedures of deductive logic (which justified us, for instance, in substituting logically equivalent statements for each other) to prove, without appeal to any premises except (α), (β), and (γ), all of which were semantical rules of *E'*, the assertion

If (*N* is true) then ((*P-or-N*) is true).

So, in accordance with the explanation of *L*-implication, we have proved,[21] as we set out to do, that

P-or-N is an *L*-implicate of *N*.

Now let us consider what advantages the semantical translation of

(1): Smith cannot be in New York without necessarily being either in Paris or New York.

as the statement

(3): *P-or-N* is an *L*-implicate of *N* in *E'*

has over the syntactical version of the linguistic thesis.

[21] Cf. the examples given by Carnap (*I.S.*, pp. 79–80). (I have deliberately tried to avoid introducing "*L*-truth" and other "*L*-terms." The criticisms of this paper would not need to be modified if account were taken of such complicating detail.)

At first sight the new formulation seems to be distinctly preferable. A major cause for disquiet concerning the validity of the syntactical version was, it will be remembered, the paradoxically arbitrary character of the relation of "consequence" in terms of which statements about logical implication were to be interpreted; this stumbling block in the path of a linguistic interpretation, at least, seems to be removed by the transition from syntax to semantics. For whether the new translation of statements involving logical implication proves on other grounds to be adequate or not, it may seem that the question, whether the derived sentence (If N is true then P-or-N is true) is deducible from the semantical rules of E' without appeal to other premises, is one that admits of a perfectly definite answer. The fact that we were able to *prove* that P-or-N is an L-implicate in E' of N suggests that the relation now offered as a substitute for logical implication has a clear and definite character.

This illusion of the superior definiteness of the new version will however be dispelled by a little reflection. We have followed Carnap in saying that the test of the truth of a statement involving logical implication requires us (according to the latest proposal) to decide whether a certain derived statement about the truth of sentences follows from (or is deducible from) the semantical rules of the language concerned. If these words "follows" and its alternative "deducible" were understood in their normal meanings, however, the proposed translation of statements involving logical implication would be guilty of the most blatant circularity; for the translation offered of statements expressed by using the word "deducible" or a synonym would itself use that very same word. In order to determine whether a statement involving logical implication were true, we should have to determine, according to the new proposal, whether some other statements (among them the semantical rules) were in the very same relation of logical implication. The proposed procedure would thus certainly *not* establish the alleged linguistic character of statements involving logical implication.

[284]

So obvious an objection has not been overlooked by Carnap, though the point, elementary as it is, is often neglected by those who urge that principles of logic are "true by definition" —i.e., are the *logical* consequences of definitions. (If there were no other reason for criticizing the proposed analysis, there would be the sufficient technical difficulty that the account of *L*-implication reproduced in this section *mentions* the language in which the semantical rules are formulated, and cannot therefore be regarded as a definition *within* that language—the semantical metalanguage—of the notion of *L*-implication.) Carnap is quite explicit on this point: "The given characterizations of *L*-concepts are not definitions of these concepts but rather requirements which the definitions to be constructed either in general or in special semantics should fulfill" [*I.S.*, p. 81].

But where does this leave us? In order to complete the account of *L*-implication, we shall need to give a definition, in the language in which the semantical rules are formulated (the semantical metalanguage) of what it means for one statement to "follow from" or "be a consequence of" another. We shall have to supply a definition which allows us to determine, for example, whether

If (*N* is true) then ((*P* or *N*) is true)

is a consequence of the rules (α), (β), and (γ), without recourse to our preconceived and unformalized notions concerning the meaning of "consequence" and the correct principles of logical deduction. And if we are to be faithful to the guiding intentions of the whole program of semantics, we 'hall have to accomplish this task in such a way that the deci:' n whether two statements are in the desired relation depend₃ only ¡pon a "typographical" relation of the sentence designs.[22] I sha not linger over the technical difficulties which hamper the execution of this program of providing a *formal* definition of consequence in the general case, where we are not concerned with

[22] Cf. for example Carnap's exemplary definition of *L*-truth in a particularly simple semantical system (*I.S.*, pp. 81–82).

a specific language of assigned structure. We may grant that the difficulty of solving this general problem does not affect the problem of providing a formal definition of "consequence" in the language E' which more closely concerns us. And we may accept Carnap's assurance that such a definition, being already available in especially simple instances of languages, may be expected with some degree of confidence in the more general case.[23]

What we have rather to notice is that the semantical version of the linguistic thesis, as we now begin to understand its import, turns out to be identical, in all essential respects, with the syntactical version which we have already rejected. For what did the latter come to in the end if not an assertion that the truth conditions of our original statement (1) consisted in the manifestation of a certain formal relation, namely that of "consequence" between the sentences N and $P\text{-}or\text{-}N$? And what does the latest proposal for the interpretation of the same statement mean if not that we must finally establish some formal, typographical, characteristic of the compound sentence

If N then $(P\text{-}or\text{-}N)$?

There is a slight difference of presentation, to be sure. In the former case we had to compare *two* sentence designs to verify the satisfaction of the alleged truth conditions; and now we are asked instead to verify the presence of a formal characteristic of a single complex sentence. But this difference is quite trivial. The very same typographical relation whose exhibition by the two sentences N and $P\text{-}or\text{-}N$ respectively will establish the second as a "consequence" of the first will likewise establish the single complex sentence

If N then $(P\text{-}or\text{-}N)$

as "L-true."

Whether we take the semantical or the syntactical version, then, we shall in either case be committed to regarding the

[23] The general problem is discussed in section 16 of *I.S.* (pp. 83–88).

truth conditions of the statement to be analyzed as consisting solely in the presence of a certain typographical relation between two sentence designs. The only appreciable difference in the later version is that the character of the truth conditions involved is masked by the introduction of the "semantic rules." We are first asked to translate the original sentence in a specified way into a complex sentence in which the word "truth" repeatedly occurs; but the semantic rules are framed in such a way as to make it possible before long to eliminate all reference to "truth"; and so we arrive, by a roundabout way, at the very same truth conditions which the earlier versions offered as the basis of an adequate analysis of statements involving logical implication.

This reduction of truth conditions of L-implication to those of the earlier presented relation of consequence is not a mere by-product of the simplicity of our language E' or the semantical rules by means of which it is defined. No matter how complex the language or languages to which reference is made in descriptive syntax, the semantical rules, so long as they conform to Carnap's specifications, will be such as to make the presence of the word "truth" appear trivially redundant in the verification of the defining conditions of L-implications; and the truth of "T_2 is an L-implicate of T_1," will always hold in just those cases where T_2 is a consequence of T_1 according to the older, syntactical version.

If this view of Carnap's later procedure is the correct one, we are in a position to understand why he passes so easily from saying that logic is identical with semantics to saying that it is also identical with syntax. For whatever differences there may be in *some* uses of the two theories (and I am not denying that there are such differences), they coincide in the uses which are here under consideration. The reason why logic is identical with both syntax and semantics is that the semantical procedures do not differ for present purposes in any significant manner from those invoked in syntax.

I conclude therefore that the later recourse to semantics

[287]

does nothing at all to strengthen the case for a linguistic interpretation of logic, and is subject to the objections already discussed in the previous section of this paper.

I believe accordingly that contemporary semantics and syntax have nothing of major importance to contribute to the philosophical question of the "nature of logic." (Perhaps there is no such "question"? But that itself is another and a wider question which I cannot discuss here.) My reasons for this conclusion should by now be sufficiently clear to the reader.

7. *Retrospect.* I began this paper by trying to formulate a precise version of a thesis of the linguistic nature of necessary truths. For this purpose, I had recourse to various statements made by Carnap in which he identified logic either with syntax or with semantics, i.e., with two branches of what has been called "semiotic." In order to determine the truth of these statements, I chose an illustrative statement that would be generally recognized to be a "necessary truth," viz., *Smith cannot be in New York without being necessarily either in Paris or New York,* which I called "(1)." I then introduced *"N"* and *"P-or-N"* as names for the *sentences* "Smith is in New York," and "Smith is in Paris or New York," respectively. Carnap must say that (1) is correctly translated or "explicated" as *"P-or-N is a consequence of N."* Call the sentence that is offered as a correct translation the sentence "(2)." I tried to make plain the various meanings that would have to be attached to (2) in "pure syntax," and in "descriptive syntax," in "pure semantics" and in "descriptive semantics."

The first step was to complete (2) by adding reference to some "language" or calculus K. If K is an uninterpreted calculus, (2) belongs to pure syntax, but is then clearly an incorrect translation of (1). But if K is a calculus modeled upon the grammatical structure of current English, the translation offered makes (1) empirical. There are further difficulties, arising from the special interpretation attached to "consequence" in the formulation of (2). When Carnap says the relation of consequence is "formal," he says that only the sentence designs and not the meanings of the sentences determine that the relation holds. I therefore said the relation was intended to be "typographical." The chief objection is that any two sentences are in *some* typographical relations: it is hard to see why only some of these should be specially regarded as "logical." We also find that the word "formal" is construed so liberally that any two sentences can be supposed to be in the formal relation of "consequence" (as evidenced by the designation of the so-called P-rules as "formal"). Finally, the proposed interpretation of the necessary statement (1) and of other necessary statements does not agree with the testing procedures actually used to accredit or discredit such statements in English or any other "natural" language. For the view criticized would seem to make the "truth" of necessary statements a matter of arbitrary convention.

On turning to descriptive semantics (pure semantics being eliminated for reasons similar to those advanced in the case of pure syntax), we are able to meet some of the above objections. For whether the sentence "P-or-N is a consequence of N" is the expression of a necessary truth (i.e., is L-true in Carnap's terminology) is now decided by determining whether the derived sentence "If N is true then P-or-N is true" follows from the so-called "semantical rules" of the language in question. This no longer seems to be a question of there being an arbitrarily designated typographical relation between the two sentence designs, but rather a question having a quite definite and "objective" answer. Further examination showed this to be only an appearance. In the end we are still required to establish a mere typographical relation between the two sentences, as before. This is why Carnap can say that logic is syntax and also that logic is semantics: there is here only *one* untenable view: that in settling logical questions we need to examine the designs of sentences and nothing more.

One of the chief points in the above can perhaps be conveyed by the following fable:

A certain man who was fond of playing chess was much troubled by philosophical doubts about the game. "Am I *really* permitted to move the king in this position," he would say, and again, "Suppose the rules of the game allow me to move the king, how am I to justify the rules themselves?"

On the advice of his friends he consulted a learned semiotician, who informed him that his condition could be improved only by learning a new game which the semiotician had just invented. Now this game proved to have the same number and kinds of pieces as were to be found in chess, arranged in the same way on the chessboard. Indeed the only difference that the man could discover was that each piece wore a little cap on its head. And the name of this game was Heterochess.

The beauty of this new game, the semiotician explained, consisted in this, that each piece moved exactly the same way as its uncapped brother in the game of chess itself. "If you are uncertain whether you may move the king," the semiotician said, "all you have to do is to refer to the other game and ask yourself whether you may in a similar position move the heteroking." "And you need worry no longer about the justification of the rules of chess," he continued, "for you will find that each of them exactly resembles a corresponding rule in heterochess. Indulge no longer in philosophical doubts, for every question about chess is answered in heterochess."

This explanation proved satisfactory to the man, who continued to play both games with equal happiness. And the semiotician assured the man's friends that in case of any relapse into metaphysical regression, he would never be at loss to invent still another game to effect a cure.

Additional Notes and References

I. THE DEFINITION OF SCIENTIFIC METHOD

1. Originally published in *Science and Civilization,* ed. Robert C. Stauffer (University of Wisconsin Press, Madison, Wis., 1949).

2. The expression "definition of concrescence," used in the original paper, has been replaced by "range definition," which I now prefer. See the second essay.

II. DEFINITION, PRESUPPOSITION, AND ASSERTION

1. Originally published in *Philosophical Review,* 61 (1952): 532–550.

2. See also P. F. Strawson, *Introduction to Logical Theory* (London, 1952), p. 175. Further discussion will be found in Wilfrid Sellars, "Presupposing," *Philosophical Review,* 63 (1954): 197–215, and P. F. Strawson, "Presupposing—A Reply to Mr. Sellars," *ibid.,* 216–231.

III. SAYING AND DISBELIEVING

1. Originally published in *Analysis,* 13 (1952): 25–33.

IV. THE LANGUAGE OF SENSE-DATA

1. Part of a symposium (with Roderick Firth), somewhat misleadingly entitled "Phenomenalism," in *Science, Language, and Human Rights* (Proceedings of American Philosophical Association, Eastern Division, vol. 1 [Philadelphia, 1952]: 21–42). The topic was suggested by Firth's contention that "we may say that the problems of perception have traditionally been formulated in the 'sense-datum language' " (*ibid.,* p. 1) and by his repeated use of the expression, "sense-datum language." His own paper is directed mainly to a consideration of the merits of the "language of appearing."

2. The reader may wish to consult G. A. Paul's "Is There a Problem about Sense-Data?" *Aristotelian Society Proceedings,* supp. vol. 15 (1936), which takes a line rather similar to my own.

[291]

V. THE IDENTITY OF INDISCERNIBLES

1. Originally published in *Mind*, 61 (1952): 152–164.

2. For further discussion see G. Bergmann, "The Identity of Indiscernibles and the Formalist Definition of 'Identity,'" *Mind*, 62 (1953): 75–79, N. L. Wilson, "The Identity of Indiscernibles and the Symmetrical Universe," *Mind*, 62 (1953): 506–511, and A. J. Ayer, "The Identity of Indiscernibles," *Proceedings of the XIth International Congress of Philosophy*, vol. 3 (Brussels, 1953): 124–129.

3. *The Definition of Identity:* See *Principia Mathematica*, 1 (Cambridge, 1910), definition 13.01. The theory of types required Whitehead and Russell to say *x* and *y* are identical if and only if the same predicative functions are satisfied by both. For a similar definition see W. V. Quine, *Mathematical Logic* (New York, 1940), definition D 10 (p. 136). See also G. Frege, *The Foundations of Arithmetic* (Oxford, 1940), p. 76.

4. *Self-evidence of the Principle:* "I think it is obvious that the principle of Identity of Indiscernibles is not true" (G. E. Moore, *Philosophical Studies* [London, 1922], p. 307). "Leibniz's 'principles of indiscernibles' is all nonsense. No doubt, all things differ; but there is no logical necessity for it" (C. S. Peirce, *Collected Papers* [Cambridge, Mass., 1933]: 4.311). "Russell's definition of '=' won't do; because according to it one cannot say that two objects have all their properties in common (even if this proposition is never true, it is nevertheless *significant*)." (L. Wittgenstein, *Tractatus Logico-Philosophicus* [London, 1922], 5.5302). See also C. H. Langford, "Otherness and Dissimilarity" in *Mind*, 39 (1930): 454–461.

5. *Bradley's remark:* Not made in connection with *this* topic. See *Ethical Studies* (2d ed.; Oxford, 1927), p. 165. Bradley affirmed what he called "the Axiom of the Identity of Indiscernibles" (*The Principles of Logic* [2d ed.; Oxford, 1928], p. 288).

6. *Identity as a relational property:* ". . . numerical identity, which is a dyadic relation of a subject to itself of which nothing but an existent individual is capable" (C. S. Peirce, *Collected Papers*, 1.461).

7. *The proof of the principle by treating identity as a property:* "It should be observed that by 'indiscernibles' he [Leibniz] cannot have meant two objects which agree as to *all* their properties,

for one of the properties of x is to be identical with x, and therefore this property would necessarily belong to y if x and y agreed in *all* their properties. Some limitation of the common properties necessary to make things indiscernible is therefore implied by the necessity of an axiom" (*Principia Mathematica*, 1: 51). Cf. K. Grelling, "Identitas indiscernibilium," in *Erkenntnis*, 6 (1936): 252–259.

8. *Counter-examples:* C. D. Broad tries to refute McTaggart's form of the principle ("The dissimilarity of the diverse") by the example of a universe consisting of two minds, without bodies, that are exactly alike in all respects. (*Examination of McTaggart's Philosophy*, 1 [Cambridge, 1933]: 176). Broad holds however, that "either spatial or temporal separation involves dissimilarity" (*ibid.*, p. 173).

9. *The argument from verifiability:* "To say that B and C are 'really' two, although they seem one, is to say something which, if B and C are totally indistinguishable, seems wholly devoid of meaning" (B. Russell, *An Inquiry into Meaning and Truth* [New York, 1940], p. 127).

10. *The distinguishability of asymmetric bodies and their mirror images:* There is a famous discussion of this in Kant's *Prolegomena*, section 13. See, for instance, H. Vaihinger, *Kommentar zur Kant's Kritik der reinen Vernunft*, 2 (2d ed.; Stuttgart, 1922): 518–532—("Anhang—Das Paradoxon der symmetrischen Gegenstände") which also contains references to Kant's discussions of the identity of indiscernibles.

VI. ACHILLES AND THE TORTOISE

1. Originally published in *Analysis*, 11 (1951): 91–101.

2. The quotation is taken by permission from Paul Valéry, "Le Cimetière Marin," in *Charmes* (Paris, Librairie Gallimard, 1926), p. 112, ll. 121–126.

3. For references to critical discussions of this essay, see the first footnote of the next essay.

VII. IS ACHILLES STILL RUNNING?

Not previously published.

VIII. THE PARADOX OF THE ARROW

Not previously published.

[293]

IX. THE PARADOX OF THE STADIUM

Not previously published.

X. "PRAGMATIC" JUSTIFICATIONS OF INDUCTION

1. Not previously published. (This essay should be read in conjunction with the two that follow, which elaborate upon points that are central to the argument.)

2. Among good previous discussions of Reichenbach's views are the following: E. J. Nelson, "Professor Reichenbach on Induction," *Journal of Philosophy*, 33 (1936): 577–580. (See also Reichenbach's reply, *ibid.*, 35 (1938): 127–130, and Nelson's retort, in the same volume, 355–360.) Isabel P. Creed's "The Justification of the Habit of Induction," *Journal of Philosophy*, 37 (1940): 85–97, makes some telling comparisons between Reichenbach's justification of induction and Pascal's wager. Reichenbach's reply appeared under the title of "On the Justification of Induction" in the same volume, 97–103.

For a more general discussion of Reichenbach's theories see E. Nagel, "Probability and the Theory of Knowledge," *Philosophy of Science*, 6 (1939): 212–253.

3. Kneale's views are discussed in C. D. Broad's "Critical Notice," *Mind*, 59 (1950): 94–115. This mainly favorable report may be contrasted with F. L. Will's "Kneale's Theories on Probability and Induction," *Philosophical Review*, 63 (1954); 19–42.

4. For a more elaborate example of a deductive clarification of an inductive notion, consider the following.

A famous problem in the philosophy of inductive inference has been that of explaining why mere *increase* in the number of confirmatory instances should have any tendency to strengthen the corresponding hypothesis. "It is only after a long course of uniform experiments in any kind, that we attain a firm reliance and security with regard to a particular event. Now, where is that process of reasoning, which, from one instance, draws a conclusion so different from that which it infers from a hundred instances that are nowise different from that single one?" (Hume, *Inquiry*, Section IV.)

Let us try the following argument: Suppose I am set the task of guessing whether all the hundred balls in a given urn are white.

[294]

If I am allowed to draw at random, it would certainly be rational to do so. For if the ball drawn should prove not to be white, I would know the correct answer to the question set. Suppose I do draw a ball and find it to be white. Then I still do not know whether all the balls are white or not, but my task has been reduced to that of discovering whether the remaining ninety-nine are white. Now if I am allowed to make a further draw, parity of reasoning demands that I should do so. For if it was rational to draw a ball to test the hypothesis about the original hundred it must be rational to do the same for the hypothesis about the remaining ninety-nine. By repetition of the same argument, it must be rational for me to draw as many balls as I am allowed. Finally, suppose I do not know the number of balls in the urn, but am set the problem of finding out whether all of them are white: clearly the above arguments will lead to the same result, since they did not depend upon the number of balls in the urn, nor upon my knowing that number.

This argument, if sound, shows that anybody committed to sampling *in the kind of situation described* is necessarily committed to taking the largest sample permitted (neglecting the need to reach a decision in a reasonably short time, etc.). This conclusion, though reached by deductive inference, is illuminating to the extent that it is unexpected. It does throw some light (though not much) on the *meaning* of "sample," "rational," etc. I do not think a plausible case can be made for saying that the writings discussed in this essay have succeeded in producing such illumination in their analysis of "primary" or "pure" induction.

XI. INDUCTIVE SUPPORT OF INDUCTIVE RULES

1. Not previously published.

2. Some puzzling questions are raised by any attempt to use inductive arguments to *discredit* or refute the rules governing those very same arguments. Consider first the position of a man who holds that the sole rule of induction is R_1, i.e., "To argue from *All examined instances of* A's *have been* B to *All* A's *are* B." Suppose an extreme case in which R_1 has *never* been found to be successful, so that every time an inductive argument conforming to R_1 used a true premise, the conclusion was subsequently found to be false. This might be thought to provide excellent experi-

ential grounds for abandoning R_1. The formal argument would run as follows, however:

(b₁): All examined instances of the use of R_1 in arguments with true premises have been instances in which R_1 has been unsuccessful.

Hence:

All instances of the use of R_1 in arguments with true premises are instances in which R_1 is unsuccessful.

Call the conclusion of this argument P. Then because (b₁) is an argument conforming to R_1 and having a true premise, P says that the conclusion of (b₁) is false. In other words, if P is true, P must be false—and hence P must be false. This shows that even in this most extreme case, where R_1 has never produced a true conclusion from a true premise, we are unable to draw the only conclusion, P, which sole reliance upon the rule of inference R_1 permits. And yet, after all, R_1, as the preceding remarks have shown, has failed in the instance (b₁) as in all the preceding ones, for (b₁)'s premise was true and its conclusion false. And, for all we know, it may continue to be unsuccessful in all cases of its application to a true premise—only we shall never be entitled to conclude that it will!

Consider next the slightly more plausible position of a man who takes R_2 to be the sole rule of inference. And suppose he finds that in most examined instances of the use of R_2 in arguments with true premises that rule has been unsuccessful (i.e., has led from true premise to false conclusion). The formal inductive argument to discredit R_2 then runs as follows:

(b₂): In most instances of the use of R_2 in arguments with true premises examined in a wide variety of conditions, R_2 has been unsuccessful.

Hence (probably):

In the next instance to be encountered of the use of R_2 in an argument with a true premise, R_2 will be unsuccessful.

Call the premise of this argument Q. If we take (b₂) itself as the "next instance" of the application of R_2, we see that if Q is true Q must be false. And here again we seem able to prove that Q must be false, even though if this is so, R_2 *is* unsuccessful in the "next instance" and may continue to be so in most instances of its application to true premises.

Is it therefore correct to say "our inductive principle is at any rate not capable of being *disproved* by an appeal to experience" (Russell, *Problems of Philosophy*, p. 106)? I find this hard to believe. Certainly it is flatly at variance with common sense: if the use of an inductive rule always—or even in most cases—led us to infer false conclusions from true premises, common sense would urge that we had a very good reason for jettisoning the rule. Now common sense may well be wrong. But before we give it permission to go and hang itself like Judas, we might do as well to consider very carefully whether common sense may not be right after all.

XII. HOW DIFFICULT MIGHT INDUCTION BE?

1. Not previously published.

2. The problem was suggested to me by Professor John Myhill, to whom I am also indebted for valuable criticism of earlier drafts of the paper. I hope his own acute discussion will be published.

XIII. FREGE ON FUNCTIONS

1. Not previously published. I am grateful to Mr. Peter Geach for generous criticism of an earlier version of this essay.

2. The critical tone of this essay should not mislead the reader into supposing I undervalue the importance of Frege's work in the philosophy of logic. My debt to him is enormous. But for all his clarity, the central ideas of Frege's theories are very difficult and a good deal of careful exposition and criticism will be needed before we can learn all that he has to teach us.

3. It has been suggested to me by Mr. Geach that the chief difficulties in Frege's theory of functions arise from supposing (as Frege did) that functions can be *named* or designated. Consider the following example: "2^3," "5^3," and "7^3" are three designations of a certain numerical function (the cube function). According to Frege, these three designations have a *common character*, sometimes represented by him as "ξ^3," that is a *name* (*Funktionsname*) of that function. This leads to the serious difficulties I have elabo-

rated in the text. Now Geach makes the ingenious suggestion that instead of regarding "ξ^3" as a name, we take it to *specify* a certain *name-function* (i.e., a function whose arguments and values are designations). Consider the function whose value for "2" (the numeral, not the number!) is "2^3" (the expression, not the number), whose value for "5" is "5^3," for "7" is "7^3," and so on. Call this name-function "K" for the moment. Then Geach proposes that the original numerical function (the cube function) be taken to be represented *by this correlated name-function, K,* and not by "ξ^3," or indeed by any other expression. This idea deserves further exploration. (It would be necessary, of course, to explain how a function can represent.)

4. There has been little serious work done on Frege hitherto. Russell's paper "The Logical and Arithmetical Doctrines of Frege" (Appendix A of *The Principles of Mathematics* [Cambridge, 1903]) is still valuable, though inaccurate in detail. Of recent discussions, the best I know are Rulon Wells, "Frege's Ontology," *Review of Metaphysics,* 4 (1951): 537–573, and William Marshall, "Frege's Theory of Functions and Objects," *Philosophical Review,* 62 (1953): 374–390.

XIV. CARNAP ON LOGIC AND SEMANTICS

1. Originally published under the title, "Logic and Semantics," in *Philosophical Studies. Essays in Memory of L. Susan Stebbing* (London, 1948). Apart from minor changes of wording, and the addition of a summary, I have left the paper unchanged. Professor Leonard Linsky was kind enough to criticize the earlier version in detail, and I owe it to him that it does not contain more mistakes. This essay was written in 1945 and no longer adequately represents my views; but I think it may still have some value for the reader.

2. The paper was reviewed by Olaf Helmer in *Journal of Symbolic Logic,* 15 (1950): 213.

3. Some of the high hopes that were held for the future of "semantics" at the time this essay was written have since evaporated, though some young philosophers, chiefly American, are still eloquent in metalanguages. But the views here examined have something more than historical importance, and I hope what I have written may help anybody who wishes or is compelled to

work his way through the intricacies of these ambitious attempts to apply mathematical methods to philosophical problems.

4. The main conclusions of this essay have been advocated by a number of other writers. See, for instance, Arthur Pap, "Are All Necessary Propositions Analytic?" *Philosophical Review,* 58 (1949): 299–320, and W. V. Quine, "Two Dogmas of Empiricism," *Philosophical Review,* 60 (1951): 20–43, especially pp. 23–34. (A revised version of this paper is reprinted in the same author's *From A Logical Point of View* [Cambridge, Mass., 1953].)

5. Carnap's later book, *Meaning and Necessity* (Chicago, 1947), is highly relevant. I have discussed it under the title, "Carnap's Semantics," *Philosophical Review,* 58 (1949): 257–264. See also the reviews by E. Nagel, *Journal of Philosophy,* 40 (1948): 467–472, G. Ryle, *Philosophy,* 24 (1949): 69–76 and C. Lewy, *Mind,* 58 (1949): 228–238.

6. On the crucial point of the need for the linguistic thesis to conform with preanalytic meanings of "logic," see Carnap's useful discussion of the notion of "explication" in Chapter 1 of his *Logical Foundations of Probability* (Chicago, 1950).

Index

Achilles and tortoise paradox, 95-126: Whitehead's solution of, 96-100
"Alpha" machine, 102-103, 110, 111
Analysis of Knowledge and Valuation, The (Lewis), 164n
Aristotle, 7, 95, 99, 107, 118n, 127, 127n 130, 131, 143n, 148, 150, 151, 154: his conception of continuity, 132; his solution of the flying-arrow paradox, 129-133; criticism of his solution, 130-133
Aristotle's Criticism of Pre-socratic Philosophy (Cherniss), 135
Aristotle's Physics (Ross), 135
Assertion, 37, 38, 42
Axiom of infinite divisibility, 124
Ayer, A. J., 72, 292

Bacon, Francis, 7
Bar-Hillel, Y., 46n
Basic statements, 60
Bergmann, G., 258n, 292
Berkeley, 257
Bernard, Claude, 14-20: his determinism, 15, 17, 18, 23; his fallibilism, 15; rationalism and empiricism synthesized by, 16; his scepticism, 23
"Beta" machine, 103-105, 110-112
Braithwaite, R. B., 201n
Broad, C. D., 71n, 73, 74, 74n, 76, 131, 190, 293, 294
Burks, Arthur, 179n

Cajori, F., 95n
Carnap, Rudolf, 255-290, 299
Clear cases, 26, 31
Cognitive inquiry and inductive policies, 173-180
Coherence with empirical theory, 166

Collected Papers of Charles Sanders Peirce, 15n, 110n
Common-sense view of the world, 120
Conant, James Bryant, 6n
Connotation, 3, 24
Constitutive factors, 26n, 29, 33, 34
Contemporary British Philosophy, 63n, 121n, 247
Context, 43
Continuity, Aristotle's conception of, 132
Continuity of motion postulate: a necessary truth, 113
Continuous magnitude, 130, 154
Convergent geometrical series, 96-98
Convergent series of acts, 115
Counter-inductionist, 178-179
Counter-inductive policy, 171-173
Couturat, L., 102n
Creed, Isabel, 294
Criteria: overlapping and interacting, 13; for application of a word, 26, 26n
Critical Realism (Dawes Hicks), 22n

"Dachshund" example, 25-32
Dawes Hicks, G., 72, 72n
De l'infini Mathématique (Couturat), 100n
Definition, 3, 24, 32: Aristotelian, 9, 23; as clarification of our language, 10; by exhibition of species, 25; by necessary and sufficient condition, 25, 26, 28; dictionary, 25; of scientific method, 3-23; *per genus et differentiam*, 9-11, 25; persuasive, 4; philosophical, 4; range, 13, 14, 19, 30, 34
"Delta" machine, 106
Demon series, 210-225

Lightning Source UK Ltd.
Milton Keynes UK
UKOW07n1135160215

246254UK00001BB/1/P